国际贸易学

International Trade
—Perspective from China

主编／吕小明

参编／陈 书 黄 森

重庆大学出版社

内容提要

本书共十章,分为三个大的板块,即"是什么""为什么"和"怎么做"。第一至第三章围绕"国际贸易是什么"展开。第一章是引言导入和事实数据,第二章是国际贸易的基本概念,第三章介绍国际贸易分析工具。第四至第七章围绕"为什么开展国际贸易"展开,这部分也是本教材的重点内容。第四章介绍了十八至十九世纪的国际贸易古典理论,第五章分析了二十世纪上半期的新古典国际贸易理论,第六章分析了二战之后的新国际贸易理论,第七章是经济增长与国际贸易。第八至第十章围绕"怎么协调国际贸易"展开。第八章和第九章侧重于分析国际贸易政策的影响,即关税和非关税贸易壁垒。第十章介绍世界经济一体化的活动。

本书简明易懂,既可作为文科高校开展教学的教科书,也可作为大学生的通俗读物。

图书在版编目(CIP)数据

国际贸易学 = International Trade—Perspective
from China / 呙小明主编. -- 重庆:重庆大学出版社,
2023.12
(四川外国语大学新文科建设系列丛书)
ISBN 978-7-5689-4042-9

Ⅰ.①国… Ⅱ.①呙… Ⅲ.①国际贸易—高等学校—
教材 Ⅳ.①F74

中国国家版本馆 CIP 数据核字(2023)第 192889 号

国际贸易学
International Trade—Perspective from China
GUOJI MAOYIXUE

主 编 呙小明

责任编辑:陈 亮 版式设计:陈 亮
责任校对:谢 芳 责任印制:赵 晟

*

重庆大学出版社出版发行
出版人:陈晓阳
社址:重庆市沙坪坝区大学城西路 21 号
邮编:401331
电话:(023) 88617190 88617185(中小学)
传真:(023) 88617186 88617166
网址:http://www.cqup.com.cn
邮箱:fxk@cqup.com.cn(营销中心)
全国新华书店经销
重庆升光电力印务有限公司印刷

*

开本:720mm×1020mm 1/16 印张:18.75 字数:535 千
2023 年 12 月第 1 版 2023 年 12 月第 1 次印刷
ISBN 978-7-5689-4042-9 定价:56.00 元

总 序

交叉融合,创新发展
——四川外国语大学新文科建设系列教材总序

四川外国语大学校长　董洪川

　　四川外国语大学,简称"川外"(英文名为 Sichuan International Studies University,缩写为 SISU),位于歌乐山麓、嘉陵江畔,是我国设立的首批外语专业院校之一。古朴、幽深的歌乐山和清澈、灵动的嘉陵江涵养了川外独特的品格。学校在邓小平、刘伯承、贺龙等老一辈无产阶级革命家的关怀和指导下创建,从最初的中国人民解放军西南军政大学俄文训练团,到中国人民解放军第二高级步兵学校俄文大队,到西南人民革命大学俄文系、西南俄文专科学校,再到四川外语学院,至 2013 年更名为四川外国语大学。学校从 1979 年开始招收硕士研究生,2013 年被国务院学位委员会批准为博士学位授予单位,2019 年经人社部批准设置外国语言文学博士后科研流动站。学校在办学历程中秉承"团结、勤奋、严谨、求实"的优良校风,弘扬"海纳百川,学贯中外"的校训精神,形成了"国际导向、外语共核、多元发展"的办学特色,探索出一条"内涵发展,质量为先,中外合作,分类培养"的办学路径,精耕细作,砥砺前行,培养了一大批外语专业人才和复合型人才。他们活跃在各条战线,为我国的外交事务、国际商贸、教学科研等各项建设做出了应有的贡献。

　　经过七十三年的发展,学校现已发展成为一所以外国语言文学学科为主,文学、经济学、管理学、法学、教育学、艺术学、哲学等协调发展的多科型外国语大学,具备了博士研究生教育、硕士研究生教育、本科教育、留学生教育等多形式、多层次的完备办学体系,主办了《外国语文》《英语研究》等有较高声誉的学术期刊。学校已成为西南地区外语和涉外人才培养以及外国语言文化、对外经济贸易、国际问题研究的重要基地。

　　进入新时代,"一带一路"倡议、"构建人类命运共同体"和"中华文化'走出去'"等国家战略赋予了外国语大学新使命、新要求和新任务。随着"六卓越一拔尖"计划2.0(指卓越工程师、卓越医生、卓越农林人才、卓越教师、卓越法治人才、卓越新闻传播人才教育培养计划 2.0 和基础学科拔尖学生培养计划 2.0)和"双万"计划(指实施一流专业建设,建设一万个国家级一流本科专业点和一万个省级一流本科专业点)的实施,"新工科、新农科、新医科、新文科"建设(简称"四新"建设)成为国家高等教育的发展战略。2021年,教育部发布《新文科研究与改革实践项目指南》,设置了6个选题领域、22个选题方向,全面推进新文科建设研究和实践,着力构建具有世界水平、中国特色的文科人才培养体系。为全面贯彻教育部等部委系列文件精神和全国新文科建设工作会议精神,加快文科教育创新发展,构建以育人育才为中心的文科发展新格局,重庆市率先在全国设立了"高水平新文科建设高校"项目。而四川外国语大学有幸成为重庆市首批"高水平新文科建设高校"项目三个入选高校之一。这就历史性地赋予了我校探索新文科建设的责任与使命。

2020年11月3日,全国有关高校和专家齐聚中华文化重要发祥地山东,共商新时代文科教育发展大计,共话新时代文科人才培养,共同发布《新文科建设宣言》。这里,我想引用该宣言公示的五条共识来说明新文科建设的重要意义。一是提升综合国力需要新文科。哲学社会科学发展水平反映着一个民族的思维能力、精神品格和文明素质,关系到社会的繁荣与和谐。二是坚定文化自信需要新文科。新时代,把握中华民族伟大复兴的战略全局,提升国家文化软实力,促进文化大繁荣,增强国家综合国力,新文科建设责无旁贷。为中华民族伟大复兴注入强大的精神动力,新文科建设大有可为。三是培养时代新人需要新文科。面对世界百年未有之大变局,要在大国博弈竞争中赢得优势与主动,实现中华民族复兴大业,关键在人。为党育人、为国育才是高校的职责所系。四是建设高等教育强国需要新文科。高等教育是兴国强国的"战略重器",服务国家经济社会高质量发展,根本上要求高等教育率先实现创新发展。文科占学科门类的三分之二,文科教育的振兴关乎高等教育的振兴,做强文科教育,推动高教强国建设,加快实现教育现代化,新文科建设刻不容缓。五是文科教育融合发展需要新文科。新科技和产业革命浪潮奔腾而至,社会问题日益综合化、复杂化,应对新变化、解决复杂问题亟需跨学科专业的知识整合,推动融合发展是新文科建设的必然选择。进一步打破学科专业壁垒,推动文科专业之间深度融通、文科与理工农医交叉融合,融入现代信息技术赋能文科教育,实现自我革故鼎新,新文科建设势在必行。

新文科建设是文科的创新发展,目的是培养能适应新时代需要、能承担新时代历史使命的文科新人。川外作为重庆市首批"高水平新文科建设高校"项目三个入选高校之一,需要立足"两个一百年"奋斗目标的历史交汇点,准确把握新时代发展大势、高等教育发展大势和人才培养大势,超前识变,积极应变,主动求变,以新文科理念为指引,谋划新战略,探索新路径,深入思考学校发展的战略定位、模式创新和条件保障,构建外国语大学创新发展新格局,努力培养一大批信仰坚定,外语综合能力强,具有中国情怀、国际化视野和国际治理能力的高素质复合型国际化人才。

基于上述认识,我们启动了"四川外国语大学新文科建设系列丛书"编写计划。这套丛书将收录文史哲、经管法、教育学和艺术学等多个学科专业领域的教材,以新文科理念为指导,严格筛选程序,严把质量关。在选择出版书目的标准把握上,我们既注重能体现新文科的学科交叉融合精神的学术研究成果,又注重能反映新文科背景下外语专业院校特色人才培养的教材研发成果。我们希望通过丛书出版,积极推进学校新文科建设,积极提升学校学科内涵建设,同时也为学界同仁提供一个相互学习、沟通交流的平台。

新文科教育教学改革是中国高等教育现代化的重要内容,是一项系统复杂的工作。客观地讲,这个系列目前还只是一个阶段性的成果。尽管作者们已尽心尽力,但成果转化的空间还很大。提出的一些路径和结论是否完全可靠,还需要时间和实践验证。但无论如何,这是一个良好的开始,我相信以后我们会做得越来越好。

新文科建设系列丛书的出版计划得到了学校师生的积极响应,也得到了出版社领导的大力支持。在此,我谨向他们表示衷心的感谢和崇高的敬意! 当然,由于时间仓促,也囿于我们自身的学识和水平,书中肯定还有诸多不足之处,恳请方家批评指正。

2023 年 5 月 30 日

写于歌乐山下

前　言

作为一名在国际经济学领域执教多年的教师，我一直感觉到编写一部更加具备中国特色的《国际贸易学》全英文版教材的必要性、紧迫性和重要性，尤其是对于我们这样的外语类院校，率先编写基于中国实践经验的国际贸易课程全英文版教材，切实推进国际贸易课程全英文教学，意义是非同小可的。

目前，高校在进行国际贸易课程全英文教学时，大多采用国外作者编写的引进版教材或影印版教材。一方面，这些教材大都为多次印刷版本，核心内容的撰写时间多在十多年前，新的版本除了部分案例和数据时间有所改进，并无本质变化，这会导致应用这些教材的教师和学生无法跟踪最前沿的理论和方法；另一方面，由于作者的文化背景和实际经历与中国教师和学生相差较大，其中的案例选取和观点阐述可能无法反映出中国对外经济活动的实际情况，难以引起中国学生的共鸣，从而学生的学习兴趣和认同感得不到有效激发。与市场上有大量中国学者编著全英文版其他类经济学教材和国际贸易实务教材的盛况相比，国际贸易学的全英文版教材编写就相形见绌了。所以，针对国际贸易理论与政策编写一本全英文版教材，并融入中国的外贸实践经验，我们中国学者需要积极参与。

《国际贸易学》（*International Trade—Perspective from China*）的编写，正是为了弥补目前国内高校国际贸易课程全英文版教材的缺憾，力争做到既能够满足本学科专业教材国际化发展的迫切需要，又能结合经典国际贸易理论及中国对外贸易案例实践，实现本土化与国际化的融合。

本教材共十章，涵盖国际贸易的基本概念、数据分析、国际贸易三大经典理论、经济增长对国际贸易的影响、国际贸易政策分析等内容，整体逻辑是以全球贸易发展轨迹为统领、全球贸易形成原因与格局分析为基础，从基础概念到指标统计，从贸易发展现状到未来预测，从贸易产生原因到贸易利益所得，依次展开，从贸易政策类型到贸易政策经济效应，由浅入深，涵盖面广，容易理解。这些章节可以大致分为三个大的板块，即"是什么""为什么"和"怎么做"。

第一至第三章围绕"国际贸易是什么"展开。第一章是引言导入和事实数据，第二章是国际贸易的基本概念，第三章介绍国际贸易分析工具。这三章将介绍国际贸易的概念和发展，帮助学生识别不同概念之间的细微差异，掌握国际贸易各种统计指标的计算方法。同时，这里还将引导学生搜索各种资源，获取与贸易相关的数据，了解全球贸易的基本事实,掌握总体发展模式。

第四至第七章围绕"为什么开展国际贸易"展开,这部分也是本教材的重点内容。第四章介绍了十八至十九世纪的国际贸易古典理论,第五章分析了二十世纪上半期的新古典国际贸易理论,第六章分析了二战之后的新国际贸易理论。第四至第六章都将集中探索这些经典国际贸易理论的发展脉络,以帮助读者了解不同国家之间为什么会发生国际贸易,他们为什么进口或者出口某种商品,以及他们通过国际贸易所能获得的收益。第七章是经济增长与国际贸易,与前面章节不同的是,本章所探讨的是在一个本来已经开放的国际环境里,当一国经济状况发生变化时,国际贸易形势会发生什么变化,这一章的内容将是对前面三章内容的一个有益补充。

第八至第十章围绕"怎么协调国际贸易"展开。第八章和第九章侧重于分析国际贸易政策的影响,即关税和非关税贸易壁垒。第十章介绍世界经济一体化的活动。这些章节通过介绍国际贸易政策,引导学生了解各国如何通过各种政策工具的组合来实现其外贸发展目标,从而促进本国经济增长和提高本国人民的福利。

本教材将国际贸易学理论与中国对外开放实践相结合,每章附有"聚焦中国案例研究",其中绝大部分是中国学者关于中国外贸问题和中国外贸政策的研究成果,相当于中国开放经济问题的一些案例研究,有助于读者进一步理解国际经济现实问题及国际经济理论在解决现实问题方面的应用。本教材力图既传授国际经济学中国际贸易的专业知识,又传授经管类专业的英语语言知识,还将着重探索中国实践和启示,便于教师在课堂上训练本学科专业的思维逻辑和分析方法,以及与国际经济学有关的英语的应用技能,着力培养出兼具世界视野和中国思维的国际化人才,也利于教师将社会主义核心价值观、实现民族复兴的理想和责任融入国际贸易课程教学之中。

我深信,本教材将为读者们提供一个新的视角来看待国际贸易。通过对中国的案例和经验的深入分析,读者们可以更好地理解中国的发展和成就,同时也可以更好地认识到全球化和国际贸易对世界各国的影响。我衷心希望,本教材能够为读者们打开一扇通往全球贸易的大门,并启迪他们进一步思考和探索。

特别说明的是,本教材是四川外国语大学国际金融与贸易学院国际贸易课程组的集体智慧成果,组员分别是陈书老师、黄森老师和邹思晓老师,他们为本教材的完成付出了极大的努力,在此表示衷心的感谢!

本教材得到了四川外国语大学新文科项目的大力资助,在本教材出版之际,我特别要感谢四川外国语大学教务处的鼓励和资助。我也要特别感谢重庆大学出版社编辑对本教材内容的细致审核和耐心指导!

由于编者水平有限,教材中难免有疏漏和错误之处,敬请广大同行批评指正。

吕小明

2023 年 6 月

Contents

Chapter 1 Introduction

Learning goals

After learning this chapter, you should be able to:

✓ understand the meaning and importance of international trade.

✓ describe the development history of international trade.

✓ understand the reality of international trade and its dimensions.

✓ identify the major international trade problems and challenges facing China and the world.

The nearly 80 years since the end of the Second World War have witnessed the unprecedented development in international trade. Over the past years, the General Agreement on Tariffs and Trade (GATT) has come into force temporarily and eight complete rounds of multilateral trade negotiations have been successfully held. Then the World Trade Organization (WTO), established in 1995, has become increasingly important in adjusting contemporary world economic and trade relations. These years after the war were also those when the economy and trade mutually promoted and developed together. International trade has become the engine of world economic growth, and economic development in turn promotes the rapid development of international trade and international capital flows. The development of multinational corporations and economic globalization are the result of the mutual promotion of economy and trade.

At the same time, with the founding of the People's Republic of China, China's economy and foreign trade have also entered an unprecedented period of historical development. Especially since the reform and opening-up in 1978, China's position in the world trade has been constantly improving. In 1978, China's total foreign trade value was only \$21.09 billion, ranking 34th in the world. However, by 2002, China's total foreign trade had risen to \$620.77 billion, becoming the 5th largest trading country in the world, and in 2003 China's total foreign trade reached \$850.99, becoming the 4th largest trading country in the world. In 2009 China's total foreign trade reached \$2,207.54 billion, ranking the 2nd in the world. And in 2013, China's total foreign trade increased to \$4,159.00 billion, surpassing the United States, becoming the world's largest trader of goods. Since 2013, China has almost always occupied the position of the world's largest trader in goods. In 2020, under the ravage of COVID-19, the global economy was deeply affected, and all major economies experienced serious economic recession. Thanks to the control of the large-scale spread of the epidemic, strong macro policy measures and the rapid recovery of production and consumption, China's economy grew against the trend and became one of the few economies in the world that maintained positive economic growth. China's foreign trade has also experienced a "V" shaped reversal due to the supply gap caused by the spread of the epidemic abroad, the shutdown of enterprises and the substantial increase in the demand for epidemic prevention materials. This is not only better than expected, but also a new historical record. In this year, China's total foreign trade reached \$4,655.92 billion, an increase of 1.7% over 2019. In 2021, China still remained the world's largest trading country with a total trade volume of \$6,051.49 billion, breaking the \$6,000 billion threshold for the first time.

The rapid development of international trade requires an independent economic discipline to study the increasingly active international economic activities, and thus International Economics has officially emerged. International Economics, as a discipline, has two major branches: One is International Trade, and the other is International Finance. It has always been an attractive and divergent research area in the field of economic analysis. This book is mainly about the discussion of the international trade. Before reading this book, you may have a lot of questions in your mind about international trade, such as: What is international trade? How should a country decide what things to sell and buy in a global market? What benefits will international trade bring to the participating countries? Why do all countries basically implement trade protection policies while at the same time they join the WTO, which advocates free trade? How will the free flow of capital and labor around the world affect the countries concerned? How can China improve its position in the world economy and trade?

Your questions may go beyond the above. Reading this book does not guarantee that you will find the completely correct and satisfactory answers to all the international economic and trade issues, but it will certainly help you to master the necessary analysis tools and frameworks to address these issues.

This chapter will give a general introduction to the concept and the development of international trade as well as the current situation, and the content arrangement of the book, so that readers can be aroused with a big interest in intentional trade issues and better understand the internal connection between the chapters.

1.1 What is international trade?

1.1.1 What is trade?

Trade is the activity of buying, selling, or exchanging goods or services between people, firms, or countries. Although the theory of trade originated from Western economics, the term "trade" was not unique to the West. In ancient China, there were already words related to trade, and ancient Chinese people were also full of the wisdom of trade.

(1) Trade behavior found in ancient China

If the government wants to raise money, food and other things from the citizens in war time, the government should offer fair price if these citizens want to trade for some daily appliances.

——"Mozi • Order" in China's Spring and Autumn Period and the Warring States Period

(2) The earliest trade war in Chinese history

Guan Zhong, a famous politician in the Spring and Autumn Period, assisted Duke Huan of Qi to succeed.

Duke Huan of Qi was the 16th monarch of Qi (reigned from 685 to 643 BCE). He was known as one of the five super-powers of the Spring and Autumn Period.

However, Qi's road to hegemony was not smooth. The neighboring State of Lu was the first opponent to be defeated. At that time, the State of Lu developed rapidly and its strength could not be underestimated. Duke Huan of Qi was worried about the threat from neighboring states and had to plan ahead for becoming a overlord, so he asked Guan Zhong, the prime minister for advice.

Many people in the State of Lu took weaving ti (a kind of coarse fabric) as their industry. Guan Zhong advised Duke Huan of Qi to do two things. Firstly, Duke Huan of Qi took the lead in wearing clothes made of ti fabric. His courtiers followed suit. Together with the common people of Qi, the whole state followed suit. Everyone wore clothes made of ti. Secondly, Duke Huan of Qi ordered the people of Qi not to produce ti fabric. As a result, the whole State of Qi had to import lots of ti fabric from the State of Lu. In order to benefit from export, the people of Lu gave up growing grain and chose to weave ti, for exporting to Qi.

One year later, the people of Lu produced a lot of ti fabric. And Guan Zhong advised Duke Huan of Qi to do another two things again. Firstly, Duke Huan of Qi began to wear clothes made of bo, a silk fabric, and led the people to wear bo clothes instead of ti clothes. Secondly, Duke Huan of Qi ordered to cut off economic exchanges with the State of Lu, stopping importing ti from Lu. The monarch of the State of Lu hurriedly ordered his people to stop weaving ti and concentrate on planting crops. But the crops could not be planted and harvested in a short time. As a result, the food price of the State of Lu soared and the people could not bear it, suffering from famine.

At this time, Guan Zhong advised to lower food price inside Qi. Finding that the food of the State of Qi was much cheaper than that of Lu, the people of Lu all fled to the State of Qi, causing the decline of Lu. Three years later, the monarch of the State of Lu also surrendered to the State of Qi.

1.1.2   What is international trade?

International trade, also known as world (global) trade, refers to the exchange of goods, technologies and services between different countries (or regions).

(1) International trade vs foreign trade

Both refer to the exchange of goods and services across national borders. However, international trade is from the overall perspective, while foreign trade is from the individual perspective.

(2) Foreign trade vs overseas trade

Both refer to the exchange of goods and services between countries or regions. However, some island countries prefer to call their foreign trade as overseas trade, such as Japan, and some landlocked countries will not call their foreign trade as overseas trade, such as Kazakhstan.

1.2   Why is international trade important?

Why does every country trade with other countries? If a country has enough resources to be self-sufficient, what is the need to trade with other countries?

1.2.1 We live in a globalized world

With the development of economy and technology, people come to realize that the contact between countries has become more and more closely frequent. Nowadays we can connect instantly with any corner of the world by cellular phones, e-mail, instant message and teleconference, and we can travel anywhere incredibly fast. Tastes are converging and many goods we consume are either made abroad or have many imported parts and components. For example, American-made clothes take imported fabrics, and most Dell's PC components are manufactured worldwide (see Table 1.1), and it is not easy to confirm a manufactured product belonging to only one nation. Many of our coffee beans and bananas also come from abroad.

Table 1.1 Locations and companies that supply specific parts and components for Dell's PCs

Part/Component	Location	Company
Monitors	Europe and Asia	Phillips, Nokia, Samsung, Sony, Acer
PCBs	Asia, Scotland, and Eastern Europe	SCI, Celestica
Drives	Asia, mainly Singapore	Seagate, Maxtor, Western Digital
Printers	Europe (Barcelona)	Acer
Box builds	Asia and Eastern Europe	Hon Hai/Foxteq
Chassis	Asia and Ireland	Hon Hai/Foxteq

According to historical investigation, globalization began in the Mediterranean nearly 1,000 years ago, and with the great geographical discovery in the 15th-16th century, the globalization process continued extensively. Economic globalization is an important form of globalization. It refers to the cross-border economic activities of countries or regions in the world, including the extensive and free cross-border flow of goods and services, capital, labor, technology, information, and other production factors in the global scope, so as to realize the effective allocation of resources and strengthen the relations and interactions among countries, who then form a relationship of mutual dependence and even restriction.

However, the connotation of economic globalization is not static, especially in the 21st century, during which time the world pattern is constantly changing, and economic globalization also shows an unprecedented new trend.

Firstly, the global industrial chain is being reorganized. Since the 1970s, the Western industrial powers have been upgrading their industries with the help of technology, and the traditional manufacturing industries have been transferred out gradually. However, some developing countries, especially China, which is carrying out reform and opening-up policy, are undertaking these industries. In addition, China has an abundant labor force. Therefore, China has developed into a huge manufacturing country. In the last two decades of the 20th century, the traditional manufacturing industry with "made in China" has become the most influential and important industry in the world. However, "made in China" does not mean that the whole chain of production is made in China. A considerable part of the production belongs to a link in the global industrial chain, but its important link or the final link of the products is in China, so it is given the name "made in China". From this point of view, China has been at the center of the global industrial chain of traditional manufacturing for a long time. However, after Donald Trump came to power in the United States in 2017, things changed. On the one hand, he implemented the manufacturing return plan to revitalize the manufacturing industry in the United States. On the other hand, in 2018, the Trump administration provoked trade frictions between China and the United States, which looked like a tariff issue, but in essence an industrial issue. The purpose was to combat the upgrading of China's manufacturing industry. In the view of the US government, there is a serious conflict between China's "Made in China 2025" plan and the revitalization of the US manufacturing industry. After several rounds of negotiations, trade friction has gradually eased, but the economic problems between China and the United States have not been fundamentally resolved. The global spread of COVID-19 in 2020 made the global manufacturing industry even worse. China, which was the center of the manufacturing industry chain, was more affected. Against the background, based on the consideration of "safety and controllability of the industrial chain", the multinational companies changed "outsourcing" to "insourcing", and took back the business which was originally subcontracted to external enterprises.

Secondly, global supply chain centers are shifting. After undertaking the traditional manufacturing industry of Western industrial countries, China has gradually become the global supply chain center of traditional manufacturing industry in a few decades. However, the transfer of global industrial centers will inevitably lead to the transfer of global supply chain centers. In order to cope with the impact of the epidemic on the economy, Western developed countries quickly adjusted their economic development strategies and began to promote the digital economy, a new economic form, with the aim of reorganizing global factor resources, reshaping the global economic structure and changing the global competition pattern. This means that the proportion of traditional manufacturing industry in the global economy will be greatly reduced, and the supply chain center of manufacturing industry will soon be replaced by the supply chain center of digital economy.

Thirdly, global value chains are being reshaped. In the traditional manufacturing industry and its industrial chain, the formation process of global value chain is mainly restricted by the manufacturing industry chain. The products in the traditional manufacturing industry are tangible. In the process of global division of labor, not only is the manufacturing process transparent, but also the value formation process is very clear. For example, the price of an iPhone from a Chinese factory is $144, but China only contributes $4 of it. Among them, $100 is from an imported Japanese hard disk, display screen and battery, and $15 is from imported American memory and processor. Of course, this also shows that for a long time, China has mainly relied on traditional factors to participate in the division of labor in the global value chain. Not only is the added value of products low, but also the brand effect is lacking. Therefore, Chinese industries are mainly concentrated in the middle and low end of the global value chain and mainly participate in the market competition with "low price and good quality". However, in the digital economy era, data is not only a means to reshape the global value chain, but also a key link of the global value chain itself. This means that more and more products are changing from the physical product forms to the digital forms.

It is difficult for us to predict what will happen in the future. China is an important participant in globalization and one of the main beneficiaries of globalization. While realizing its own development, China has also been feeding the world back and becoming the engine of world economic growth. Standing at the crossroads of globalization, China is trying to explore a path to promote inclusive and equitable development of globalization. By giving play to China's advantages and characteristics, China can inject new impetus into the development of globalization.

1.2.2　We live in a diversified world

The world is rich and colorful. Diversity is the charm of human civilization and the source of vitality and power for world development.

With the improvement of socio-economic and cultural development level, people's values, aesthetic views and living needs are constantly diversified due to the stimulation of social environmental conditions and the change of people's internal needs. Firstly, the enrichment and improvement of material and spiritual life provide subjective and objective conditions for the pursuit of diversity. In the era of shortage economy, due to the limitation of material conditions, people mainly pursue the quantity of material conditions, and rush for food and clothing. The value orientation is determined by the quantity of material, and the pursuit of life is relatively simple. The abundance of material life makes people get rid of the shackles of economic conditions and have the time, energy and ability to pursue in many aspects. As the basic material needs have been met, the pursuit of a broader spiritual life has been constantly strengthened, leading to the diversification of life pursuit and lifestyle. Secondly, the improvement of science pushes the production technology, and enterprises enjoy continuous enhancement of means and ability to meet social needs. Thus the continuous emergence of new products and the gradual shortening of product life cycle have stimulated people's new consumption pursuit.

Take agricultural products as an example. As China's largest agricultural product import source, the United States is China's important agricultural product trade partner. In 2017, China imported \$24.12 billion of agricultural products from the United States, ranking first among China's 179 import sources. The amount of agricultural products imported from the United States accounted for 19% of China's total agricultural product imports. More than 30% of the soybeans in the United States were sold to China, and the corn and wheat imported by China were mainly from the United States. Today, China has become the world's largest importer of agricultural products, accounting for 1/10 of the world's agricultural product trade, and the total net import of grain, cotton, oil, sugar, meat and milk and other major agricultural products. At present, about 70% of China's agricultural product imports come from the United States, Brazil, ASEAN, the European Union (EU) and Australia. However, China's agricultural product imports from countries along the Belt and Road are growing rapidly. The next step is to strengthen agricultural trade cooperation with countries along the Belt and Road, improve trade policies and expand import channels. Increasing imports, especially the import of differentiated products to supplement domestic production, is the demand of people's increasingly improved living standards. Under the current conditions of insufficient supply, it is a wise choice to appropriately increase imports to optimize resource allocation and adjust surplus and shortage globally.

Take the automobile products as another example. Because of different design styles, development levels and emphasis directions, the industrial production of automobile has formed different automobile factions according to the differences of countries or regions, which leads to some people's preference for automobile brands in a certain country or region. For example, most of the models produced by American automobile brands are rough-looking and straightforward, because Americans pursue freedom. South Korean automobile brands also pursue beautiful appearance like their nationals. French cars pursue romantic design elements. Japan is an island country with very scarce natural resources. Therefore, the use of resources goes deep into the minds of Japanese automobile brand designers. Every designer wants to maximize the use of resources in their own models, which makes Japanese cars emphasize cost control. In addition, the reputation of Japanese cars for fuel economy is well-known. By contrast, as the birthplace of automobiles, German automobile brands, like Volkswagen, Audi or BMW, have all demonstrated their outstanding technical content. This is also inseparable from the low-key and stable character of the Germans. German cars generally give consumers the impression that they are solid and of good quality. This is also one of the factors for German cars to dominate the Chinese market. In addition, the materials used for German cars are quite good. The manufacturers' sincerity to consumers can be seen in some visible and invisible parts of their cars. Comparatively speaking, German cars pay more attention to the use of technology and materials and Japanese cars are more durable and fuel-efficient. The cars of the different countries have their own advantages and disadvantages. Consumers can buy according to their own preferences.

1.3　The origin of international trade

International trade originated and developed under certain historical conditions. The emergence of international trade must meet the following conditions: There are surplus products available for exchange due to productivity development and the exchange of products is between different states. Therefore, fundamentally speaking, the development of social productive forces and the expansion of social division of labor are the basis for the emergence and development of international trade.

There are three social divisions of labor in human history. In the early stage of primitive society, people used simple and crude production tools such as wooden sticks and stones. On the basis of natural division of labor, they engaged in gathering, hunting and fishing to maintain a minimum living. In the middle stage of the savage period of the primitive society, some tribes learned to domesticate animals to obtain milk, meat and other means of life. With the formation of large-scale herds, these tribes mainly engaged in animal husbandry, separating themselves from the rest of the barbarians and becoming nomadic tribes. The means of living produced by nomadic tribes were different from those of other tribes, and the number was large, which promoted the development of exchange and made regular exchange possible. Herding a group of livestock required only a few people. Therefore, individual labor has replaced group labor. Accordingly, private ownership has emerged, and families have also changed. Animal husbandry by men has become the main means of livelihood. Men have gained a dominant position in the family. Later, agriculture and handicrafts also developed. Grain became the food of mankind. Looms and bronzes appeared. People began to master ore smelting and metal processing. The increase in production in all sectors enabled the human labor force to produce more products than necessary for the labor force. So the prisoners of war were no longer killed, but were absorbed into labor and became slaves. Thus, slavery appeared sporadically. Through the first social division of labor, the society was divided into two classes: masters and slaves, namely exploiters and the exploited.

The second social division of labor appeared in the advanced stage of the savage period of the primitive society. The use of iron tools and the progress of production technology promoted the development of agriculture and the improvement of labor productivity, and also diversified the handicraft industry. Such diversified activities could no longer be carried out by one person, so the second social division of labor occurred, and handicraft industry was separated from agriculture. With the second social division of labor, commodity production with the direct purpose of exchange emerged. With the development of exchange, precious metal has become a dominant currency commodity. Once monetary wealth appeared in the society, it would become the object of people's pursuit and important purpose of life. Some people would try to accumulate wealth. With the gradual increase of surplus products, the value of human labor force has been improved. In the previous stage, slavery was a scattered phenomenon, and it has become an essential part of the social system.

The third social division of labor took place at the threshold of the civilized era, also called the late slave society. Due to the development of commodity exchange, a merchant class that was not engaged in production but only engaged in exchange emerged. As intermediaries between producers, they exploited producers and gained the leadership of production. The need for exchange development produced metal currency. Money lending, interest and usury also appeared gradually. The private right of land has been firmly established, and the land has become private property, which could be inherited, mortgaged and even sold. In addition to the difference between free people and slaves, there was a difference between the rich and the poor. This was a new class division with the new division of labor. The wealth became more concentrated, the number of slaves increased, and the forced labor of slaves became the economic foundation of the whole society. As a result of class antagonism, the form of states came into being.

Social division of labor is the foundation of commodity economy, and market is the expression of social division of labor in commodity economy. The development of social division of labor determines the depth, breadth and mode of exchange, as well as the scale and content of the market. On the contrary, the type, quantity and market scale of exchange will also affect the development of production and division of labor.

Similarly, international division of labor is the foundation of international trade and world market. Without international division of labor, there would be no international commodity exchange and no world market. International trade and world market develop with the development of international division of labor. The development level of international division of labor determines the depth, breadth and mode of international exchange activities, and also determines the scale and content of the world market. On the contrary, international exchange and world market are the means to realize international division of labor, and their development will inevitably affect and restrict the development of international division of labor.

Case 1.1　International division of labor between China and the United States

In April 2018, the US government released a list of Chinese goods that might be subjected to new tariffs, and the Chinese government quickly counterattacked and decided to impose tariffs on the US origin soybeans, automobiles, chemicals and other goods, which initiated the US-China trade war. Soybeans, as a very important bulk agricultural product in the US-China trade, unfortunately become the sacrifice of the trade war between the two countries.

With a population of more than 1.4 billion, China is the world's biggest market for agricultural products. Among other agro-products, China has a high demand for soybeans, as it is the source of tofu, soymilk, soybean oil and even animal feed. China alone is expected to create one-third of the global demand for soybeans.

In 2017, China bought 56.9 percent of US soybean exports, almost eight times more than Mexico (7.4 percent), which was followed by Japan (4.5 percent), Indonesia (4.3 percent) and the Netherlands (3.6 percent). US Commerce Department data show soybeans have been one of the top US exports to China in recent years, just behind civilian aircraft and cars.

China is expected to import 89 million tons of soybeans this year (2019), according to a report from the China Grain and Oils Information Center. But the US media reported that China is dramatically cutting the purchase of soybeans from the United States.

The US Soybeans Export Council issued a report on December 27 last year saying the United States exported soybeans worth more than $12.25 billion to China in 2017, but in the first 10 months of 2018, thanks to the escalating trade conflicts between Beijing and Washington, the exports declined sharply to around $3.1 billion. The council said that if the trade conflicts triggered by the United States continue, China could stop buying soybeans from the United States and find substitute suppliers to meet its domestic demand.

Countries such as Brazil and Argentina with suitable climate and soil have expanded the cultivation areas for soybean production in recent years. Brazil surpassed the United States as the world's largest soybean exporter in 2012 and has maintained its leading position since then. In 2018, for example, Brazil exported 66.1 million tons of soybeans to China, far more than the United States. And Argentina has exported 5 million to 10 million tons of soybeans to China a year in the past years. So if US soybean exports to China stop, Brazil and Argentina can step in to fill the gap.

Russia, too, has been making efforts to increase soybean exports to China. China's trade data show the amount of Russian soybean exports to China has increased more than tenfold in the last four years, reaching 1 million tons last year.

Although Russia contributes just 1 percent to China's soybean imports and its geographical conditions, especially low temperatures in the Far East, restrict its per hectare crop yield to less than half that of the United States and it is unlikely to become a leading soybean exporter, the country still has great potential to expand its soybean production and increase its exports given its vast territory and proximity to China, which considerably reduces freight costs.

Thanks to strong bilateral relations, Beijing and Moscow are investing capital and technologies to boost agricultural production in Russia's Far East. Russia's soybean export to China is estimated to reach 2 million tons in the next few years, and could become an important source of soybeans for the Chinese market in the long run.

Besides, owing to the huge domestic demand for soybeans, the Chinese government has been encouraging more Chinese farmers to grow soybeans in order to raise their incomes. The total area of soybean production in China has increased this year and the output is expected to reach 16.8 million tons, 1.6 million tons more than in 2018.

Besides, as substitutes for soybeans are available, China can help reduce its citizens' reliance on soybeans, for instance, by reducing soybeans in livestock rations, and using more colza oil and sunflower oil instead of soybean oil.

No one knows what will be the consequences of the escalating US-China trade conflicts, but one thing is certain that US soybeans will lose the Chinese market if the US administration doesn't give up its unilateral policies.

1.4   The development of international trade

The development of international trade can be divided into three stages, which are international trade in the slave society, international trade in the feudal society, international trade in the capitalist society.

The slave society was dominated by the natural economy, and the direct purpose of production was mainly consumption. Commodity production was still insignificant in the whole economic life. Few commodities entered the circulation. In addition, production technology was backward and transportation tools were simple. The scope of foreign trade in each country was greatly limited. Although the international trade of slave society was limited, the development of handicraft industry was greatly promoted, which promoted the progress of social production to a certain extent. In the slave society, the goods in international trade were mainly luxuries pursued by slave owners, such as gems, decorations, various fabrics, spices, etc. At that time, Athens, Greece was one of the centers of the slave trade.

After the feudal society replaced the slave society, international trade had a great development. In particular, from the middle of the feudal society, the land rent in kind was changed into the land rent in money, the scope of the commodity economy was gradually expanded, and international trade was further increased. In the late feudal society, with the further development of urban handicrafts, capitalist factors had begun to breed and grow, and the commodity economy and foreign trade had a significant development compared with the slave society. The development of urban handicrafts was an important factor to promote the development of international trading countries at that time. The development of international trade has promoted the progress of economy and the development of capitalist factors. In this period, generally speaking, the natural economy still dominated, and the role of international trade in economic life was still quite small. In China, in the Western

Han Dynasty in the 2nd century BCE, China opened up the Silk Road from Xinjiang to the Middle East and Europe through Central Asia. China's silk, tea and porcelain were exported to Europe through the Silk Road. Zheng He of the Ming Dynasty led his fleet to the West for seven times and expanded the sea trade.

The international division of labor and the world market are the historical products of the capitalist mode of production, formed and developed on the basis of the capitalist large machine industry. Only in a capitalist society can international trade truly become worldwide. International trade under the capitalist mode of production can be further divided into the following four stages.

1.4.1 The period of preparation of capitalist production mode: late 15th to mid-18th century

The great geographical discoveries in the late 15th and early 16th centuries were an important factor in promoting the transition from feudal society to capitalist society. At that time, the development of Western Europe's commodity economy, centered on handicrafts, required an expanding market. During this period, Turks and Arabs controlled the East-West trade channel, and Europeans urgently needed to find a new route to the East. At the same time, Europeans heard that there was a large amount of gold and silver in the East, which prompted Western European countries to send many fleets to explore the ocean, find new routes and open up new markets. In 1492, Italian navigator Christopher Columbus set out from Spain and discovered the American continent via the Atlantic Ocean. In 1498, Vasco da Gama, a Portuguese, bypassed the Cape of Good Hope from Europe and arrived in India. From 1519 to 1522, Portuguese Ferdinand Magellan completed his first voyage around the earth. These famous geographical discoveries in history led to the plundering of overseas colonies and the slave trade, which was one of the important sources of the original accumulation of capital in Western Europe. Karl Heinrich Marx and Friedrich Engels pointed out, "The discovery of the America and the navigation around Africa opened up new places for the emerging bourgeoisie to engage in activities. The markets of East India and China, the colonization of the America, the trade with the colonies, the increase of means of exchange and general commodities made commerce, navigation and industry unprecedented active." The discovery of geography has brought the world market into its infancy.

At the same time, since the rise of overseas colonization, the nobles of Western Europe have established many colonial farms overseas to develop overseas trade, thus driving the development of foreign capitalism. Many landlords found that the rent for renting out land was far less than that for developing aquaculture. Therefore, in the late 18th century, the bourgeoisie and new feudal nobles in Britain, Germany, France, the Netherlands, Denmark and other countries drove farmers away from the land, thus triggering a tragic "Enclosure Movement". Among them, the British Enclosure Movement was the most famous, where sheep "ate" man. Countless farmers drifted in this movement. Although the Enclosure Movement sacrificed farmers, Britain obtained the primitive accumulation of capital, provided cheap wage labor and a domestic market for capitalism, which laid the most solid material foundation for the development of Britain, especially the establishment of maritime hegemony.

Generally speaking, the commodities circulating in the world market during this period were mainly colonial tropical and subtropical native products or luxury goods and European handicrafts. The backward means of transportation still severely restricted the entry of bulk commodities into the international exchange field. The discovery of geography has expanded international trade and the world market, but because the era of big machine industry has not yet arrived, the international division of labor and the world market are still in the embryonic stage.

1.4.2 The period of free competition capitalism: 1760s-1870s

From the beginning of the Industrial Revolution to the end of the period of free competition capitalism, that is, from the second half of the 18th century to the second half of the 19th century, it was the stage of the formation of the international division of labor of capitalism and the establishment of the world market.

In the 1760s, Britain first started the Industrial Revolution. The revolution began with the textile industry. It was mainly manifested in the invention and improvement of textile machines and looms, which were popularized and widely adopted. The invention and promotion of the steam engine in the 1780s began the era of using machines to produce machines. Machines gradually spread across many industrial sectors such as mining, metallurgy, machine manufacturing and transportation. In the 19th century, following Britain, France, Germany, the United States and other countries also successively realized Industrial Revolution, established large machine industry, and finally established the capitalist mode of production. In this period, the international division of labor between industrial countries and agricultural countries, that is, suzerain countries and colonies, was basically centered on Britain. As Britain was the first country to complete the Industrial Revolution, it became the most developed country at that time and the industrial center of the world, known as the "factory of the world".

With the development of international division of labor, international trade has grown rapidly, and the commodity structure of international trade has changed greatly. Trade in industrial products, especially textiles, increased significantly. The position of coal, metal and machinery in international trade was gradually rising. Grain, cotton, wool, wood and other raw materials have become bulk trade commodities. Countries and regions participating in international trade have spread all over the world. International trade has become world trade and the world market has also taken shape.

1.4.3　The period of monopoly capitalism: 1870s-1930s

The second scientific and technological revolution, represented by the invention and application of electricity and the innovation of steel, chemistry and transportation industry, which began in the 1870s, made the capitalist economy develop by leaps and bounds in the last 30 years of the 19th century. The wide application of science and technology, such as generators, motors and new steel-making methods, has led to the emergence of many new industrial sectors, such as the steel industry, smelting industry, automobile manufacturing industry and chemical industry. The new scientific and technological progress marks another great increase in social productive forces and another profound change in the international division of labor and the world market.

Due to the development of emerging industries such as electric power, steel, chemical industry and automobile manufacturing, the proportion of heavy industry in the original industrial countries has gradually increased, and it has replaced light industry to occupy the dominant position. During this period, the development of science, technology and productive forces in capitalist countries was unbalanced. At the end of the 19th century, the United States and Germany developed rapidly economically, while Britain developed slowly. Britain's original position as the "world factory" was increasingly challenged by the United States and Germany. The center of division of labor changed from one country in Britain to a group of countries. The industrial production of these industrial countries had different emphasis, forming an international division of labor dominated by economic sectors.

The world economic crisis in 1873, first in Germany and the United States, marked the end of the free capitalism. At the end of the 19th century and the beginning of the 20th century, capitalism entered the monopoly stage. Capital export is one of the basic economic characteristics of imperialism. In the past, although colonial and semi-colonial countries had been involved in capitalist commodity exchange, they had not been involved in capitalist production. And then, through the export of capital, imperialist countries set up various enterprises in the colonies to develop the industrial raw materials, food and primary processing industries needed by imperialist countries. As a result, most countries in Asia,

Africa and Latin America developed abnormally, and their production and export were often limited to one or two or a few products. As the world was divided by a few imperialist powers, capitalist production relations expanded to all corners of the world, and the whole world economy became a capitalist world economic system. In short, the transition from free competition capitalism to monopoly capitalism, the tremendous economic impact brought about by the second scientific and technological revolution, and the formation and improvement of the international division of labor have given decisive impetus to the final formation of a unified international market.

In this period, although the trade volume has increased, the growth rate is relatively lower than that in the period of free competition. The proportion of primary products and manufactured goods in the world trade commodity structure has remained stable.

1.4.4 The period of state-monopoly capitalism: 1940s-1990s

After the Second World War, there emerged the third scientific and technological revolution, which was mainly marked by the development and application of atomic energy, electronic computers and space technology. The progress of science and technology has led to the emergence of a series of new energy, new materials and new processes and the establishment of a series of new industrial departments, which has greatly promoted the development of productive forces. With the continuous strengthening of production specialization and internationalization, the interdependence between countries is deepening, and the international division of labor has entered a new period of deepening development.

Profound changes have taken place in the international division of labor: The antagonism and division of labor between the world's cities and the world's countryside, which were formed in the 19th century, still exist, but have been weakened and increasingly replaced by the division of labor dominated by world industry—the international division of labor has gradually developed from the traditional division of labor based on natural resources to the division of labor based on modern technology. The vertical division of labor has developed into horizontal division of labor, the division of labor among various industrial departments into the division of labor inside various industrial departments, and into the new international division of labor based on product specialization, the division of labor according to products into the division of labor according to production factors, the division of labor determined by the spontaneous forces of the market into the direction of organized division of labor, especially organized by multinational companies.

During this period, unprecedented growth in international trade has occurred, and developed countries continue to dominate international trade, but the position of developing countries in international trade has been strengthened. The ratio of industrial manufactured products exceeds that of primary products, and trade in services and technology has developed rapidly.

1.5   The current situation of international trade

1.5.1   Trade in goods

Entering the 21st century, the global trade in goods continued to grow. Especially China's entry into the WTO in 2001 greatly contributed to the growth of global trade. Before the outbreak of the global financial crisis in 2008, the global trade in goods showed a good trend of steady growth. After the crisis and until 2015, the global trade in goods also grew slowly in fluctuations, but the growth rate declined.

In 2015, the total value of global trade in goods fell by 13.8% in US dollars, the first contraction since 2009. Excluding price factors, the global trade volume increased by 2.5% in 2015, but it was still lower than the 3.1% growth rate of the global economy. Before the world financial crisis in 2008, the growth rate of global trade volume was almost twice that of economic growth. Since 2011, the trade growth rate has been equal to or even lower than the economic growth rate. The main reason for the decline in global trade value in 2015 was the decline in demand from developing economies, and the trade value of developing countries represented by China declined. As an important indicator of global freight trade, the Baltic Dry Index (BDI) has fallen to the lowest value in history. China, the world's largest importer and exporter of goods, saw a double-digit decline in its import and export value in January, while Brazil was experiencing the worst economic recession in a century. In January, imports from China fell by 60%. The main reason is that the fluctuation of the currency value and the decline of the price of bulk commodities have led to a decline in the import and export value of various regions in the world. Among them, the export value of the United States in 2015 fell by 6.3% under the influence of the strong dollar, while the export value of the Middle East and Africa fell by 41.4% under the influence of the fall in oil prices.

In 2017, global trade began to recover, but the good times were not long. In 2019, under the complex and changeable situation of rising unilateralism and protectionism, escalating trade frictions, the uncertainty of Brexit, surging non-tariff measures, increasing dependence on bulk commodities, unbalanced development of the digital economy, tense geopolitical situation, impending climate crisis and the WTO falling into reform disputes, global trade once again fell into a weak situation. In 2019, the global merchandise trade value decreased by 0.1%, and the trade volume also decreased by 0.4%, which was the first time that the trade volume decreased in 2010. The policy shift of some countries is an important reason for the weakness of international trade. For example, the US Trump administration pursued the "US First" policy, withdrew from the Trans-Pacific Partnership Agreement, and other practices, so that the United States moved away from trade liberalization, toward protectionism, and spread trade barriers to more regions.

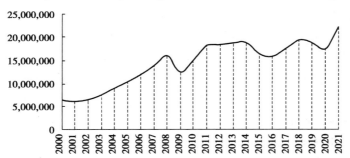

Figure 1.1   WTO data: world total merchandise exports (million USD)

The spread of the COVID-19 epidemic in the world continued to hit global trade in 2020. Fortunately, global trade rebounded in 2021, reaching a record high of $28.5 trillion, up 25% and 13% respectively over 2020 and 2019. On the whole, the global trade in goods remained strong in 2021. From a regional perspective, the trade growth of developing countries was faster. In the fourth quarter of 2021, the imports and exports of all major trading economies were higher than the same period in 2019, but compared with developed countries, the growth of developing countries' trade in goods was stronger. Compared with the same period in 2020, the exports of developing countries and developed countries increased by about 30% and 15% respectively. Affected by the relaxation of epidemic restrictions, the weakening of the economic stimulus plan, the shortening of the supply chain and the diversification of suppliers, it was predicted that the growth of global trade in 2022 would be lower than expected.

1.5.2　Trade in services

At the beginning of the development of international trade, the proportion of service trade was very small, so it was not taken seriously by people. After the Second World War, with the further expansion of economic globalization and the progress of information and communication technology, the simple trade in goods could no longer fully meet people's needs, so the proportion of services has gradually increased. Entering the 21st century, the tourism trade, transportation, finance and commercial services, have all flourished, showing a stronger growth momentum than trade in goods.

Overall speaking, the value of world trade in services is increasing. The period from 2005 to 2008 was a period of rapid development of world service trade. After 2008, affected by the global financial crisis, the growth of trade in services slowed down, and the total service trade value fell in 2009, basically the same as that in 2007, and after 2010, it showed a rapid growth momentum again. This growth momentum ended in 2015. In 2015, world service trade exports amounted to $4.7 trillion, down 6%. This trend is very similar to that of global trade in goods, which indicates that both trade in goods and trade in services were affected by the global economic downturn that year.

Similar to the global trade in goods, the service trade also regained growth in 2016, and the growth began to disappear in 2019. In 2020, compared with the trade in goods, the trade in services was more severely hit by the epidemic, and the trade value has fallen to the level of the 1990s, with a year-on-year decrease of 15.4%. The hit is particularly prominent in traditional service trade fields that rely on cross-border movement of people, such as travel. But in the long run, the epidemic has also greatly accelerated the digitalization of service trade, brought new opportunities for the structural adjustment of service trade and the development of new service trade, spawned some new business forms and modes such as telemedicine, shared platform and collaborative office, and expanded the development space of global service trade.

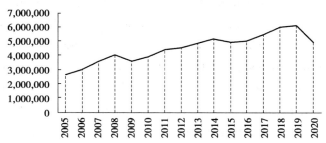

Figure 1.2　WTO data: world total trade in services (million USD)

Service trade barriers

Due to the concealment and non-quantitative nature of barriers to trade in services, the liberalization of trade in services is much more complex than the liberalization of trade in goods. There are more than 2,000 kinds of barriers to international trade in services, which can be roughly divided into four types.

①Barriers to people movement

International trade in services is usually inseparable from the cross-border movement of people between different countries. The barriers to personnel movement in international trade in services include restrictive policies for foreign workers to enter the domestic service market, namely immigration restrictions and various cumbersome entry and exit procedures. The movement of service providers or consumers across national borders is an indispensable part of the completion of transactions in international trade in services, especially in the forms of personnel movement such as commercial presence, cross-border consumption and the movement of natural persons. Restrictions on the cross-border movement of people will affect international trade in services. For example, the United Kingdom has restricted the number of foreigners going to its country by modifying the relevant entry policies.

②Barriers to product movement

The main form of service product movement barrier is to restrict the movement of service products. Usually, the government of a country will set the maximum amount of services provided. If the services provided by foreign service product providers exceed this maximum amount, their service products will be refused to enter the country for sale or circulation. Barriers to the movement of service products usually include government behavior, intellectual property protection, unfair technical standards, product quantity restrictions, product quality requirements, etc. For example, Canada and Switzerland restrict the import of foreign advertisements or data communications into their own countries. Intellectual property barriers mainly include patent technical barriers, trademark barriers and international technical standard barriers. As China's intellectual property system is not mature enough, it is at a disadvantage in breaking intellectual property barriers, and all parties need to work together to achieve a breakthrough in international intellectual property barriers.

③Barriers to capital movement

International settlement is an inevitable problem in both trade in goods and trade in services. As for service trade, most of it cannot be stored, which has to involve international direct investment. Since investment is involved, foreign exchange, inward and outward remittance will inevitably be involved. There are three types of capital movement barriers: foreign exchange control, floating exchange rate and restrictions on the remittance of investment income. Among them, foreign exchange control is the most important means, which can protect the country's emerging industries and develop the national economy.

④Barriers to the right of establishment

The barrier of business opening right is also known as the barrier of production and entrepreneurship. On the one hand, a country allows investors from other countries to set up production and operation institutions in its territory, but on the other hand, it restricts all aspects of the production and operation institutions it sets up, such as the location of institutions, the form of capital contribution, the proportion of ownership, the mode of operation, the scope of operation, and so on. A survey shows that more than 60% of US service industry investors believe that production and entrepreneurship barriers are the main obstacles to their trade in services.

1.5.3 Gravity model of trade

The idea of the gravity model of trade originates from the law of universal gravitation proposed by Isaac Newton in physics, which is that the mutual gravitation between two objects is proportional to the mass of two objects and inversely proportional to the distance between two objects. Jan Tinbergen in 1962 and Poyhonen P. in 1963 were the first to use the gravity model to study international trade. They independently used the gravity model to study and analyze bilateral trade flows and reached the same result: The scale of bilateral trade between the two countries is directly proportional to their total economic volume and inversely proportional to the distance between the two countries.

The basic form of the gravity model of trade is:

$$T_{ij} = A \times \frac{Y_i Y_j}{D_{ij}}$$

In which the T is the trade flow between country i and country j, Y the economic masses of countries, and D the distance between country i and country j, and A the gravitational constant.

Take the logarithm on both sides:

$$\ln(T_{ij}) = \beta_0 + \beta_1 \ln GDP_i + \beta_2 \ln GDP_j + \beta_3 \ln DIST_{ij} + \varepsilon$$

Since the gravity model was introduced into the study of measuring bilateral trade flows in the 1960s, it has been continuously expanded and improved. More and more literature use the gravity model to conduct empirical research on international trade. In the expanded gravity model, two types of variables are often added. One is to add dummy variables, such as if sharing a common language, a common border, a common colonial history, a common religion, and so on. The other is to add system quality indicator variables, such as whether they belong to the same preferential trade agreement or regional economic integration organization, government governance quality, contract implementation guarantee, etc.

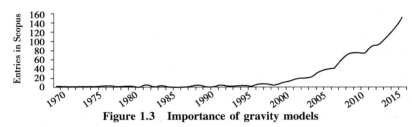

Figure 1.3　Importance of gravity models

Note: Show the number of entries in Scopus when using the search term "gravity model"

in the "economics" field

1.6　Brief introduction to the course

1.6.1　Learning objectives of this course

◆ Students can understand various analysis charts and tables related to international trade.

◆ Students can collect data related to international trade and make basic analysis.

◆ Students can understand the analysis of other factors affected by international trade, and remain sensitive to such articles.

◆ Students can understand the analytical text of the factors affecting international trade, and remain sensitive to such articles.

◆ Students can understand the text of international trade policy analysis and remain sensitive to such articles.

◆ Students should be able to read and be sensitive to articles on the impact of international trade on international political situation.

1.6.2　Contents of the course

　　Chapter 1 is an introduction to the course. Chapter 2 introduces basic concepts of international trade. These two chapters will introduce the concepts and development of international trade, help students identify the subtle differences between different concepts, and master the calculation methods of various statistical indicators of international trade. At the same time, the two chapters will also guide students to search various resources to obtain trade-related data, to understand the basic facts of global trade, and grasp the general development patterns. Chapter 3 introduces the analysis tools for standard theory of international trade.

　　Chapter 4 analyzes the classical theory of international trade. Chapter 5 analyzes the neo-classical theory of international trade, and Chapter 6 introduces new theory of international trade. All these chapters will concentrate on theories of international trade to find out why international trade can happen among countries and their gains through trade. Chapter 7 analyzes economic growth and international trade, trying to tell why international trade situation would change when economic development occurs.

Chapter 8 and Chapter 9 focus on trade policies, namely the tariffs and non-tariff trade barriers. Chapter 10 briefly introduces the economic integration of the world. Through the introduction of international trade policies, these chapters guide students to understand how countries achieve their foreign trade policy goals through various combinations of government tools, so as to promote their own economic growth and enhance the welfare of their own people.

1.6.3 The source disciplines of this course

◆ Philosophy: The development of the discipline of International Trade can be traced back to the origin of ancient philosophy. In ancient Greece, philosophers began to explore the essence of trade, currency, and exchange, which laid the foundation for later international trade theories. Over time, philosophers' views on trade gradually merged with those of economists. In the 17th and 18th centuries, many philosophers began to pay attention to the growth of national wealth and the impact of trade on national prosperity. The ideas of these philosophers provided important insights for the formation of modern international trade theory.

◆ Economics: The discipline of International Trade is an important branch in the field of economics, and can be said to be a derivative of Economics. The discipline of International Trade is based on the theories and methods of Economics to study the exchange behavior of goods and services in the international market and explain the underlying laws.

◆ International Economics (International Trade and International Finance): International Trade is one of the compulsory courses and one of the core basic courses for students majoring in economics and management. It is also the professional subject in the entrance examination for postgraduates majoring in finance and economics in many colleges and universities.

1.6.4 Relations with other courses

◆ Pre-courses: Macroeconomics and Microeconomics, especially Microeconomics. The relationship between Microeconomics and International Trade: They all study the allocation of resources by price mechanism, but Microeconomics is mainly aimed at one closed economy, and International Trade is aimed at open economies, which leads to differences in mobility of production factors and differences in obstacles from policies.

◆ Parallel courses: International Finance, International Marketing, Introduction to World Economy, International Business Negotiation, International Investment.

◆ Follow-up courses: International Trade Practice, WTO, International Transportation and Insurance, Import and Export Customs Declaration and Commodity Inspection, Foreign Exchange Business, Operation and Management of Multinational Corporations.

China-perspective case study

2022 China International Fair for Trade in Services

China International Fair for Trade in Services (CIFTIS), co-hosted by the Ministry of Commerce of the People's Republic of China and the People's Government of Beijing Municipality, is the world's first state-level, international and comprehensive and the first and by far the global largest comprehensive fair for trade in services. It is also an important window for the opening-up of China´s service industry. Since it was officially launched, CIFTIS has attracted 495 overseas institutions and business associations, and more than 1.7 million visits of attendees and exhibitors from 195 countries and regions.

The CIFTIS is positioned as a national, international and comprehensive trade fair in services. It is the only comprehensive service trade trading platform in the world that covers the 12 major areas of service trade defined by the WTO (including business services, communication services, construction and related engineering services, financial services, tourism and travel related services, entertainment, culture and sports services, transportation services, health and social services, education services, distribution services, environmental services, and other services).

The 2022 China International Fair for Trade in Services was held in Beijing from August 31 to September 5. The number, scale and internationalization rate exceeded the previous one. Another 10 countries were added, including the United Arab Emirates, Switzerland, Italy, Australia and other countries. The reason why CIFTIS can attract so many countries is that the scale of China's market is very large. According to relevant data, in the past 10 years, China's accumulated imports of services have exceeded $4 trillion. This is a huge market and a huge business opportunity, which is good for enterprises from all over the world, so it attracts foreign enterprises to participate in the exhibition.

At the annual CIFTIS, a signal of openness and cooperation can be sent to the world through speeches by national leaders, keynote speeches and policy releases by relevant ministries and commissions. The CIFTIS is an important platform for "introducing inside" and "going outside". On the one hand, China brings in foreign high-quality services and technologically advanced services, so that consumers and domestic enterprises can see and cooperate with them. At the same time, the fair also promotes and publicizes China's high-quality services and related enterprises that can represent China's service brands, so that partners and consumers around the world can know that we have such an excellent service brand. From these two aspects, China can improve the openness of China's service industry and service trade by holding the CIFTIS.

Key concepts

international trade	foreign trade	overseas trade	globalization
global supply chain	diversified world	division of labor	world market
capitalist mode of production	trade barriers	gravity model of trade	
International Trade (discipline)			

Summary

1. International trade, also known as world (global) trade, refers to the exchange of goods, technologies and services between different countries (or regions).

2. International trade is important for every country trades with other countries. We live in a globalized as well as a diversified world, where international trade is a necessity.

3. The emergence of international trade must meet the following conditions: There are surplus products available for exchange due to productivity development and the exchange of products is between different states. Therefore, fundamentally speaking, the development of social productive forces and the expansion of social division of labor are the basis for the emergence and development of international trade.

4. The development of international trade can be divided into three stages, which are international trade in the slave society, international trade in the feudal society, international trade in the capitalist society. Only in a capitalist society can international trade truly become worldwide. International trade under the capitalist mode of production can be further divided into four stages.

5. Entering the 21st century, the global trade in goods continues to grow. Especially China's entry into the WTO in 2001 greatly contributed to the growth of global trade. Before the

outbreak of the global financial crisis in 2008, the global trade in goods showed a good trend of steady growth. After the crisis and until 2015, the global trade in goods also grew slowly in fluctuations, but the growth rate declined.

6. After the Second World War, with the further expansion of economic globalization and the progress of information and communication technology, the proportion of services has gradually increased. Entering the 21st century, tourism trade, transportation, finance and commercial services, have all flourished, showing a stronger growth momentum than trade in goods.

7. The gravity model of trade suggests that the scale of bilateral trade between the two countries is directly proportional to their total economic volume and inversely proportional to the distance between the two countries.

Exercises

1. Go through your daily newspaper and identify two or three news items of international trade, and tell the importance or effect of these information on Chinese economy, as well as to you personally.

2. What are the causes of the emergence of international trade?

3. What is the main impact of the Industrial Revolution on international trade? What is the difference between international trade after the Industrial Revolution and that before the Industrial Revolution?

4. Is the geographical feature of China's foreign trade in accord with the gravity model of trade?

5. Please list some websites where you can find detailed international trade data.

Chapter 2 Basic Concepts

Learning goals

After learning this chapter, you should be able to:

✓ learn to calculate statistical indicators reflecting international trade situations.

✓ understand the economic implications behind these statistical indicators.

✓ grasp the meaning of basic concepts related to international trade.

✓ distinguish the subtle differences between concepts related to international trade.

This chapter focuses on the common statistical indicators and basic classification of international trade. When students study international trade issues, it is necessary to understand the basic types and classifications of international trade. People often use some basic statistics in analyzing and studying the development of world economy and trade. These are all important tools to study the international economic and trade issues. As we introduce these tools, we will use some specific examples of how these indicators reflect the changes and development of international trade. This chapter hopes to lay a good foundation for students to understand the international trade reality.

2.1 Statistical indicators

2.1.1 Trade value and trade volume

(1) Trade value

Trade value is the foreign trade scale of a country in a certain period expressed in monetary amount. Generally speaking, the export of one country is the import of another country. It should be true that the total world export is equal to the total import. But most countries (regions) calculate the export at FOB price, and the import at CIF price. CIF price is higher than FOB price in terms of freight and insurance, and the total world export is often less than the total world import.

trade value of a country = export value + import value

trade value of a country = merchandise trade value + service trade value

After the impact of the epidemic in 2020, global trade recovered strongly in 2021. According to the report issued by the WTO, the global trade grew by 26.1% in 2021, and the total amount rose to $44.803 trillion. Data shows that in 2021, China's total trade value exceeded $6 trillion, reaching $6.051 trillion, an increase of nearly 30%. China remained the world's largest trading country, and its share of global trade has increased to 13.51%.

(2) Trade volume

Foreign trade scale of a country in a certain period is expressed in constant prices, excluding the impact of price changes. The value of foreign trade expressed in currency is often affected by price changes, so it can not accurately reflect the actual scale of a country's foreign trade, let alone directly compare the value of foreign trade in different periods. It usually takes a certain year as the base period, divides the import and export price index by the import and export value, and then excludes the price change factor to obtain the trade value calculated at the constant price, that is, the foreign trade volume.

export trade volume = export trade value / export price index

2.1.2   Trade commodity structure

The structure of trade commodities refers to the proportion of the trade value of various commodities in the total trade value.

Composition of international trade commodities refers to the composition of various categories of commodities in the whole international trade within a certain period, that is, the trade value of various categories of commodities, expressed in proportion to the export trade value of the whole world.

Composition of foreign trade commodities refers to the composition of various commodities in a country's import and export trade within a certain period, that is, the ratio of import and export trade of a certain commodity to the total import and export trade volume, expressed in shares.

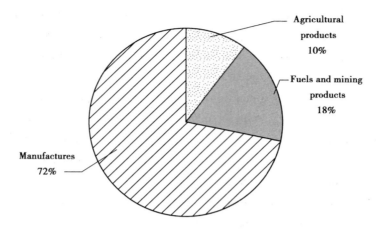

Figure 2.1　Commodity structure of global exports in 2021

2.1.3　Trade geographical structure

The geographical structure of world trade refers to the position of countries, continents and groups of countries in international trade in a certain period of time. It is usually expressed by the proportion of their exports or imports in the total world exports or imports. It can also calculate the proportion of countries' total imports and exports in the total international trade (total world imports and exports).

The geographical structure of foreign trade refers to the position of each country in the foreign trade of a country in a certain period, usually expressed by its proportion to the total imports, exports or imports of the country. The geographical direction of foreign trade indicates the source of imports and the destination of exports of a country, thus reflecting the degree of economic and trade ties between the country and other countries. In addition to historical reasons, the geographical direction of a country's foreign trade often depends to a large extent on its foreign policy. The geographical direction of foreign trade is used to indicate the position of countries, groups of countries or continents in international trade. The geographical direction of a country's foreign trade is often studied in combination with the structure of its import and export commodities, which is of great significance for identifying the whereabouts of different types of commodities in the country's exports and the sources of different types of commodities in imports.

For the United States, its main trade partners include China, Japan, Canada, Mexico and EU countries. And China's major trade partners include the United States, Japan and EU countries. According to the analysis of the proportion of individual trade volume of some major trade alliances in the total trade volume, China maintained about 60%, while the United States maintained 30%. It can be seen from this that the geographical direction of US foreign trade reflects a certain degree of diversification and enrichment, while China's current geographical direction of trade is relatively concentrated.

If there are cracks in cooperation and diplomatic relations between countries, or trade frictions caused by other policies, serious risks will arise. The centralization of trade geographical direction will bring many unstable factors to the country's foreign trade. If the import and export countries have an economic crisis or launch the import and export restriction policy, China will suffer serious economic losses, and the diversified and decentralized development of trade geography can better share the risks and losses.

2.1.4　Balance of foreign trade

Trade surplus occurs when the total export value of a country is greater than the total import value.

Trade deficit occurs when the total export value of a country is smaller than the total import value.

Trade balance occurs when the total export value of a country is equal to the total import value.

Case 2.1　China's trade surplus

Entering the 21st century, China has maintained a huge trade surplus in goods. In 2019, China's total import and export value of goods trade was 31.54 trillion yuan, an increase of 3.4% over 2018, among which, exports were 17.23 trillion yuan, an increase of 5% and imports were 14.31 trillion yuan, an increase of 1.6%. The trade surplus was 2.92 trillion yuan, an increase of 25.4%.

The trade surplus of China has the following characteristics. Firstly, lots of trade surplus comes from processing trade. The trade surplus of China's processing trade began to expand rapidly in 2004. By 2019, the export volume reached 5,267.6 billion yuan, while the import volume was 3,109.7 billion yuan, and the trade surplus was 2,157.9 billion yuan. Processing trade used to be the main source of China's trade surplus, but in recent years, with the increase in the proportion of general trade, the situation has changed.

Secondly, China's trade surplus is mainly concentrated in the field of labor-intensive products, and there is a trade deficit in the service trade. In 2019, the export value of service trade was 1,756.8 billion yuan, and the import volume was 3,474.4 billion yuan. Its trade deficit reached 1,708.6 billion yuan. It can be seen from this that China's foreign trade has the problem of unbalanced development, of which the foreign trade surplus is dominated by labor-intensive products.

Thirdly, China's processing trade surplus is geographically concentrated in developed countries and regions. China's trade surplus is concentrated in the EU, the United States, etc. Take the year 2006 as an example. China's trade surplus with the EU was $91.66 billion, the trade surplus with the United States $144.26 billion, with year-on-year growth of 30.7% and 26.2% respectively. During the same period, China's trade with other major trading partners showed a deficit, for example, the deficit with Japan was $24.08 billion, South Korea was $45.25 billion, and ASEAN was $18.22 billion. In 2018, observing several major trade provinces in China, we found that Zhejiang's trade surplus was $214.422 billion, of which the trade surplus with Europe and the United States accounted for more than half of the total trade surplus; Guangdong's foreign trade surplus was $201.497 billion, and its trade surplus with Europe and the United States accounted for more than 80%; Jiangsu's trade surplus with Europe and the United States is $130.533 billion, which is $13.3 billion higher than the total trade surplus.

Fourthly, China's processing trade surplus is mainly contributed by private and foreign-funded enterprises. For example, in 2006, China's total export value reached $969.07 billion, of which the export value of state-owned enterprises was $191.34 billion, accounting for 19.71% of the total. The export value of foreign-funded enterprises was $563.83 billion, accounting for 58.2% of the total. The private enterprises amounted to $213.9 billion, accounting for 22.1% of the total. In recent years, the proportion of private enterprises has increased, but the situation that foreign-funded enterprises and private enterprises jointly dominate China's foreign trade surplus still exists.

2.1.5 Net export and net import

If exports of a certain kind of goods in a certain period of time exceed imports, the difference is called net exports of the country. If imports exceed exports, the difference is called net imports.

Case 2.2   US soybean net exports

According to the data released by the US Department of Agriculture, in September 2022, the amount of soybeans exported by the United States to Chinese mainland reached 574,500 tons, a year-on-year decrease of 36.1%, accounting for 27.06% of the total US soybean exports.

In September 2022, the US soybean export volume was 2122900 tons, with a year-on-year growth of 1.2%. China was one of its major export markets.

From January to September 2022, the cumulative amount of soybeans exported by the United States to Chinese Mainland reached 11.1449 million tons, up 28.5% year on year, accounting for 37.81% of the total cumulative amount of soybeans exported by the United States, up 0.63 percentage points over the same period last year.

From January to September 2022, the cumulative export volume of American soybeans reached 29.4735 million tons, a year-on-year increase of 26.3%, and the contribution rate of the Chinese Mainland market to its soybean export growth reached 40.2%.

From October 2021 to September 2022, the cumulative amount of soybeans exported by the United States to Chinese Mainland reached 29.675 million tons, a year-on-year decrease of 5.3%, accounting for 50.51% of the total cumulative amount of soybeans exported by the United States, a year-on-year decrease of 5.45 percentage points.

From October 2021 to September 2022, the cumulative export volume of American soybeans reached 58,745,300 tons, a year-on-year increase of 3.8%.

2.1.6   Degree of dependence upon foreign trade

Degree of dependence upon foreign trade is also known as the foreign trade coefficient, referring to the proportion of a country's total foreign trade value (the sum of exports and imports) in the country's GDP.

Case 2.3   China's dependence on foreign trade

Since the 1980s, with the integration of China's economy into the world economy, foreign trade has grown rapidly. With the growth of foreign trade, China's dependence on foreign trade is also increasing.

From 1985 to 1990, with the gradual expansion of China's opening-up, exports grew slowly. In 1985, China's dependence on foreign trade was 23.1%, including 9.02% on exports and 14.08% on imports. In 1990, China's dependence on foreign trade reached 30% for the first time, including 16.05% on exports and 13.84% on imports. China's exports slowly caught up with and surpassed imports. At this stage, due to the shortage of domestic resources and the import of a large number of technical equipment, the import dependence was higher than the export dependence for many consecutive years.

From 1990 to 2000, during this period, China adopted a series of macroeconomic control measures, resulting in an average annual growth rate of 12.4% in export volume, which exceeded the average annual GDP growth rate of 8.8%. The rise of labor-intensive industries and the development of processing trade have led to a rapid growth of exports, with the degree of export dependence exceeding the degree of import dependence, promoting the steady rise of foreign trade. China's dependence on foreign trade also exceeded 40% in 1994.

Since 2001, China's accession to the WTO, economic globalization has further deepened, and the role of foreign trade in economic growth has become increasingly obvious. The growth rate of China's foreign trade is far higher than the growth of China's GDP and world trade. China's dependence on foreign trade has increased rapidly, exceeding 50% in 2002, reaching 63% in 2005, and reaching a high point of 67% in 2006. Since then, affected by China's economic transformation, domestic and foreign demand structural adjustment and the international financial crisis, China's dependence on foreign trade has gradually decreased since 2007, from 60.2% in 2008 to 50.1% in 2011 and 31.5% in 2020. It may further decrease in the future.

In terms of provinces and cities, Shanghai has the highest degree of dependence on foreign trade in China since 2000. In 2007, Shanghai's dependence on foreign trade reached 172.22% (the highest year). In addition to Shanghai, other provinces and cities with a high degree of dependence on foreign trade in China include Beijing, Guangdong, Tianjin, Zhejiang and Jiangsu.

2.1.7 Terms of trade

Terms of trade (TOT) refer to the proportion of how many units of foreign imported goods can be exchanged for each unit of goods exported by a country in a certain period of time, or the exchange rate. TOT can reflect the economic benefits of a country's foreign trade.

TOT = (export price index/import price index) × 100%

If the terms of trade index is greater than 1, it means that the export price is relatively higher than the import price, and the same amount of exported goods can be exchanged for more imported goods than before. The country's terms of trade in that year are better than the base period. That is, they are improved. If the terms of trade index is less than 1, it means that the export price is relatively lower than the import price, and the number of imported goods that can be exchanged for the same amount of exports is less than the original. The country's terms of trade in that year are more unfavorable than the base period, that is, worse.

However, it should be noted that even if the terms of trade of Country A are improved, we cannot judge that the trade situation of Country A has improved while that of Country B has deteriorated. Because changes in terms of trade are the result of the joint action of many forces that have an impact on the country and the rest of the world, we cannot determine the net impact of these forces on the welfare of a country solely by relying on changes in terms of trade.

Table 2.1 gives the terms of trade of the G7 for selected years from 1972 to 2014. The terms of trade were measured by dividing the index of export unit value by the index of import unit value, taking 2000 as 100. Table 2.1 shows that the terms of trade of the G7 countries fluctuated very widely over the years and were much lower in 2014 than in 1972 for the United States, Germany, and especially for Japan; a little lower for the United Kingdom, France, and Italy; and much higher in the past decade for Canada (primarily because of the sharp increase in the price of petroleum and of other commodities, of which Canada is a major primary exporter).

Table 2.1 Terms of trade of the G7

	1972	1974	1980	1985	1990	1995	2000	2005	2010	2014	Change (1972−2014)
United States	127	107	90	103	101	103	100	97	97	96	−31
Canada	96	109	107	94	97	97	100	117	120	122	26
Japan	109	81	59	66	84	115	100	83	68	59	−50
Germany	118	105	98	94	110	108	100	105	103	102	−16
United Kingdom	107	82	103	102	101	100	100	105	103	102	−5

continued

	1972	1974	1980	1985	1990	1995	2000	2005	2010	2014	Change (1972−2014)
France	101	89	90	89	100	107	100	111	100*	100*	−1*
Italy	106	80	78	78	94	96	100	101	99	103	−3

* Refers to 2008 and 1972−2008.

Table 2.2 gives the terms of trade of industrial countries, developing countries as a whole, as well as African, Asian, European, Middle Eastern, and Western Hemispheric developing countries for selected years from 1972 to 2014. The terms of trade were measured by dividing the index of export unit value by the index of import unit value, with 2000 as 100.

Table 2.2 shows that the terms of trade of industrial countries declined from 1972 to 1985 but then rose until 1995, and they were 98 in 2014, as compared with 110 in 1972. For developing countries, the terms of trade rose sharply from 1972 to 1980 primarily as a result of the very sharp increase in the terms of trade of Western Hemispheric countries, but they then declined until 1985 and they were 95 in 2014, as compared with 61 in 1972. The terms of trade of Africa increased from 85 in 1972 to 127 in 2012. From 1972 to 2014, the terms of trade of Asia declined sharply from 101 to 70 and for European developing countries from 112 to 96. The terms of trade rose sharply for the Middle East from 94 in 1972 to 124 in 2014 and for the Western Hemisphere from 39 in 1972 to 100 in 2014.

Although the terms of trade of industrial and developing countries reflected to a large extent the large fluctuations in the price of petroleum over the period examined, other forces were also clearly at work (note, for example, that the largest fluctuation was in the terms of trade of the Western Hemisphere, whose exports were mostly non-petroleum and that the terms of trade of the Middle East as a whole declined between 1972 and 1974 because many Middle Eastern countries did not export petroleum).

Table 2.2　Terms of trade of advanced and developing countries

	1972	1974	1980	1985	1990	1995	2000	2005	2010	2014
Industrial countries	110	97	89	87	100	105	100	101	100	98
Developing countries	61	86	107	101	103	102	100	99	106	95
Africa	85	118	117	115	100	103	100	108	104	127*
Asia	101	101	101	98	103	107	100	92	92	70

continued

	1972	1974	1980	1985	1990	1995	2000	2005	2010	2014
Europe	112	101	69	64	69	106	100	102	98	96
Middle East	94	75	90	80	109	68	100	140	134	124
Western Hemisphere	39	110	194	189	130	107	100	104	98	100

* = 2012

2.2　Basic classifications

2.2.1　By moving direction of goods

（1）Export trade

Export trade refers to the export of domestically produced or processed goods to overseas markets. The general process of export includes market research, quotation of export products, establishment of business relations, inquiry, offer, counter offer and acceptance, conclusion of contract, and performance of contract.

（2）Import trade

Import trade refers to the import of foreign goods into the domestic market for sale, generally including market research, signing of import contracts, completion of delivery procedures, settlement of all customs clearance fees, payment of foreign exchange for verification.

（3）Transit trade

Transit trade of Country C refers to the trade in which goods pass through Country C on the way from the producing Country A to the consuming Country B.

Transit trade can be divided into direct transit trade and indirect transit trade. Direct transit trade means that foreign goods arrive at a domestic port, and then, they leave the country from other ports through the domestic transportation under the direct supervision of the customs. Sometimes, they transit directly without unloading or changing the means of transportation. Indirect transit trade means that the foreign goods arrive at a domestic port, and before leaving the country, then they may be stored in the customs bonded warehouse, or may be re-selected or sorted, their packages may be changed.

Transit trade usually occurs between those landlocked countries adjacent to each other.

Transit duties/tariff, also known as "passage tax", refers to a tariff imposed by a country on foreign goods passing through its customs territory. In 1994, in accordance with the provisions the GATT, in addition to charging part of the service management fees for transit goods, the transit tariffs shall be exempted. At present, transit countries do not charge transit tariffs for transit trade.

If the trading commodities are carried flying over the airspace of a third country, the third country will not include them in its transit trade. Because crossing the airspace does not require customs clearance and inspection, but needs the permission of the Ministry of Foreign Affairs and the Ministry of National Defense of the country.

If transit trade is included in a country's total foreign trade statistics depends on the statistical standards of various countries. As far as China is concerned, goods passing through China should be included in the statistics of China's foreign trade.

Case 2.4　China-Europe Railway Express and transit trade

China-Europe Railway Express refers to the international railway trains running between China and Europe and countries along the Belt and Road according to fixed train numbers, lines and other conditions. There are three routes for China-Europe Railway Express. The western route from the central and western regions of China exits China via Alashankou (Khorgas) Xinjiang, the central route from north China exits China via Erenhot in Inner Mongolia, and the eastern route from northeast China exits China via Manzhouli (Suifenhe City) in Heilongjiang. In March 2011, the first China-Europe Railway Express train was sent from Chongqing China to Duisburg Germany, which opened a prelude to the innovative development of China-Europe Railway. Over the past 10 years, China-Europe Railway Express trains have exceeded 40,000 in total, with a total value of more than $200 billion. It has opened 73 operating lines and reached more than 160 cities in 22 countries in Europe. In these 10 years, the China-Europe Railway Express trains have opened a new chapter in the land transport between Asia and Europe and forged a bridge for mutual benefit and win-win cooperation between countries along the line.

China-Europe Railway Express trains pass through many countries, and transit trade often occurs. For example, the goods exported from Chongqing China to Germany are transported by the China-Europe Railway Express (Chengdu-Chongqing) train, creating transit trade for Kazakhstan, Russia, Belarus and Poland on the way. Although it transits many countries, goods from Chongqing are transported through the China-Europe Railway Express (Chengdu-Chongqing) train can enjoy mutual recognition of customs clearance and supervision along the way. All information can be shared by route countries, and only one declaration, one inspection and one release are required for the whole transportation process, which greatly saves transportation time and improves trade efficiency.

2.2.2   By forms of goods

（1）Tangible trade

Tangible trade refers to the import and export trade of commodities, or called merchandise trade. According to the 4th Revision of Standard International Trade Classification (SITC) by the United Nations (UN), tangible goods are assembled in 262 groups, 67 divisions and 10 sections, which contains 3,993 basic headings and subheadings. The SITC sections are as follows：

Section 0-Food and live animals；

Section 1-Beverages and tobacco；

Section 2-Crude materials, inedible, except fuels；

Section 3-Mineral fuels, lubricants and related materials；

Section 4-Animal and vegetable oils, fats and waxes；

Section 5-Chemicals and related products, n.e.s；

Section 6-Manufactured goods classified chiefly by material；

Section 7-Machinery and transport equipment；

Section 8-Miscellaneous manufactured articles；

Section 9-Commodities and transactions not classified elsewhere in SITC.

Generally speaking, the first five sections belong to primary products, and the last five sections belong to manufactured products.

Case 2.5   China's trade commodity structure

Due to the lack of capital and the relatively low level of technology, China's trade has experienced a pattern of exchanging industrial manufactured products from developed countries through the export of primary products. Because primary products are basically resource-intensive, their output does not have strict requirements on technology. At the initial stage of economic development,

China's rich natural resources endow it with comparative advantages over industrial finished products in the production of primary products. However, with the improvement of China's production technology, the gap between the production efficiency of industrial manufactured products and that of developed countries has gradually narrowed. At the same time, the high level of savings has made China's capital accumulation speed very high, and the capital stock has expanded rapidly, which has changed the basic situation of China's factor endowment to a great extent, and further led to fundamental changes in China's trade commodity structure.

Before 1994, China's primary product trade was always in surplus, and the surplus level began to decline after reaching its peak in 1985. In 1995, China's primary product trade showed a deficit for the first time, and since 1995, the deficit of primary product has been expanding. At present, China has become a major importer of primary products, especially in energy products and food products. However, China's trade in manufactured goods was in deficit before 1989, and the deficit level began to decline after reaching its peak in 1985. In 1990, China's industrial manufactured goods had a trade surplus for the first time. After that, except for the deficit in 1993, China's industrial manufactured goods were in a trade surplus in all years, and the trade surplus continued to expand. Therefore, the fundamental transformation of China's trade commodity structure began in the late 1990s. After that, China has changed to a net importer of primary products, and a net exporter of manufactured products.

As the main body of China's foreign trade and an important indicator to measure the industrial level, trade in industrial manufactured goods plays an important role in China's economic growth. Entering the 21st century, the commodity structure of China's import and export of manufactured products is gradually optimized. The proportion of high-tech products represented by machinery and transportation is rising. The proportion of low-tech products represented by textiles and rubber products is gradually decreasing. The main trade manufactured products are transitioning from labor-intensive products to capital and technology-intensive products. This also shows that China's overall competitiveness in foreign trade is gradually rising. China's light textile products have always maintained high competitiveness, and with the continuous export of mechanical transport products, the competitiveness of these capital and technology-intensive products in the international market has also steadily increased.

（2）Intangible trade

Intangible trade refers to the international exchange activities of buying and selling all goods without physical form. The goods used for exchange include various services related or unrelated to the occurrence of tangible trade. Intangible trade can also be called service trade in general. Because of the universality of service trade and the complexity of its occurrence, the definition of service trade can only be illustrative rather than normative.

At present, the definition of the General Agreement on Trade in Services （GATS） is quite authoritative and widely accepted by all countries. According to GATS, trade in services has four forms: cross-border supply, consumption abroad, commercial presence and movement of natural persons.

The cross-border supply means that people provide services inside their own territory to people inside the territory of other countries. Its characteristic is that service providers and consumers are located in different countries, and in the process of providing services, the service content itself has crossed the national border. For example, a consulting company in one country provides legal, management, information or other professional services to a customer in another country.

The consumption abroad refers to a country's service provider offering services within its territory to service consumers from any other countries in order to obtain remuneration. Its characteristic is that service consumers accept services in the territory of other countries. For example. The patients go abroad for medical treatment. Tourists travel abroad to receive tour services. Students and scholars go abroad to study.

The commercial presence, the most important way of providing services in GATS, refers to that a country's service provider establishes a commercial organization （affiliated enterprise or branch） in any other country's territory to provide services to consumers for remuneration. For example, if a telecommunications company of a country sets up a telecommunications operation institution abroad to participate in the competition in the telecommunications service market of the target country where it is located, it belongs to a "commercial existence". It is characterized by service providers （individuals, enterprises or economic entities） opening business abroad, such as investing in the establishment of joint ventures, cooperative or wholly-owned service enterprises （bank branches, restaurants, retail stores, accounting firms, law firms, etc.）.

Movement of natural persons refers to a country's natural person （service provider） providing services in any other country's territory for remuneration. Its characteristic is that service providers inside foreign countries provide services to service consumers. For example, experts and professors go abroad to give lectures and give technical advice and guidance, and cultural and art practitioners go abroad to provide cultural and entertainment services. For another example, Mr. X is a lawyer of member Country A. After he came to Country B, he did not set up his own law firm but directly provided legal advisory services.

The common ground between the movement of natural persons and commercial presence is that service providers provide services in the territory of the country where consumers are located. The difference is that the former service is provided through the movement of natural persons, and the service provider does not set up a commercial institution or professional institution in the territory of the country where the consumer is located. This kind of service is individual and temporary.

According to service industry characteristics, service trade can generally be divided into two big categories in statistics, one is commercial services and the other is government-provided services. Among them, commercial services occupy an absolutely important position, which can be further divided into four categories, namely goods-related services, transport, travel and other commercial services.

Technology trade is also a kind of service trade. Because of the particularity of technology compared with other ordinary service types, technology trade can also be listed separately for analysis. Technology trade is the transfer of a certain technology (the right to use patents, trademarks, know-how, or management techniques) by the technology exporter to the importer in the form of transaction.

Main modes of international technology trade include licensing trade, franchise, and technical service and consultation.

Licensing trade refers to a technology transaction in which the owner of intellectual property or know-how, as the licensor, signs a license contract with the licensee (the importer), grants the technology the licensor owns to the licensee, allows the licensee to use the technology, produce or sell contract products according to the conditions agreed in the contract, and the licensee pays a certain amount of technology use fee.

Franchise is a new type of technology transfer mode that has developed rapidly in the past 20 to 30 years. It refers to the technology trade behavior in which an enterprise that has obtained successful experience transfers its trademark, trade name, service mark, patent, know-how, mode or experience of operation and management to another enterprise for use, and the latter enterprise (the franchisee) pays a certain amount of royalties to the former enterprise (the franchisor).

Technical service and consultation refers to the activities in which independent experts or expert groups or consulting institutions, as service providers, provide high-knowledge services to the client on a specific technical subject at the request of the client, and the client pays a certain amount of technical service fees. The scope and content of technical services and consulting are quite wide, including product development, achievement promotion, technical transformation, engineering construction, science and technology management, etc., ranging from the engineering design and feasibility study of large-scale engineering projects to the improvement of a certain equipment and the control of product quality.

2.2.3 By the statistical scope of national foreign trade

According to the difference in statistical scope of national foreign trade in different countries, foreign trade can be divided into a general trade system and a special trade system, which is the exclusive concept of trade in goods. How a country counts products as its exports or imports depends on whether the country is adopting the general trade system or the special trade system.

A country adopts a general trade system if this country's goods value is included in its foreign trade when the goods cross the "national geographic border".

A country adopts a special trade system if this country's goods value is included in its foreign trade when the goods cross the "customs border". At the "customs border", the customs formalities for the goods are cleared.

As for "national geographic border" and "national customs border", the three situations are as follows:

Situation 1: "national geographic border" = "national customs border"

In general, the customs border is consistent with the national geographic border. Especially before the Second World War, the customs borders and the national geographic borders of most countries were consistent.

Situation 2: "national geographic border" > "national customs border"

Some countries have set up free trade zones or bonded zones inside their geographic territory, which are not within the customs territory but within the national geographic boundary.

Situation 3: "national geographic border" < "national customs border"

Some countries establish a customs union with each other, connecting the geographic territories of the countries participating in the customs union. At this time, the customs territory is larger than the national geographic territory. Customs union refers to the conclusion of an agreement between two or more countries to establish a unified customs territory. The contracting countries in the unified customs territory reduce or cancel tariffs among themselves, and implement common tariff rates and foreign trade policies for imports of goods from countries or regions outside the customs territory.

At present, there are about 90 countries and regions adopting the general trade system, including Japan, Britain, Canada, the United States, Australia, etc. About 83 countries and regions have adopted a special trade system, including Germany, Italy, France, etc.

Due to the different methods used by countries in compiling the trade data, the foreign trade volume data of countries published by the UN generally indicate the trade system adopted. China and the United States both adopt the general trade system.

2.2.4 By if participated by a third country

(1) Direct trade

The transaction of goods is directly between producing countries and consuming countries. The producing country is doing direct export and the consuming country is doing direct import.

(2) Indirect trade

The transaction of goods is between a producing country and a consuming country through a third country. The producing country is doing indirect export, and the consuming country is doing indirect import.

(3) Entrepot trade

The transaction of goods is between a producing country and a consuming country through a third country. For the third country, it is entrepot trade (intermediary trade). In entrepot trade, goods can be transported directly or indirectly.

The difference between entrepot trade and transit trade is whether the ownership of goods has been transferred. In transit trade, the ownership of goods has not been transferred, the third country is not involved in commodity transactions, and the third country cannot make commercial profits through a transit trade. In entrepot trade, the ownership of goods has been transferred, the third country is directly involved in commodity transactions, and the third country can make huge profits through entrepot trade.

Because entrepot trade may earn high profits, and it does not necessarily require transportation and warehousing, namely, the operation cost is not high, entrepot trade is very active in practice.

The exporters choose a third party for entrepot trade when exporting countries encounter huge trade barriers from importing countries.

Case 2.6　"Made in China" encounters anti-dumping and entrepot trade solutions

In recent years, the rise of "made in China" has set off a wave of Chinese products circulating around the world. However, opportunities come with challenges. When more "made in China" goes to the world, it encounters serious anti-dumping obstacles. At present, the global anti-dumping cases are generally on the rise, and China is the first to be affected. Many countries have begun to collect large tariffs on many products made in China, resulting in local enterprises not wanting to import products from China, which is a large loss for Chinese manufacturers who have developed foreign markets. Many Chinese manufacturers have no choice but to turn to entrepot trade in third countries, export through Southeast Asian countries for example. It can help Chinese sellers continue to export, maintain old foreign customers and keep foreign markets. It can also reasonably solve the problem of high tariffs.

For example, a batch of Chinese goods are exported to the United States when the United States imposes high tariffs on China. Since the United States does not impose high tariffs on Malaysia, the specific methods to solve the problems of high tariffs are:

Step 1: Normal export from Chinese ports to Malaysia.

Step 2: Unload the goods after they arrive in Malaysia.

Step 3: Export the cabinet from Malaysia to the destination country, the United States.

Step 4: Provide a full set of customs clearance documents such as the certificate of origin of the third country in Malaysia.

Through these four steps, the origin identification will be successfully converted to the origin of being made in Malaysia.

The exporters choose a third party for entrepot trade also when exporting enterprises need the help of a third party to develop unfamiliar foreign markets.

The exporters choose a third party for entrepot trade also when exporting enterprises want to take advantage of opportunities to make extra profits: by tax avoidance and avoiding the risk of exchange rate fluctuations.

The above third reason induces the arbitrage motive for domestic enterprises to conduct entrepot trade. Entrepot trade has the characteristics of "both ends are abroad". The domestic enterprise, also the third party, only acts as a middleman, and both the seller and the buyer are overseas. As it is a cross-border trade, the trade background is easy to "forge" and the authenticity is difficult to identify. Besides, entrepot trade has the characteristics of a mismatch between cargo logistics and capital flow. The exporting goods do not pass through domestic ports, and there is no official data such as customs declaration or entry record list, which provides convenience for enterprises to fabricate.

Enterprises obtain cross-border income through fictitious entrepot trade background, which is the behavior of making use of interest rate difference and exchange rate difference between domestic and overseas to earn profits. Enterprises use the channels of banks to avoid the policy red line and realize arbitrage, which is not illegal, but taking advantage of the loopholes of polices frequently is easy to commit crimes. It is not recommended anyway.

For the country or region where the intermediary (the third party) is located, the entrepot trade generally must meet two conditions. Firstly, natural conditions, that is, the port of the intermediary country must be a deep-water port with strong handling capacity, superior geographical location, and located in the traffic hub between countries or the main international route. Secondly, artificial conditions, that is, the intermediary countries are required to adopt special tariff preferential policies and trade policies, such as free ports and free trade zones, so that the entrepot trade costs will not be too high. At the same time, it is required that the infrastructure, transportation, finance, information and other service systems of this place be developed and complete, so as to facilitate the entrepot trade.

Malaysia, for example, has become one of the best choices of entrepot trade for overseas businessmen. Firstly, Malaysia's superior geographical location makes it a world-class maritime and shipping transportation hub. Secondly, the Malaysian government has signed free trade agreements with many countries, issuing open foreign investment policy and various tax preferential policies. Thirdly, Malaysia has high-quality human resources, reasonable labor costs, sound infrastructure, convenient road transportation, reliable customs documents and global shipping routes. Fourthly, Malaysia has a stable political system, economic and trade environment, and harmonious relations among all ethnic groups.

2.2.5　By modes of freight transportation

（1）Trade by ocean transportation

In the international trade, seaway (ocean) transportation is the most important mode of transportation, accounting for more than 80% of the total international cargo transportation. The reason why ocean transportation is so widely used is that compared with other modes of transportation, it has the obvious advantages: large capacity and low freight.

(2) Trade by land transportation

Land transportation of international goods mainly includes railway transportation and roadway transportation, in which, railway transport is the main mode of transport next to ocean transport. Most of the import and export goods transported by sea are concentrated and evacuated by railway transport. Railway transportation is generally not affected by climate conditions, which can ensure normal transportation throughout the year. Besides, it has large volume, fast speed and high continuity. The disadvantage is that the initial investment of the railway is large. On the contrary, the roadway transportation has the characteristics of flexibility, speed and convenience, especially in the realization of "door-to-door" transportation. However, road transportation also has some shortcomings, such as limited cargo capacity, high transportation cost, and easy to cause cargo damage accidents.

(3) Trade by air transportation

Air transportation is a modern mode of transportation, which has the advantages of fast transportation speed, high cargo quality, and not limited by ground conditions. It is most suitable for transporting emergency supplies, precision instruments and valuables.

(4) Trade by pipeline transportation

Pipeline transportation is a special mode of transportation. It is a mode of transportation in which goods are transported to the destination by means of the pressure of the high-pressure air pump in the pipeline, which is mainly applicable to the transportation of liquid and gas goods. It has the characteristics of large fixed investment and low transportation cost after completion.

(5) Trade by multimodal transport

International multimodal transport of goods refers to the form of transport organization in which the multimodal transport operator is responsible for transporting goods from the place where the goods are received in one country to the place where the goods are delivered in another country by two or more modes of transport in accordance with the multimodal transport contract. This multimodal transport mode combines different modes of transport into a comprehensive integrated transport. Through only one consignment, one billing, one document and one insurance, the carriers in each transport section jointly complete the whole transport of goods. International multimodal transport is developed on the basis of container transport in the 1960s.

In the 1960s, the United States was the first country to pilot multimodal transport, which was welcomed by cargo owners. Subsequently, international multimodal transport was adopted in North America, Europe and the Far East. In the 1980s, international multimodal transport has been gradually implemented in developing countries. At present, international multimodal transport has become a new and important mode of international container transport, which has been widely valued by the international shipping community. The UN Convention on International Multimodal Transport came into being at the UN meeting held in Geneva in May 1980. The convention entered into force one year after 30 countries ratified and acceded to it. Its entry into force has a positive impact on the future development of international multimodal transport.

There are many advantages in developing international container multimodal transport, mainly in the following aspects:

Firstly, it can simplify the procedures of consignment, settlement and claim settlement, and save manpower, material resources and related expenses. Under the international multimodal transport mode, no matter how far the goods are transported, it is completed by several modes of transport together, and no matter how many times the goods are changed during the transportation, all transportation matters are handled by the multimodal transport operator. The shipper only needs to handle one consignment, sign a transportation contract, pay the fees and insurance once, thus saving the shipper much inconvenience in handling the consignment procedures. At the same time, because multimodal transport uses a single freight document and unified billing, it can also simplify the procedures of document preparation and settlement, saving manpower and material resources. In addition, once goods are damaged or damaged during transportation, the multimodal transport operator is responsible for the whole transportation, which can also simplify the claim settlement procedures and reduce the claim settlement costs.

Secondly, it can shorten the transportation time of goods, reduce the inventory, reduce the accidents of goods damage and difference, and improve the quality of goods. Under the mode of international multimodal transport, each transport link and various means of transport cooperate closely, link up tightly, transfer goods quickly and timely wherever they go, greatly reducing the stay time of goods in transit, thus fundamentally ensuring the safe, rapid, accurate and timely delivery of goods to the destination, thus reducing the inventory volume and inventory cost of goods accordingly. At the same time, multimodal transport uses containers as the transportation unit for direct transportation. Although the freight has to be changed many times on the way, because professional machinery is used for loading and unloading, and the goods in the tank are not involved, the accidents of damage and difference of goods are greatly reduced, which greatly improves the transportation quality of goods.

Thirdly, it can reduce the transport costs and save various expenses. Since multimodal transport can carry out door-to-door transport, for the cargo owner, after the goods are handed over to the first carrier, he can obtain the cargo documents and settle foreign exchange according to them, thus advancing the time of settlement of foreign exchange. This not only accelerates the turnover of funds occupied by goods, but also reduces the expenditure of interest. In addition, since the goods are transported in containers, in a sense, the expenses of packaging, tallying and insurance of the goods can be correspondingly saved.

2.2.6 By numbers of participating countries

(1) Bilateral trade

Bilateral trade refers to the trade between two countries or regions.

(2) Multilateral trade

Multilateral trade refers to the trade between governments of multiple countries under agreed trade rules and regulatory mechanisms. For example, the trade carried out by countries in the WTO belongs to multilateral trade.

2.2.7 By settlement instruments

(1) Spot exchange trade

The spot exchange trade is also called free-liquidation trade, referring to trade settlement in international currencies. The payment currencies should be convertible currencies in the international financial market.

(2) Barter trade

The barter trade is to trade goods or services without the exchange of money. Barter trade, with the help of modern information technology, through many efficient and practical barter platforms, effectively integrates the remaining assets and realizes the rapid exchange of resources. It has become an important means for enterprises to break through regional restrictions, achieve free docking, and solve the shortage of funds and overstocked products. It also can realize the exchange of various advertising resources, so as to enhance the status and brand value of the enterprise.

(3) Compensation trade

The compensation trade, also known as product resale, means that one party to the transaction imports equipment on the basis of the credit provided by the other party, and then uses the products produced by the equipment to offset the price and interest of the imported equipment in installments.

For compensation trade and barter trade, both are direct exchanges between the buyer and the seller, generally no currency circulation occurs, and currency is only a means of pricing in these trade. However, they have big differences. Barter trade is the exchange of goods, usually one-time, and the transaction is completed at the same time. Compensation trade is the repayment by instalments. It is a multiple buying and selling behavior that lasts for a long time. This leads to a comparatively high risk in compensation trade.

Besides, in barter trade, there is generally no connection between the commodities exchanged, but there may be a connection between the commodities exchanged in compensation trade. Moreover, the party providing technology and equipment generally provides assistance and participates in the production process in order to make the technology and equipment put into production smoothly. This leads to a higher responsibility for compensation trade.

Therefore, compared with the re-popularity of barter trade, compensation trade is gradually declining. At present, the lease trade, instead, is very active. The lease trade refers to that the lessor delivers the goods to the lessee for use within a certain period of time in the form of lease and collects the rent on schedule. Similar to compensation trade, movable property is the target goods, which is relatively expensive, such as electronic computers, aircraft, ships, automobiles, mining equipment, textile machinery, agricultural machinery, etc. In recent years, it has been expanded to complete sets of factories and large complete sets of equipment. The lease trade has lower risk, lower cost and higher flexibility than compensation trade.

Case 2.7　Internationalization of RMB

Internationalization of RMB refers to the process that RMB can cross national boundaries, circulate abroad, and become the internationally recognized pricing, settlement and reserve currency. Although the circulation of RMB overseas does not mean that the RMB has been internationalized, the expansion of the circulation of RMB overseas will eventually lead to the internationalization of RMB and make it become the world currency.

The cross-border trade RMB settlement pilot launched by China in 2009 has opened a new chapter of RMB internationalization. At the end of 2015, the RMB was approved to be included in the Special Drawing Right (SDR) basket by the Executive Board of the IMF, marking the international acceptance and recognition of the internationalization of the RMB. Since then, although the domestic stock market and foreign exchange market have been shaken, the internationalization of

RMB has been steadily promoted.

By the end of 2020, the central banks of more than 75 countries and regions had included RMB in their foreign exchange reserves. By the end of May 2022, the inter-bank bond market had attracted 77 foreign central bank institutions. By the end of May 2020, 230 institutions including the IMF and 15 countries and regions had received a total RQFII investment of 723 billion yuan. By the end of June 2022, a total of 40 overseas central bank institutions had signed bilateral local currency swap agreements with the People's Bank of China, with a total agreement value of 3.66 trillion yuan.

By the end of 2020, the People's Bank of China had authorized 27 overseas RMB clearing banks, covering 25 countries and regions. The rapid development of RMB offshore business in London and New York further demonstrates the potential of RMB as a global international currency.

The People's Bank of China said that in the next stage, it will adhere to the principle of meeting demand and "natural conditions", adhere to market-driven and enterprise-independent choice, further improve the policy support system and infrastructure arrangements for cross-border use of RMB, promote two-way opening of financial markets, develop the offshore RMB market, create a more convenient environment for market players to use RMB, and further improve the prudent management framework for cross-border capital flows, and keep the bottom line of no systemic risk.

2.2.8   By types of trade policies

(1) Free trade

The state government does not intervene and restrict import and export trade activities in free trade.

(2) Protective trade

The state government restricts imports through high tariffs, import licenses, foreign exchange controls and other measures. At the same time, it gives subsidies and preferential treatment to its export commodities to encourage exports.

2.2.9   By types of trade documents

(1) Documentary trade

Payment based on the exchange of documents and other commercial documents in international trade.

（2）Electronic data interchange

Trade information such as transaction, transportation, insurance and customs can be exchanged and shared between relevant departments through an electronic information system.

Case 2.8　China's efforts and achievements in trade facilitation

The year 2021 marks the 20th anniversary of China's accession to the World Trade Organization (WTO). In the past twenty years, China has been a firm supporter of, an active participant in and an important contributor to the multilateral trading system. China has fully delivered on its accession commitments. By 2010, China had fulfilled all of its tariff reduction commitments, reducing the average tariff level from 15.3% in 2001 to 9.8%. China's further voluntary moves to cut tariffs brought its overall tariff level further down to the current 7.4% in 2021.

China has focused trade facilitation on the following areas:

First, China fully implements the WTO Trade Facilitation Agreement. Since the Trade Facilitation Agreement came into effect in February 2017, the Chinese government has actively implemented various trade facilitation measures required by the Agreement. In January 2020, China notified the WTO that it implemented measures in the Agreement ahead of schedule, such as the establishment and publication of average release times. China has 100% implemented various measures under the Trade Facilitation Agreement.

Second, China continues to reduce the time to clear import and export through customs. In June this year, the time to clear import through customs was 36.7 hours, 62.3% lower than that of 2017. The time to clear export through customs was 1.8 hours, 85.2% shorter than that of 2017.

Third, China continues to reduce the number of documents required by regulation during import and export. Relevant departments have reduced the items for approval during import and export and improved regulatory requirements in accordance with law. In July this year, the number of documents to be verified during import and export required by regulation was reduced from 86 in 2018 to 41, a decrease of 52.3%.

Fourth, FTAs and PFTZs have effectively promoted trade facilitation. To date, China has signed 19 FTAs with 26 countries and regions, covering transparency, release of goods, customs cooperation and other provisions, playing a positive role in streamlining customs procedures, improving clearance efficiency and facilitating cross-border movement of goods. PFTZs have actively explored trade facilitation and have replicated and promoted 79 institutional innovations of trade facilitation across China.

Fifth, enhancing and expanding the "single window" for international trade. Currently, many import and export certificates, including automatic import licenses and export licenses, go 100% paperless in application.

The Chinese government will continue to promote trade liberalization and facilitation, unswervingly advance high-level opening-up, and boost high-quality development of trade to share its own development opportunities with the world, realizing win-win and common development for a community with a shared future for mankind.

2.2.10　By technical level of traded goods

(1) Horizontal trade

Exchange between commodities at a similar technical level usually occurs between countries with roughly the same economic level.

(2) Vertical trade

Exchange of products with different technical levels generally occurs between countries or regions with different economic levels.

Through trade liberalization, developing economies have improved the level of vertical specialization, occupied a place in the global value chain, and promoted their own industrial development and industrial upgrading.

2.2.11　By ways of selling

(1) Exclusive sales

The exporter and the foreign distributor reach an agreement to grant the exclusive right to sell the designated goods in the designated area to the distributor within a certain period of time. The distributor promises not to sell the same or replaceable goods from other sources.

For exporters, the main purpose of adopting exclusive sales is to establish a stable and developing market in a specific region by using the funds and sales capacity of the exclusive sellers. As far as the underwriters (exclusive distributors) are concerned, they are in a favorable position in the sales of designated commodities because they have obtained the monopoly right, thus avoiding the situation of price reduction and profit reduction caused by multi-head competition. Therefore, the exclusive distributor has high business enthusiasm and can make more investment in advertising promotion and after-sales service.

As the exclusive distributor buys out the goods and then sells them by himself, the distributor needs to have a certain capital investment and bear the sales risk. If the distributor is short of capital or sales capacity, it may form a dilemma of sales failure. Therefore, for exporters, choosing a suitable distributor is the key to the successful adoption of exclusive sales.

(2) Agency

Within the agreed region and time limit, the agent is engaged in trade-related business on a commission basis in the name and capital of the principal. The agent only acts on behalf of the principal, such as looking for customers, signing sales contracts, handling the goods, receiving payment for goods, etc.

According to the different authorities granted by the principal to the agent, the sales agent can be divided into three types: general agent, exclusive agent, and commission agent.

General agent is the representative of the client. Represent customers in sales and other large commercial transactions in specific fields.

Exclusive agent has exclusive rights to the specified goods within the time range and region specified in the agency agreement. The principal shall not sell on its own or on behalf of any other party within the scope specified above.

Commission agent has no exclusive franchise rights. The principal can entrust the sales of the same product to multiple agents in the same region at the same time. The range of his commission is the amount of his own transactions. There can be multiple commission agents in the same region.

(3) Consignment

The consignor first transports the goods to the place of consignment, and entrusts a foreign consignee to sell the goods on behalf of the consignor according to the conditions stipulated in the consignment agreement. After the goods are sold, the consignee settles the payment with the consignor.

(4) Fair and sales

Exhibitions, expositions and other trade fairs are held to exhibit and sell commodities. The advantages of the exhibition are mainly shown in four aspects: Firstly, it is conducive to publicizing export products, expanding influence, attracting potential buyers and promoting transactions. Secondly, it is conducive to establishing and developing customer relations and expanding the sales area and scope. Thirdly, it is beneficial to carry out market research, hear consumers' opinions, improve commodity quality and enhance export competitiveness. Fourthly, at the same time of purchasing and selling goods, the exhibitors will display the full picture of their economic achievements and exchange economic information.

2.2.12　By modes of trade

(1) General trade

General trade refers to the trade of unilateral import or unilateral export by enterprises with import and export management rights in China. General trade is a trade mode opposite to processing trade.

(2) Processing trade

The enterprises import all or part of raw and auxiliary materials, parts and components, and re-export finished products after processing or assembly. The processing trade is normally classified into two categories.

Processing with given materials: The production materials and parts are provided by overseas enterprises free of charge. Processing or assembly are carried out according to the requirements of overseas enterprises, and only the processing fees are charged. Finished products are sold by overseas enterprises. Producing enterprises do not bear economic risks, and there is no transfer of ownership of raw materials and finished products.

Processing with imported materials: The production materials and parts shall be imported by the producing enterprise, and the finished products shall be exported by the producing enterprise. The importing enterprise may have a sales contract signed or unsigned when importing the materials.

——— *China-perspective case study* ———

China's processing trade

Since China's reform and opening-up, processing trade has gone through the development process of "three supplies and one compensation", "processing with imported materials" and "processing and export with foreign capital", and has always occupied an important position in China's exports. Processing trade has played an important role in promoting China's industria-lization, introducing foreign capital, driving employment and upgrading the industrial structure.

China's processing trade policy has gone through five stages: preliminary exploration, encouraging standardization, strengthening supervision, policy improvement and innovative development. The exploration, guidance and standardization of the development of processing trade in the early stage laid a good foundation for China to participate in the international division of labor and integrate into the global production system. After China's entry into WTO, the regulatory policy of processing trade tends to be strict, and the processing trade has entered a stable development stage.

Specifically, the development of China's processing trade experienced a stable development stage from 2000 to 2006 and a deep adjustment stage from year 2007 to 2014. The proportion of processing trade exports decreased from 55.2% in 2000 to 32.7% in 2014. The trade pattern structure of China's export products has changed from a pattern of common development of general trade and processing trade to a pattern dominated by general trade patterns.

In the process of transformation and upgrading of processing trade, the proportion of imported processing exports has decreased significantly, but imported processing exports have always been the main production and operation mode of China's processing trade. The proportion of processing exports with supplied materials has fluctuated at 10% since 2005, indicating that a certain proportion of China's export products are still produced and exported in the form of simple processing and assembly with supplied materials.

In terms of the distribution of export regions, China's coastal and inland regions have obvious structural imbalances in the development of foreign trade. From 2000 to 2006, China's coastal areas contributed about 90% of the export share, and the export of coastal areas accounted for more than 97% of the export products of processing trade, occupying an absolute leading position. Since 2007, the opening-up level of inland areas has improved, and the export share has increased from 15.2% in 2007 to 23% in 2014. As there is a big gap between inland areas and coastal areas in terms of industrial supporting facilities and transport costs, the mechanism for the transfer of processing trade from eastern coastal areas to inland areas needs to be established and improved, which is an urgent problem to be solved in the transformation and upgrading of China's processing trade.

In terms of the types of export entities of processing trade, foreign-funded enterprises dominated the export business entities of China's processing trade from 2000 to 2006. China's accession to the WTO has provided opportunities for foreign-funded enterprises to carry out processing trade in China. The export share of processing trade of wholly foreign-owned enterprises has increased year by year, from 38% in 2000 to 61% in 2006. The proportion of processing trade exports of foreign-funded enterprises increased from 70% in 2000 to 84% in 2006. Since 2007, the proportion of domestic enterprises and foreign-funded enterprises in the composition of processing trade operators has been relatively balanced. Domestic-funded processing trade enterprises accounted for about 40%. Among them, the ability of private enterprises to participate in international production division has been significantly enhanced, and the export share of processing trade has increased from 4% in 2006 to 18% in 2014.

Key concepts

trade value	trade volume
trade commodity structure	trade geographical structure
trade surplus	trade deficit
net export	net import
terms of trade	merchandise trade
trade in services	transit trade
general trade system	special trade system
entrepot trade	barter trade
lease trade	trade by exclusive sales
trade by agency	processing trade

Summary

1. The value of foreign trade expressed in currency is often affected by price changes, so it can not accurately reflect the actual scale of a country's foreign trade. Trade volume is the foreign trade scale of a country in a certain period expressed in constant prices,

excluding the impact of price changes.

2. Entering the 21st century, China has maintained a huge trade surplus in goods, but has the trade deficit in services.

3. Since the 1980s, with the integration of China's economy into the world economy, foreign trade has grown rapidly. With the growth of foreign trade, China's dependence on foreign trade is also increasing.

4. Terms of trade refer to the proportion of how many units of foreign imported goods can be exchanged for each unit of goods exported by a country in a certain period of time, or the exchange rate. TOT can reflect the economic benefits of a country's foreign trade.

5. Transit trade of Country C refers to the trade in which goods pass through Country C on the way from the producing Country A to the consuming Country B. Transit trade can be divided into direct transit trade and indirect transit trade.

6. According to the 4th Revision of Standard International Trade Classification (SITC) by the United Nations (UN), tangible goods are assembled in 262 groups, 67 divisions and 10 sections, which contains 3,993 basic headings and subheadings. Generally speaking, the first five sections belong to primary products, and the last five sections belong to manufactured products.

7. According to GATS, trade in services has four forms: cross-border supply, consumption abroad, commercial presence and movement of natural persons.

8. According to the difference of statistical scope of national foreign trade in different countries, foreign trade can be divided into general trade system and special trade system, which is the exclusive concept of trade in goods.

9. The difference between entrepot trade and transit trade is that whether the ownership of goods has been transferred. In transit trade, the ownership of goods has not been transferred, the third country is not involved in commodity transactions, and the third country cannot make commercial profits through a transit trade. In entrepot trade, the ownership of goods has been transferred, the third country is directly involved in commodity transactions, and the third country can make huge profits through entrepot trade.

10. In the international trade, seaway (ocean) transportation is the most important mode of transportation, accounting for more than 80% of the total international cargo transportation.

11. Compared with the re-popularity of barter trade, compensation trade is gradually declining. At present, the lease trade, instead, is very active.

12. According to the different authorities granted by the principal to the agent, the sales

agent can be divided into three types: general agent, exclusive agent and commission agent.

13. The processing trade is that the enterprises import all or part of raw and auxiliary materials, parts and components, and re-export finished products after processing or assembly. The processing trade is normally classified into two categories: processing with given materials and processing with imported materials.

Exercises

1. In a year, the world's export trade value of goods was \$3.2 trillion, and the import trade value was \$3.3 trillion. The international trade value of goods in that year was _____ .
   A. \$0.1 trillion   B. \$3.2 trillion
   C. \$6.5 trillion   D. \$3.3 trillion

2. Xiao Zhang works in a machine equipment Company A in China. Company A has sold a large number of equipment to Company B in the United States. Now Company B has problems using this batch of equipment. Company A sends Xiao Zhang to Company B in the United States for investigation and equipment maintenance. This belongs to _____ .
   A. cross-border delivery   B. consumption abroad
   C. commercial presence   D. movement of natural persons

3. The similarities between exclusive sales and exclusive agents are _____ .
   A. Both are "buying and selling" relations
   B. Both are agency relations
   C. Both enjoy franchise rights
   D. Both are to earn price difference
   E. Both commodities are restricted to a fixed time and a fixed region

4. True or false question: Direct trade cannot be transported indirectly, while entrepot trade can be transported directly.   (   )

5. True or false question: China has maintained a huge trade surplus in services in the 21st century.   (   )

Chapter 3 / The Analysis Tools of International Trade Theories

Learning goals

After learning this chapter, you should be able to:

✓ review the general equilibrium analysis in microeconomics using the production possibility curve and the indifference curve.

✓ understand the general equilibrium in isolation and openness.

✓ show how the equilibrium price at which trade takes place is determined.

✓ show how the equilibrium price at which trade takes place is determined with offer curves.

As the extension and expansion of microeconomics under the open conditions, the analysis tool of international trade theory also mainly adopts the microeconomic analysis method. People are motivated by international trade, as much as domestic trade, for their own interests. That is, consumers pursue personal utility maximization and manufacturers pursue profit maximization. Therefore, the theory of manufacturer and theory of consumer behavior in microeconomics are very beneficial to the analysis of problems related to international trade. One difference is that in the absence of trade, the domestic market is called closed market, and the equilibrium price is determined by domestic supply and demand; In the case of international trade, the domestic market is called open market, and the equilibrium price is affected by domestic supply and demand, and also by foreign supply and demand, namely import and export.

The analysis of international trade theory relies on some mathematical tools to explain various economic relations more accurately. In order to make readers understand these common analytical methods before formally learning international trade theory, the main analytical tools used in this book are briefly introduced.

3.1　Three key questions in international trade

International trade theory is in a dynamic process of continuous development, and there are many kinds of theories. However, all theories are trying to answer at least the following three questions:

(1) What is the basis for trade?

The basis of international trade is equal to the question that why international trade occurs. What is the motivation of each country to move from the initial closed state to the open state? What triggered the emergence of international trade behavior?

(2) What is the pattern of trade?

The pattern of international trade is also called the mode of international trade, trying to answer what goods countries export and import, with whom.

(3) What are the gains from trade?

The gains from international trade refer to what benefits countries have gained, or what losses countries have suffered, from participating in international trade. Other questions that need to be answered include how much these benefits and losses are, and how they are divided among trading countries.

3.2　Production possibility curve

Production possibility curve or production possibility frontier is the combination of the maximum quantity of various commodities that can be produced by the economy under the given resources and technical conditions.

Production possibility curve normally has the following assumptions:

- Only two goods are produced.
- At a certain time, the number of various factors of production available is fixed.
- In the production process, all production factors have been fully used, and there are no idle resources.
- Within the time range of consideration, production technology, that is, the ability to convert input into output, is fixed.

It can be seen from Figure 3.1 that the productivity possibility curve is a curve with negative slope and concave to the origin. Its economic meaning can be explained as follows.

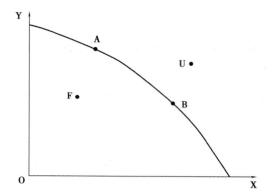

Figure 3.1　Production possibility curve

The production possibility curve reveals the law of scarcity. No economy can produce unlimited quantities, and the points outside the production possibility frontier represent the output com-binations that are impossible to achieve under modern conditions.

Any economy must make a choice. But it is impossible to select two different points at the same time. At the same time, deciding to produce at a certain point on the production possibility curve means deciding the allocation of resources.

The choice has to pay a price, and the slope of the production possibility curve is negative, indicating that it is necessary to reduce the output of another product in order to increase the production potential of one product.

The price paid for selection is the opportunity cost. The slope of any point on the production possibility curve represents the opportunity cost of X at the output level. The production possibility curve concave to the origin reflects the law of increasing opportunity cost. It means that as the output of product X increases, the output of product Y that needs to be abandoned for each unit of product X increases, or the opportunity cost of product X increases with the increase of its output.

Why can the law of increasing opportunity cost hold? The key is that in most cases, economic resources are not fully adapted to other alternative uses, that is, asset specificity. Of course, if resources can completely adapt to the production of product X and product Y, or if resources are completely replaceable, then the opportunity cost will be a certain constant. The production possibility curve would be a straight line with a negative slope.

The production possibility curve can also be used to illustrate the problem of potential and excess. Any point within the production possibility curve indicates that there is still potential for production. That is, there are still resources that are not fully utilized and idle. Any point beyond the production possibility is beyond the reach of existing resources and technical conditions. Only the point on the production possibility curve is the most efficient point of resource allocation.

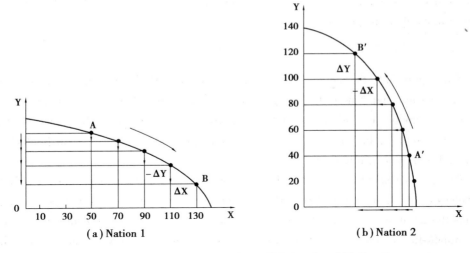

Figure 3.2   Production frontiers of Nation 1 and Nation 2

Figure 3.2 shows the hypothetical production frontier of commodities X and Y for Nation 1 and Nation 2. Both production frontiers are concave from the origin, reflecting the fact that each nation incurs increasing opportunity costs in the production of both commodities.

Suppose that Nation 1 wants to produce more of commodity X, starting from point A on its production frontier. Since at point A the nation is already utilizing all of its resources with the best technology available, the nation can only produce more of X by reducing the output of commodity Y.

Figure 3.2 shows that for each additional batch of 20X that Nation 1 produces, it must give up more and more Y. The increasing opportunity costs in terms of Y that Nation 1 faces are reflected in the longer and longer downward arrows in the figure, and result in a production frontier that is concave from the origin.

Nation 1 also faces increasing opportunity costs in the production of Y. This could be demonstrated graphically by showing that Nation 1 has to give up increasing amounts of X for each additional batch of 20Y that it produces. However, instead of showing this for Nation 1, we demonstrate increasing opportunity costs in the production of Y with the production frontier of Nation 2 in Figure 3.2.

Moving upward from point A′ along the production frontier of Nation 2, we observe leftward arrows of increasing length, reflecting the increasing amounts of X that Nation 2 must give up to produce each additional batch of 20Y. Thus, concave production frontiers for Nation 1 and Nation 2 reflect increasing opportunity costs in each nation in the production of both commodities.

The marginal rate of transformation (MRT) is another name for opportunity cost. The value of MRT is given by the slope of the production possibility frontier. The MRT increases as more units of X are produced.

$$\text{opportunity cost} = \text{MRT}_{XY} = \left|\frac{\Delta Y}{\Delta X}\right|$$

If in Figure 3.2, the slope of the production frontier, MRT, of Nation 1 at point A is 1/4, this means that Nation 1 must give up 1/4 of a unit of Y to release just enough resources to produce one additional unit of X at this point. Similarly, if the slope, or MRT, equals 1 at point B, this means that Nation 1 must give up one unit of Y to produce one additional unit of X at this point.

Thus, a movement from point A down to point B along the production frontier of Nation 1 involves an increase in the slope, MRT, from 1/4 (at point A) to 1 (at point B) and reflects the increasing opportunity costs in producing more X. This is in contrast to the case of a straight-line production frontier, where the opportunity cost of X is constant regardless of the level of output and is given by the constant value of the slope, MRT, of the production frontier. The opportunity cost can be constant, increasing and decreasing, as Figure 3.3 shows.

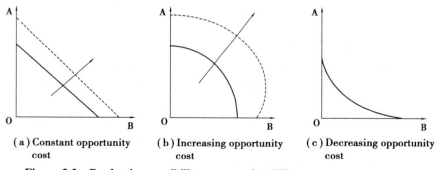

(a) Constant opportunity cost   (b) Increasing opportunity cost   (c) Decreasing opportunity cost

Figure 3.3   Production possibility curve under different opportunity costs

3.3   Community indifference curve

The indifference curve is used to indicate that the utility provided to consumers by different combinations of two commodities is the same. It shows that under the conditions of fixed income and commodity price, in order to obtain the same degree of satisfaction, consumers must increase the consumption of one commodity and reduce the consumption of another commodity.

A community indifference curve shows the various combinations of two commodities that yield equal satisfaction to the community or nation. Higher curves refer to greater satisfaction, lower curves to less satisfaction. Community indifference curves are negatively sloped and convex from the origin. To be useful, they must not cross. (Readers familiar with an individual's indifference curves will note that community indifference curves are almost completely analogous.)

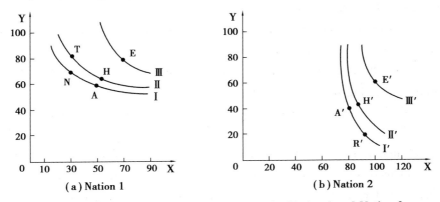

Figure 3.4   Community indifference curves for Nation 1 and Nation 2

Figure 3.4 shows three hypothetical indifference curves for Nation 1 and Nation 2. They differ on the assumption that tastes, or demand preferences, are different in the two nations.

Points N and A give equal satisfaction to Nation 1, since they are both on indifference curve I. Points T and H refer to a higher level of satisfaction, since they are on a higher indifference curve II. Even though T involves more of Y but less of X than A, satisfaction is greater at T because it is on indifference curve II. Point E refers to still greater satisfaction, since it is on indifference curve III. For Nation 2, A' = R' < H' < E'.

Note that the community indifference curves in Figure 3.4 are negatively sloped. This is always the case because as a nation consumes more of X, it must consume less of Y to have the same level of satisfaction (i.e., remain on the same level of satisfaction). Thus, as Nation 1 moves from N to A on indifference curve I, it consumes more of X but less of Y. Similarly, as Nation 2 moves from A' to R' on indifference curve I', it consumes more of X but less of Y. If a nation continued to consume the same amount of Y as it increased its consumption of X, the nation would necessarily move to a higher indifference curve.

The marginal rate of substitution (MRS) of X for Y in consumption refers to the amount of Y that a nation could give up for one extra unit of X and still remain on the same indifference curve. This is given by the (absolute) slope of the community indifference curve at the point of consumption and declines as the nation moves down the curve. For example, the slope, or MRS, of indifference curve I is greater at point N than at point A (see Figure 3.4). Similarly, the slope, or MRS, of indifference curve I is greater at point A' than at R'.

$$MRS_{XY} = \left| \frac{\Delta Y}{\Delta X} \right|$$

The decline in MRS or absolute slope of an indifference curve is a reflection of the fact that the more of X and the less of Y a nation consumes, the more valuable to the nation is a unit of Y at the margin compared with a unit of X. Therefore, the nation can give up less and less of Y for each additional unit of X it wants.

Declining MRS means that community indifference curves are convex from the origin. Thus, while increasing opportunity cost in production is reflected in concave production frontiers, a declining MRS in consumption is reflected in convex community indifference curves.

Law of diminishing of MRS exists due to diminishing marginal utility. With the continuous increase of the consumption of X, the marginal utility of this commodity is decreasing, and the number of Y that can be replaced by an additional unit of X is decreasing. That is, the number of Y that consumers are willing to give up in order to get a unit of X is decreasing.

$$MRS_{XY} = \frac{MU_X}{MU_Y} = \left| \frac{\Delta Y}{\Delta X} \right|$$

3.4 Budget line and consumer equilibrium

The budget line is the trajectory of various commodity combinations that consumers may purchase with a given income under a given price level. It is sometimes called budget constraint or consumption possibility line or price line.

The budget line equation is:

$$I = P_X Q_X + P_Y Q_Y$$

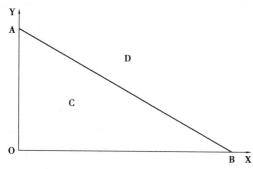

Figure 3.5 Budget line

In which, I represents the fixed income of consumers, P_X and P_Y represent the price of goods X and Y respectively, and Q_X and Q_Y represent the quantity of goods X and Y respectively.

The budget line AB divides the planar coordinate map into three areas. First, any point in the area outside the budget line AB, point D for example, is a combination point where consumers can't purchase goods with all their income. Second, any point in the area within the budget line AB, such as point C, means that income of the consumer still remains after purchasing the product portfolio at that point. Only any point on the budget line AB is the point where consumers spend all their income on the goods they can buy.

The budget line in the figure is a straight line inclined downward to the right, with a slope of $-P_X/P_Y$. This is an important feature. In addition, the position and shape of the budget line are determined by the income level I of the consumer and the prices (P_X, P_Y) of the two commodities. With the change of the price and income level, two kinds of change effects will occur: horizontal movement and slope change.

$$Q_Y = \frac{I}{P_Y} - \frac{P_X}{P_Y}Q_X$$

If the prices P_X and P_Y of the two commodities remain unchanged, the consumer's income I changes. At this time, the position of the corresponding budget line will shift parallelly. If the consumer's income I remains the same, the prices P_X and P_Y of the two commodities will change in the same proportion and direction. At this time, the position of the corresponding budget line will also shift parallelly. When the income I of the consumer is unchanged, the price P_X of the commodity X changes and the price P_Y of the commodity Y remains unchanged, then the slope of the budget line changes and the intercept of the budget line changes. If the consumer's income I changes in the same proportion and direction as the prices P_X and P_Y of the two commodities, at this time, the budget line does not change.

Consumer equilibrium is to study how a single consumer allocates his limited monetary income to the purchase of various goods to obtain the maximum utility. It can also be said that it is the equilibrium condition for a single consumer to achieve maximum utility under a given income.

The indifference curve represents the subjective attitude of consumers towards different product combinations, while the budget line constraint shows the objective conditions for consumers to consume goods with the ability to pay. Putting the two together can determine the final choice of consumers. If the indifference curve and the budget line are combined in a graph, the budget line must be tangent to one of the indifference curves at the same point, and consumer equilibrium is achieved at this tangent point, as the point E in Figure 3.6 shows.

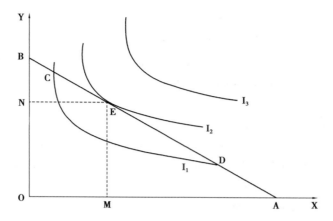

Figure 3.6   Consumer equilibrium 1

Why can the consumer equilibrium be achieved only at this tangent point E? The utility represented by the indifference curve I_3 farther from the origin is greater than I_2, but the budget line AB is neither intersecting nor tangent to it, which indicates that the quantity combination of X goods and Y goods that reach the I_3 utility level cannot be realized under the condition that the income and price are fixed. On the indifference curve I_1 closer to the origin, although the budget line AB has two intersections C and D with it, it shows that the quantity of X goods and Y goods purchased at points C and D is also the largest combination under the condition of fixed income and price. But the combination of X goods and Y goods in C and D cannot achieve the maximum utility.

Suppose the marginal utility of goods X and Y is MU_X and MU_Y, at equilibrium we have:

$$MRS_{XY} = \frac{P_X}{P_Y} = \frac{MU_X}{MU_Y} = \left| \frac{\Delta Y}{\Delta X} \right|$$

If $MRS_{XY} > P_X/P_Y$, with constant goods price, what will consumers who seek to maximize utility do? When $MRS_{XY} > P_X/P_Y$, since $MRS_{XY} = MU_X/MU_Y$, consumers can increase MU_Y and decrease MU_X, meaning to decrease consumption of Y and increase consumption of X. The combination point will move down along the budget line.

Question: If Xiao Zhang's income is 600 yuan, and he only consumes two products X and Y. It is known that the prices of these two products $P_X = 2$ yuan and $P_Y = 4$ yuan, and the utility function is $TU = X^{0.5} Y^{0.5}$. Solving, what is the consumption of X and Y at equilibrium?

$$MU_X = \frac{\partial TU}{\partial X} = 0.5X^{-0.5} Y^{0.5}$$

$$MU_Y = \frac{\partial TU}{\partial Y} = 0.5X^{0.5} Y^{-0.5}$$

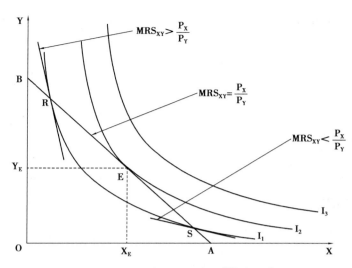

Figure 3.7   Consumer equilibrium 2

At equilibrium:

$$MRS_{XY} = \frac{P_X}{P_Y} = \frac{MU_X}{MU_Y}$$

So:

$$\frac{X}{Y} = \frac{2}{4}$$

The budget line is:

$$2X + 4Y = 600$$

So:

$$X = 150, \ Y = 75$$

3.5   General equilibrium in isolation and openness

In the above sections we have discussed the production or supply, as well as the consumption. Next we will see how the interaction of these forces of demand and supply determines the equilibrium point, or point of maximum social welfare in a nation in isolation, or in the absence of international trade.

❯ 3.5.1   General equilibrium in isolation

In the absence of international trade, a nation is in equilibrium when it reaches the highest indifference curve possible given its production frontier. This occurs at the point where a community indifference curve is tangent to the nation's production frontier. The common slope of the two curves at the tangency point gives the internal equilibrium-relative commodity price in the nation and reflects the nation's comparative advantage. Let us see what all this means.

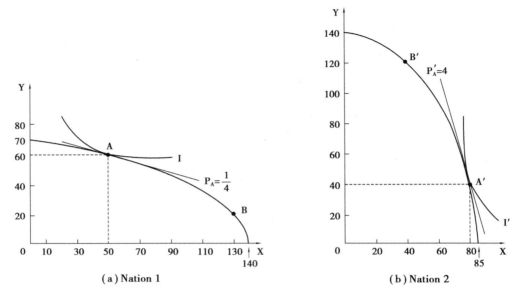

Figure 3.8　Equilibrium in isolation

Figure 3.8 brings together the production frontiers and the community indifference curves. We see in Figure 3.8 that indifference curve I is the highest indifference curve that Nation 1 can reach within its production frontier. Thus, Nation 1 is in equilibrium, or maximizes its welfare, when it produces and consumes at point A in the absence of trade, or autarky. Similarly, Nation 2 is in equilibrium at point A, where its production frontier is tangent to indifference curve I'.

Note that since community indifference curves are convex from the origin and drawn as nonintersecting, there is only one such point of tangency, or equilibrium. Furthermore, we can be certain that one such equilibrium point exists because there are an infinite number of indifference curves (i.e., the indifference map is dense). On one hand, points on lower indifference curves are possible but would not maximize the nation's welfare. On the contrary, the nation cannot reach higher indifference curves with the resources and technology presently available.

The equilibrium-relative commodity price in isolation is given by the slope of the tangent common to the nation's production frontier and indifference curve at the autarky point of production and consumption. Thus, the equilibrium-relative price of X in isolation is $P_A = P_X/P_Y = 1/4$ in Nation 1 and $P_A' = P_X/P_Y = 4$ in Nation 2 (see Figure 3.8). Relative prices are different in the two nations because their production frontiers and indifference curves differ in shape and location.

Since in isolation $P_A < P'_A$, Nation 1 has a comparative advantage in commodity X and Nation 2 in commodity Y. It follows that both nations can gain if Nation 1 specializes in the production and export of X in exchange for Y from Nation 2.

Figure 3.8 illustrates that the forces of supply (as given by the nation's production frontier) and the forces of demand (as summarized by the nation's indifference map) together determine the equilibrium-relative commodity prices in each nation in autarky. For example, if indifference curve Ⅰ had been of a different shape, it would have been tangent to the production frontier at a different point and would have determined a different relative price of X in Nation 1. The same would be true for Nation 2. This is in contrast to the case of constant costs, where the equilibrium P_X/P_Y is constant in each nation regardless of the level of output and conditions of demand, and is given by the constant slope of the nation's production frontier. Table 3.1 gives the comparative advantage of the largest advanced and emerging market economies in manufactured products.

Table 3.1　Comparative advantage of the largest advanced and emerging economies in 2015

United States	Chemicals other than pharmaceuticals, aircraft, integrated circuits, non-electrical machinery, and scientific and controlling instruments
European Union	Iron and steel, chemicals (including pharmaceuticals), automotive products, aircrafts, all types of machinery other than office and telecom equipment, and scientific and controlling instruments
Japan	Iron and steel, chemicals other than pharmaceuticals, all types of machinery other than office and telecom equipment, automobiles and other transport equipment, and scientific and controlling instruments
China	Iron and steel, office and telecom equipment, and most other types of machinery other than integrated circuits, transport equipment other than automobiles, power generating and electrical machinery, textiles and clothing, and personal household goods
Brazil	Iron and steel, and personal and household goods
South Korea	Iron and steel, chemicals other than pharmaceuticals, office and telecom equipment, integrated circuits, automotive products, and textiles

▶ 3.5.2　General equilibrium in openness

A difference in relative commodity prices between two nations is a reflection of their comparative advantage and forms the basis for mutually beneficial trade. The nation with the lower relative price for a commodity has a comparative advantage in that commodity and a comparative disadvantage in the other commodity, with respect to the second nation. Each nation should then specialize in the production of the commodity of its comparative advantage (i.e., produce more of the commodity than it wants to consume domestically) and exchange part of its output with the other nation for the commodity of its comparative disadvantage. However, as each nation specializes in producing the commodity of its comparative advantage, it incurs increasing opportunity costs. Specialization will continue until relative commodity prices in the two nations become equal at the level at which trade is in equilibrium. By then trading with each other, both nations end up consuming more than in the absence of trade.

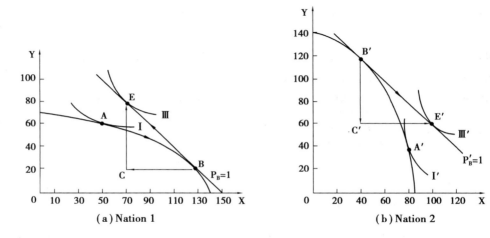

Figure 3.9　Gains from trade

We have known that in the absence of trade the equilibrium-relative price of X is $P_A = 1/4$ in Nation 1 and $P'_A = 4$ in Nation 2. Thus, Nation 1 has a comparative advantage in commodity X and Nation 2 in commodity Y.

Suppose that trade between the two nations becomes possible (e. g., through the elimination of government obstacles to trade or a drastic reduction in transport costs). Nation 1 should now specialize in the production and export of commodity X in exchange for commodity Y from Nation 2. How this takes place is illustrated by Figure 3.9.

Starting from point A (the equilibrium point in isolation), as Nation 1 specializes in the production of X and moves down its production frontier, it incurs increasing opportunity costs in the production of X. This is reflected in the increasing slope of its production frontier. Starting from point A′, as Nation 2 specializes in the production of Y and moves upward along its production frontier, it experiences increasing opportunity costs in the production of Y. This is reflected in the decline in the slope of its production frontier (a reduction in the opportunity cost of X, which means a rise in the opportunity cost of Y).

This process of specialization in production continues until relative commodity prices (the slope of the production frontiers) become equal in the two nations. The common relative price (slope) with trade will be somewhere between the pre-trade relative prices of $1/4$ and 4, at the level at which trade is balanced. In Figure 3.9, this is $P_B = P'_B = 1$.

With trade, Nation 1 moves from point A down to point B in production. By then exchanging 60X for 60Y with Nation 2 (see trade triangle BCE), Nation 1 ends up consuming at point E (70X and 80Y) on its indifference curve Ⅲ. This is the highest level of satisfaction that Nation 1 can reach with trade at $P_X/P_Y = 1$. Thus, Nation 1 gains 20X and 20Y from its no-trade equilibrium point. (Compare point E on indifference curve Ⅲ with point A on indifference curve Ⅰ.) Line BE is called the trade possibility line or, simply, trade line because trade takes place along this line.

Similarly, Nation 2 moves from point A' up to point B' in production, and by exchanging 60Y for 60X with Nation 1 (see trade triangle B'C'E'), it ends up consuming at point E' (100X and 60Y) on its indifference curve Ⅲ'. Thus, Nation 2 also gains 20X and 20Y from specialization in production and trade.

Note that with specialization in production and trade, each nation can consume outside its production frontier (which also represents its no-trade consumption frontier).

The equilibrium-relative price with trade is the common relative price in both nations at which trade is balanced. In Figure 3.9, this is $P_B = P'_B = 1$. At this relative price, the amount of X that Nation 1 wants to export (60X) equals the amount of X that Nation 2 wants to import (60X). Similarly, the amount of Y that Nation 2 wants to export (60Y) exactly matches the amount of Y that Nation1 wants to import at this price (60Y).

Any other relative price could not persist because trade would be unbalanced. For example, at $P_X/P_Y = 2$, Nation 1 would want to export more of X than Nation 2 would be willing to import at this high price. As a result, the relative price of X would fall toward the equilibrium level of 1. Similarly, at a relative price of X lower than 1, Nation 2 would want to import more of X than Nation 1 would be willing to export at this low price, and the relative price of X would rise. Thus, the relative price of X would gravitate toward the equilibrium price of 1. The same conclusion would be reached in terms of Y.

The equilibrium-relative price in Figure 3.9 was determined by trial and error; that is, various relative prices were tried until the one that balanced trade was found. There is a more rigorous theoretical way to determine the equilibrium-relative price with trade. This makes use of either the total demand and supply curve of each commodity in each nation or the so-called offer curves and it will be discussed later.

In this figure, the equilibrium-relative price of X with trade ($P_B = P'_B = 1$) results in equal gains (20X and 20Y) for Nation 1 and Nation 2, but this need not be the case. Of course, if the pre-trade relative price had been the same in both nations (an unlikely occurrence), there would be no comparative advantage or disadvantage to speak of in either nation, no specialization in production, or mutually beneficial trade.

Please note that under increasing opportunity costs, there is incomplete specialization in production in both nations. For example, while Nation 1 produces more of X (the commodity of its comparative advantage) with trade, it continues to produce some Y (see point B in Figure 3.9). Similarly, Nation 2 continues to produce some X with trade (see point B' in Figure 3.9).

The reason for this is that as Nation 1 specializes in the production of X, it incurs increasing opportunity costs in producing X. Similarly, as Nation 2 produces more Y, it incurs increasing opportunity costs in Y (which means declining opportunity costs of X). Thus, as each nation specializes in producing the commodity of its comparative advantage, relative commodity prices move toward each other (i.e., become less unequal) until they are identical in both nations.

At that point, it does not pay for either nation to continue to expand production of the commodity of its comparative advantage.

Table 3.2 Specialization and export concentration in selected countries in 2014

Countries	Main products	Percentage of total exports
United State	Chemicals	13.7
Europe	Chemicals	18.0
South Korea	Office and telecommunications equipment	19.0
Japan	Automotive products	21.2
China	Office and telecommunications equipment	33.2
Brazil	Food	35.0
Argentina	Food	51.6
Kuwait	Fuels	90.7

Because of increasing costs, no nation specializes completely in the production of only one product in the real world, as Table 3.2 shows. The closest to complete specialization in production and trade that any nation comes is Kuwait, where petroleum exports represented 90.7 percent of the total value of its exports in 2014. For Argentina, another developing nation with highly specialized natural resources, food exports represent 50 percent of its total exports. Table 3.2 shows that the largest export product for the United States, Europe, and South Korea represents less than 20 percent of their total exports. The figure is between 21 and 34 percent for Japan and China, and it is 35 percent for Brazil.

3.5.3 The small-country case

We can still use Figure 3.9 to illustrate the small-country case with increasing costs. Let us assume that Nation 1 is now a very small country, which is in equilibrium at point A (the same as before) in the absence of trade, and that Nation 2 is a very large country or even the rest of the world. (The diagram for Nation 2 in Figure 3.9 is to be completely disregarded in this case.)

Suppose that the equilibrium-relative price of X on the world market is 1 ($P_W = 1$), and it is not affected by trade with small Nation 1. Since in the absence of trade, the relative price of X in Nation 1 ($P_A = 1/4$) is lower than the world market price, Nation 1 has a comparative advantage in X. With the opening of trade, Nation 1 specializes in the production of X until it reaches point B on its production frontier, where $P_B = 1 = P_W$. Even though Nation 1 is now considered to be a small country, it still does not specialize completely in the production of X (as would be the case under constant costs).

By exchanging 60X for 60Y, Nation 1 reaches point E on indifference curve Ⅲ and gains 20X and 20Y (compared with its autarky point A on indifference curve I). Note that this is exactly what occurred when Nation 1 was not considered to be small. The only difference is that now Nation 1 does not affect relative prices in Nation 2 (or the rest of the world), and Nation 1 captures all the benefits from trade (which now amount to only 20X and 20Y).

3.5.4 Gains from Trade

A nation's gains from trade can be broken down into two components: the gains from exchange and the gains from specialization.

Gains from exchange: Some products are traded at international prices rather than domestic prices under the condition that the resource allocation is unchanged, the output is unchanged, and the product specialization division is not implemented.

Gains from specialization: the reallocation of resources according to comparative advantages.

Figure 3.10 illustrates this breakdown for small Nation 1. Suppose that, for whatever reason, Nation 1 could not specialize in the production of X with the opening of trade but continued to produce at point A, where MRT = 1/4. Starting from point A, Nation 1 could export 20X in exchange for 20Y at the prevailing world relative price of $P_W = 1$ and end up consuming at point T on indifference curve II. Even though Nation 1 consumes less of X and more of Y at point T in relation to point A, it is better off than it was in autarky because T is on higher indifference curve II. The movement from point A to point T in consumption measures the gains from exchange.

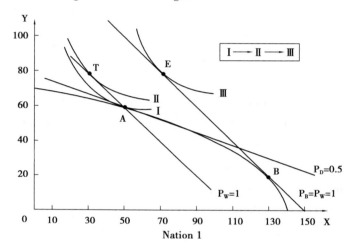

Figure 3.10 Gains from exchange and from specialization

If subsequently Nation 1 also specialized in the production of X and produced at point B, it could then exchange 60X for 60Y with the rest of the world and consume at point E on indifference curve III (thereby gaining even more). The movement from T to E in consumption measures the gains from specialization in production.

In sum, the movement from A (on indifference curve I) to T (on indifference curve II) is made possible by exchange alone. This takes place even if Nation 1 remains at point A (the autarky point) in production. The movement from point T to E (on indifference curve III) represents the gains resulting from specialization in production.

Note that Nation 1 is not in equilibrium in production at point A with trade because MRT < P_W. To be in equilibrium in production, Nation 1 should expand its production of X until it reaches point B, where $P_B = P_W = 1$. Nation 2's gains from trade can similarly be broken down into gains from exchange and gains from specialization.

3.6   Isoquant curve

The isoquant curve is the trajectory of all different combinations of the inputs of two factors (K for capital and L for labor) of production that produce the same output under the condition that the technical level is unchanged.

The characteristics of isoquant curve are as follows:

Firstly, the isoquant curve is inclined downward to the right, with a negative

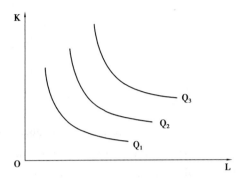

Figure 3.11   Isoquant curve

slope. This shows that, under the condition that the producer's resources and the price of the factor of production are fixed, in order to achieve the same output, when one factor of production is increased, the other factor of production must be reduced. The simultaneous increase of the two factors of production cannot be realized when resources are limited. The simultaneous reduction of the two factors of production cannot maintain the same level of output.

Secondly, there can be countless isoquant curves. The same isoquant curve represents the same output, and different isoquant curves represent different output levels. The farther the isoquant curve from the origin, the higher the output level, and the closer the isoquant curve from the origin, the lower the output level.

Thirdly, any two isoquant curves cannot intersect, because the two isoquant curves at the intersection represent the same yield level, which is contradictory to the second feature.

Fourthly, the isoquant curve is convex to the origin, which is determined by the decreasing marginal rate of technical substitution (MRTS).

On the premise that the output remains unchanged, the increase of the quantity of one factor can be replaced by another factor.

$$MRTS_{LK} = -\frac{\Delta K}{\Delta L} = -\frac{dK}{dL}$$

Law of diminishing MRTS refers to that under the condition of keeping the production level unchanged, the decrease of K decreases with the increase of L, or with the increase of L, the amount of K that can be replaced by one unit of L will be smaller and smaller.

The existence of diminishing MRTS is the law of diminishing marginal product (MP).

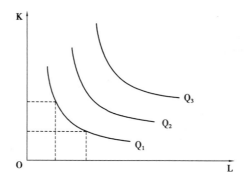

Figure 3.12　Marginal rate of technical substitution

In the long term, with the continuous increase of labor input, its marginal product (MP_L) is decreasing. In this way, the amount of capital that can be replaced by each additional unit of labor becomes less and less. That is, if the increase of labor is unchanged, the decrease of capital becomes smaller and smaller.

The relation between MRTS and MP:

$$MRTS_{LK} = -\frac{\Delta K}{\Delta L} = \frac{MP_L}{MP_K}$$

3.7　Isocost line and producer equilibrium

In real life, all kinds of production factors have prices. For example, if you hire workers, you need to pay their wages. To borrow money from a bank, you need to pay interest to the bank. To run a factory, you need to rent land, pay rent, etc. If a manufacturer wants to buy these factors of production, it must have certain monetary expenditure, which constitutes the manufacturer's production cost. If a manufacturer wants to pursue maximum profit, it must consider cost.

The isoquant curve tells us that a certain number of certain products can be produced in a variety of factor combinations, and the production of a certain number of factor combinations is also limited by the total budget expenses and factor prices paid by producers. That is, it should be restricted by the total cost and factor price. Therefore, the concept of isocost line needs to be introduced.

Isocost line is under the given cost and the given factor price, the trajectory of the different maximum quantity combinations of the two factors that a producer can purchase.

Suppose that the given cost is C, the known price of labor, that is, the wage rate, is w, and the known price of capital, that is, the interest rate, is r, from which we can obtain the isocost line. The cost equation is:

$$C = wL + rK$$

$$K = -L \times \frac{w}{r} + \frac{C}{r}$$

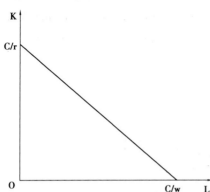

Figure 3.13   Isocost line

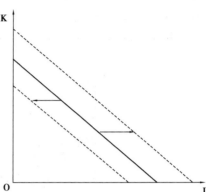

Figure 3.14   Movement of isocost line

Since the cost equation is linear, the isocost line must be a straight line. The point C/w on the horizontal axis represents the quantity when all the costs of a given enterprise purchase labor, and the point C/r on the vertical axis represents the quantity when all the costs of a given enterprise purchase capital. The line segment connecting these two points is the isocost line. It represents various combinations of labor and capital that can be purchased at a given total cost.

The slope of the equal cost line is $-w/r$. That is, the ratio of the prices of the two factors of production is negative. Any point in the area within the isocost line means that all the given costs are used to purchase the combination of labor and capital at that point, and there is still surplus. Any point in the area outside the isocost line means that the combination of labor and capital at that point is not enough to be purchased at the given total cost. Only any point on the isocost line represents the combination of labor and capital that can just be purchased with the given total cost.

If the prices of the two input factors change, the isocost line will also change. Let wage rise, namely, w rise, so that the maximum number of labor that can be employed at the same cost decreases. That is, the intercept of the isocost line on the L-axis decreases. Since r is constant, the intercept of the isocost line on the K-axis is constant, so the isocost line will rotate. In some cases, the prices of the two factors may change in proportion, which will cause the parallel movement of the isocost line.

A producer is in equilibrium when it maximizes output for a given cost outlay (i.e., when it reaches the highest isoquant possible with a given isocost). This occurs where an isoquant is tangent to an isocost (i.e., $MRTS = P_L/P_K$). In Figure 3.15, the producer is in equilibrium at point A_1, producing 1X with the lower isocost, and at point A_2, producing 2X with the higher isocost. Note that isoquant 2X, which involves twice as much output as isoquant 1X, is twice as far from the origin, and requires twice as much outlay of K and L to be reached. The straight line from the origin connecting equilibrium points A_1 and A_2 is called the expansion path and shows the constant $K/L=1/4$ in producing 1X and 2X.

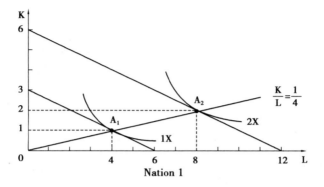

Figure 3.15   Isoquants, isocosts, and equilibrium

The equilibrium condition of the manufacturer is:

$$MRTS_{LK} = \frac{w}{r} = \frac{MP_L}{MP_K} = -\frac{\Delta K}{\Delta L}$$

When $MRTS_{LK} > \dfrac{w}{r}$, the manufacturer will constantly replace capital with labor, with the total output unchanged and the total cost reduced (like point a in Figure 3.16).

When $MRTS_{LK} < \dfrac{w}{r}$, the manufacturer will constantly use capital to replace labor, with the total output unchanged and the total cost reduced (like point b in Figure 3.16).

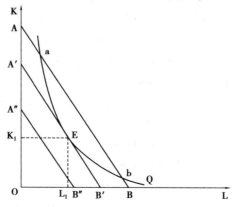

Figure 3.16   Minimum cost under given output

3.8 Supply curve, demand curve and partial equilibrium

The supply curve is a geometric representation of the functional relationship between the price of a commodity and the quantity supplied. Supply refers to the quantity that an individual manufacturer is willing to sell a commodity under certain conditions within a certain period of time. The supply curve slopes upward to the right because under the same other conditions, the higher the price means the more the supply. The supply curve may be either a straight line or a curve.

The demand curve represents the quantity of goods required at each price. Demand curve is a curve showing the relationship between price and demand. It refers to the quantity of goods that buyers are willing to buy at each price level when other conditions are the same.

Generally speaking, the demand quantity of goods is inversely proportional to the price. If the price increases, the quantity demanded decreases, and if the price decreases, the quantity demanded increases.

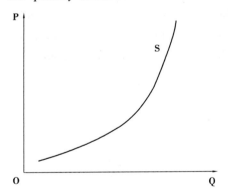

Figure 3.17 Supply curve

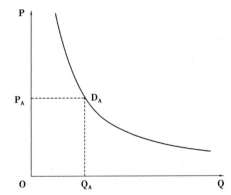

Figure 3.18 Demand curve

The slope of the demand curve reflects the sensitivity of demand to price changes, which can be called price elasticity of demand. It is usually expressed as the percentage ratio of the change in demand to the change in price, that is, the price elasticity coefficient of demand. The price elasticity of demand can be divided into point elasticity and arc elasticity.

The main factors affecting the elasticity of demand for products are: ①The importance of products to people's lives. Generally, the demand elasticity of necessities is small, and the demand elasticity of luxury goods is large. ② Substitutability of commodities. The demand elasticity of goods that are difficult to replace is small, and the demand elasticity of goods that are easy to replace is large. ③How much the product is used for. The elasticity of demand for a single use is small, while the elasticity of demand for a wide range of uses is large. ④Product popularity. The demand elasticity of products that have been popularized and saturated in society is small, and the demand elasticity of products with low popularity is large.

elasticity of demand = percentage of demand change ÷ percentage of price change

When the change percentage of demand is greater than the price change percentage and the demand elasticity coefficient is greater than 1, it is called elastic or highly elastic demand. When the change percentage of demand is equal to the change percentage of price and the demand elasticity coefficient is equal to 1, it is called the unitary elasticity of demand. When the change percentage of demand is less than the change percentage of price and the elasticity coefficient of demand is less than 1, it is called lack of elasticity or low elasticity of demand.

Figure 3.19 shows how the equilibrium-relative commodity price with trade is determined by partial equilibrium analysis. Curves Dx and Sx in the left and right panels of Figure 3.19 refer to the demand and supply curves for commodity X of Nation 1 and Nation 2, respectively. The vertical axes in all three panels of Figure 3.19 measure the relative price of commodity X (i.e., P_X/P_Y, or the amount of commodity Y that a nation must give up to produce one additional unit of X). The horizontal axes measure the quantities of commodity X.

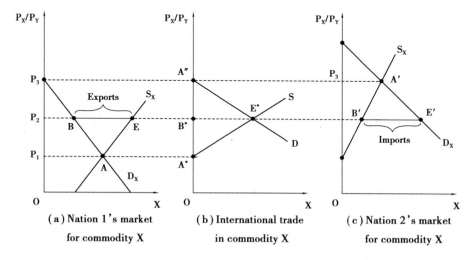

(a) Nation 1's market for commodity X　　(b) International trade in commodity X　　(c) Nation 2's market for commodity X

Figure 3.19　Equilibrium-relative commodity price with trade with partial equilibrium analysis

The left panel of Figure 3.19 shows that in the absence of trade, Nation 1 produces and consumes at point A at the relative price of X of P_1, while Nation 2 produces and consumes at point A′ at P_3. With the opening of trade, the relative price of X will be between P_1 and P_3 if both nations are large. At prices above P_1, Nation 1 will supply (produce) more than it will demand (consume) of commodity X and will export the difference or excess supply (see the left panel). Alternatively, at prices below P_3, Nation 2 will demand a greater quantity of commodity X than it produces or supplies domestically and will import the difference or excess demand (see the right panel).

Specifically, the left panel shows that at P_1, the quantity supplied of commodity X (QS_X) equals the quantity demanded of commodity X (QD_X) in Nation 1, and so Nation 1 exports nothing of commodity X. This gives point A^* on curve S (Nation 1's supply curve of exports) in the middle panel. The left panel also shows that at P_2, the excess of BE of QS_X over QD_X represents the quantity of commodity X that Nation 1 would export at P_2. This is equal to B^*E^* in the middle panel and defines point E^* on Nation 1's S curve of exports of commodity X.

The right panel shows that at P_3, $QD_X = QS_X$ (point A′), so Nation 2 does not demand any imports of commodity X. This defines point A″ on Nation 2's demand curve for imports of commodity X (D) in the middle panel. The right panel also shows that at P_2, the excess B′E′ of QD_X over QS_X represents the quantity of commodity X that Nation 2 would import at P_2. This is equal to B^*E^* in the middle panel and defines point E^* on Nation 2's D curve of imports of commodity X.

At P_2, the quantity of imports of commodity X demanded by Nation 2 (B′E′ in the right panel) equals the quantity of exports of commodity X supplied by Nation 1 (BE in the left panel). This is shown by the intersection of the D and S curves for trade in commodity X in the middle panel. Thus, P_2 is the equilibrium-relative price of commodity X with trade. From the middle panel, we can also see that at $P_X/P_Y > P_2$, the quantity of exports of commodity X supplied exceeds the quantity of imports demanded, and so the relative price of X (P_X/P_Y) will fall to P_2. On the contrary, at $P_X/P_Y < P_2$, the quantity of imports of commodity X demanded exceeds the quantity of exports supplied, and P_X/P_Y, will rise to P_2.

The same could be shown with commodity Y. Commodity Y is exported by Nation 2 and imported by Nation 1. At any relative price of Y higher than equilibrium, the quantity of exports of Y supplied by Nation 2 would exceed the quantity of imports of Y demanded by Nation 1, and the relative price of Y would fall to the equilibrium level. On the contrary, at any P_Y/P_X below equilibrium, the quantity of imports of Y demanded would exceed the quantity of exports of Y supplied, and P_Y/P_X would rise to the equilibrium level.

Table 3. 3 shows the international price of petroleum in nominal and real (i. e., inflation-adjusted) terms from 1972 to 2014.

Table 3.3 Demand, supply, and the international price of petroleum

Year	1972	1973	1974	1978	1979	1980	1985	1986
petroleum prices ($/barrel)	2.89	3.24	11.60	13.39	30.21	36.68	27.37	14.17
real petroleum prices ($/barrel)	2.89	3.00	9.51	7.70	15.82	17.14	9.34	4.69
Year	1990	1998	2000	2005	2008	2010	2013	2014
petroleum prices ($/barrel)	22.99	13.07	28.23	53.40	97.04	73.03	104.07	96.35
real petroleum prices ($/barrel)	6.51	2.90	5.73	8.99	14.83	11.90	13.89	12.44

Table 3.3 shows that the price of petroleum fluctuated widely from 1972 to 2014. As a result of supply shocks in 1973 and in 1979−1980, the Organization of Petroleum Exporting Countries (OPEC) was able to increase the price of petroleum from an average of $2.89 per barrel in 1972 to $11.60 in 1974 and to $36.68 per barrel in 1980. This stimulated energy conservation and expanded exploration and petroleum production by non-OPEC countries. In the face of excess supplies during the 1980s and 1990s, OPEC was unable to prevent the price of petroleum from falling to a low of $14.17 in 1986 and $13.07 in 1998. The price of petroleum then rose to $28.23 in 2000 to $97.04 in 2008 (the all-time monthly high was $132.60 in July 2008, before falling to $55.50 in December of the same year), and it was $79.03 in 2010 and $96.35 in 2014 (it fell from $115 in June 2014 to $62 in December).

If we consider, however, that all prices have risen over time, we can see from Table 3.3 that the real (i.e., inflation-adjusted) price of petroleum rose from $2.89 per barrel in 1972 to $9.51 in 1974 and to $17.14 in 1980; it then fell to $4.69 in 1986 and $2.90 in 1998, but it subsequently rose to $5.73 in 2000 and $14.83 in 2008, and it was $11.90 in 2010 and $12.44 in 2014. Thus, the real price of petroleum was 4.30 times higher (12.44/2.89) in 2014 than in 1972, rather than 33.34 times in nominal prices over the same period.

3.9 Producer surplus and consumer surplus

Producer surplus refers to the additional income brought to producers due to the difference between the minimum supply price of production factors and products and the current market price, that is, the price obtained by sellers from selling a good or service minus the lowest acceptable price of sellers.

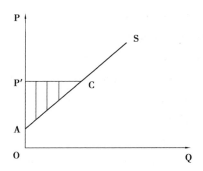

If a film company provides a film and sells it at a price of not less than 10 yuan, and consumers are willing to pay 40 yuan for it, and the film company finally sells it at a price of 40 yuan, then the producer's surplus is 30 yuan. Geometrically, it is equal to the area of the triangle above the supply curve and below the market price, as shown in Figure 3.20.

Figure 3.20   Producer surplus for the market

In a perfectly competitive market, the demand curve of a manufacturer is a horizontal straight line, so the marginal profit is equal to the product price ($MR = P$). Therefore, as long as the price P is higher than the marginal cost (MC), the manufacturer can obtain the producer surplus when it produces. At this time, the total price or total payment actually accepted by the manufacturer is the total income below the price line, and the minimum total price or total payment that the manufacturer is willing to accept is the total marginal cost below the marginal cost line. If represented graphically, the area enclosed by the price straight line and the marginal cost curve is the producer surplus, as shown by the shaded area in the left panel of Figure 3.21.

In the short term, producer surplus can also be measured by the difference between the manufacturer's total income and total variable cost. Because in the short term, the fixed cost of the manufacturer cannot be changed, and the total marginal cost must be equal to the total variable cost. The area of the shaded rectangular CP'EB in the right panel of Figure 3.21 is the producer surplus, which is equal to the total revenue minus the total variable cost.

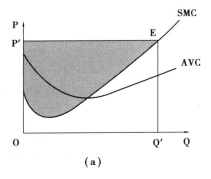

(a)

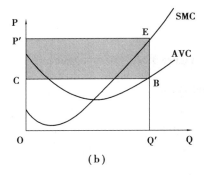

(b)

Figure 3.21   Firm's producer surplus in a short term

Consumer surplus, also known as the net income of consumers, refers to the difference between the maximum total price that consumers are willing to pay and the total price that they actually pay when they buy a certain number of certain goods. Consumer surplus measures the extra benefits that buyers feel they have gained. The total surplus of consumers can be expressed by the area of the triangle formed by the demand curve, the price line and the price axis.

If the price rises, the consumer surplus decreases; otherwise, if the price falls, the consumer surplus increases. If the demand curve is flat, the consumer surplus is 0.

The purpose of putting forward the concept of consumer surplus is to tell every consumer that what we pay is always less than what we get. We always get extra benefits from the transaction, and the total welfare of our society always grows in the transaction.

The reasons for consumer surplus are: firstly, the law of diminishing marginal utility; secondly, the price that consumers are willing to pay according to their evaluation of the marginal utility of specific products or services is often higher than the market price that they actually pay determined by the market supply and demand relationship.

It should be noted that consumer surplus is not an increase in real income, but a psychological feeling. In addition, the consumer surplus of daily necessities is large. Because consumers have a high evaluation of the utility of such goods and are willing to pay a high price, the market price of such goods is generally not high.

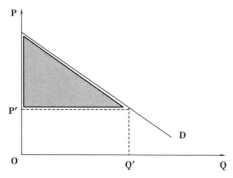

Figure 3.22 Consumer surplus

Both buyers and sellers hope to gain profits from market activities. One is called consumer surplus, and the other is called producer surplus. The sum of the two is called total surplus.

consumer surplus = the highest price the buyer is willing to pay − the actual price the buyer pays

producer surplus = income received by the seller − actual cost of the seller

total surplus = consumer surplus + producer surplus = the highest price the buyer is willing to pay − the actual cost of the seller

Using the concepts of consumer surplus, producer surplus and total surplus, we can analyze the impact of government intervention in the market (such as setting the upper and lower price limits).

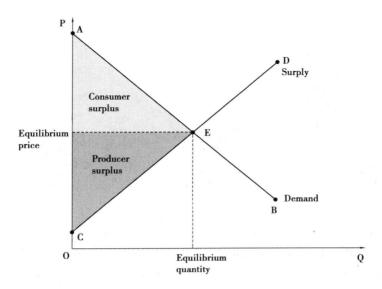

Figure 3.23　Total surplus

3.10　Offer curve

Offer curves (sometimes referred to as reciprocal demand curves) were devised and introduced into international economics by Alfred Marshall and Ysidro Edgeworth, two British economists, at the turn of the twentieth century. Since then, offer curves have been used extensively in international economics, especially for pedagogical purposes.

The offer curve of a nation shows how much of its import commodity the nation demands for it to be willing to supply various amounts of its export commodity. As the definition indicates, offer curves incorporate elements of both demand and supply. Alternatively, we can say that the offer curve of a nation shows the nation's willingness to import and export at various relative commodity prices.

The offer curve of a nation can be derived rather easily and somewhat informally from the nation's production frontier, its indifference map, and the various hypothetical relative commodity prices at which trade could take place.

In the left panel of Figure 3.24, Nation 1 starts at the no-trade (or autarky) point A. If trade takes place at $P_B = P_X / P_Y = 1$, Nation 1 moves to point B in production, trades 60X for 60Y with Nation 2, and reaches point E on its indifference curve III. This gives point E in the right panel of Figure 3.24.

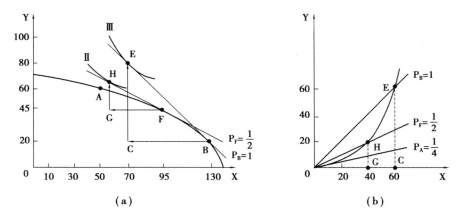

Figure 3.24   Derivation of the offer curve of Nation 1

At $P_F = P_X/P_Y = 1/2$ (see the left panel of Figure 3.24) , Nation 1 would move instead from point A to point F in production, exchange 40X for 20Y with Nation 2, and reach point H on its indifference curve II. This gives point H in the right panel. Joining the origin with points H and E and other points similarly obtained, we generate Nation 1's offer curve in the right panel. The offer curve of Nation 1 shows how many imports of commodity Y that Nation 1 requires to be willing to export various quantities of commodity X.

To keep the left panel simple, we omitted the autarky price line $P_A = 1/4$ and indifference curve I tangent to the production frontier and P_A at point A. Note that P_A, P_F, and P_B in the right panel refer to the same P_X/P_Y as P_A, P_F, and P_B in the left panel because they refer to the same absolute slope.

The offer curve of Nation 1 in the right panel of Figure 3.24 lies above the autarky price line of $P_A = 1/4$ and bulges toward the X-axis, which measures the commodity of its comparative advantage and export. To induce Nation 1 to export more of commodity X, P_X/P_Y must rise. Thus, at $P_F = 1/2$, Nation 1 would export 40X, and at $P_B = 1$, it would export 60X. There are two reasons for this: Nation 1 incurs increasing opportunity costs in producing more of commodity X (for export) and the more of commodity Y and the less of commodity X that Nation 1 consumes with trade, the more valuable to the nation is a unit of X at the margin compared with a unit of Y.

In the left panel of Figure 3.25, Nation 2 starts at the autarky equilibrium point A'. If trade takes place at $P'_B = P_X/P_Y = 1$, Nation 2 moves to point B' in production, exchanges 60Y for 60X with Nation 1, and reaches point E' on its indifference curve III'. Trade triangle B'C'E' in the left panel of Figure 3.25 corresponds to trade triangle O'C'E' in the right panel, and we get point E' on Nation 2's offer curve.

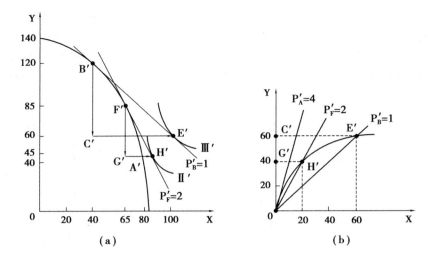

Figure 3.25 Derivation of the offer curve of Nation 2

At $P'_F = P_X/P_Y = 2$ in the left panel, Nation 2 would move instead to point F' in production, exchange 40Y for 20X with Nation 1, and reach point H' on its indifference curve Ⅱ'. Trade triangle F'G'H' in the left panel corresponds to trade triangle O'G'H' in the right panel, and we get point H' on Nation 2's offer curve. Joining the origin with points H' and E' and other points similarly obtained, we generate Nation 2's offer curve in the right panel. The offer curve of Nation 2 shows how many imports of commodity X Nation 2 demands to be willing to export various quantities of commodity Y.

Once again, we omitted the autarky price line $P'_A = 4$ and indifference curve Ⅰ' tangent to the production frontier and P'_A at point A'. Note that P'_A, P'_F, and P'_B in the right panel refer to the same P_X/P_Y as P'_A, P'_F, and P'_B in the left panel because they refer to the same absolute slope.

The offer curve of Nation 2 in the right panel of Figure 3.25 lies below its autarky price line of $P'_A = 4$ and bulges toward the Y-axis, which measures the commodity of its comparative advantage and export. To induce Nation 2 to export more of commodity Y, the relative price of Y must rise. This means that its reciprocal (i.e., P_X/P_Y) must fall. Thus, at $P'_F = 2$, Nation 2 would export 40Y, and at $P'_B = 1$, it would export 60Y. Nation 2 requires a higher relative price of Y to be induced to export more of Y because ①Nation 2 incurs increasing opportunity costs in producing more of commodity Y (for export) and ②the more of commodity X and the less of commodity Y that Nation 2 consumes with trade, the more valuable to the nation is a unit of Y at the margin compared with a unit of X.

The intersection of the offer curves of the two nations defines the equilibrium-relative commodity price at which trade takes place between them. Only at this equilibrium price will trade be balanced between the two nations. At any other relative commodity price, the desired quantities of imports and exports of the two commodities would not be equal. This would put pressure on the relative commodity price to move toward its equilibrium level. This is shown in Figure 3.26.

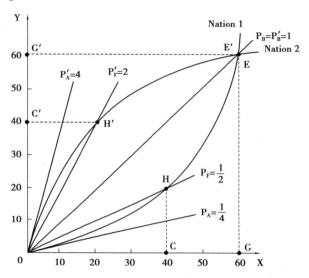

Figure 3.26　Equilibrium-relative commodity price with trade

The offer curves of Nation 1 and Nation 2 in Figure 3.26 are those derived in Figures 3.24 and 3.25. These two offer curves intersect at point E, defining equilibrium $P_X/P_Y = P_B = P'_B = 1$. At P_G, Nation 1 offers 60X for 60Y (point E on Nation 1's offer curve), and Nation 2 offers exactly 60Y for 60X (point E' on Nation 2's offer curve). Thus, trade is in equilibrium at P_B.

At any other P_X/P_Y, trade would not be in equilibrium. For example, at $P_F = 1/2$, the 40X that Nation 1 would export (see point H in Figure 3.26) would fall short of the imports of commodity X demanded by Nation 2 at this relatively low price of X. (This is given by a point, not shown in Figure 3.24, where the extended price line P_F crosses the extended offer curve of Nation 2.)

The excess import demand for commodity X at $P_F = 1/2$ by Nation 2 tends to drive P_X/P_Y up. As this occurs, Nation 1 will supply more of commodity X for export (i.e., Nation 1 will move up its offer curve), while Nation 2 will reduce its import demand for commodity X (i.e., Nation 2 will move down its offer curve). This will continue until supply and demand become equal at P_B. The pressure for P_F to move toward P_B could also be explained in terms of commodity Y and arises at any other P_X/P_Y, such as $P_F \neq P_B$.

Note that the equilibrium-relative commodity price of $P_B = 1$ with trade (determined in Figure 3.26 by the intersection of the offer curves of Nation 1 and Nation 2) is identical to that found by trial and error in Figure 3.24. At $P_B = 1$, both nations happen to gain equally from trade (refer to Figure 3.9).

--------- *China-perspective case study* ---------

More than 70% of the world's toys are produced in China

China is the largest toy producer and exporter in the world. More than 70% of toys on the global market are produced in China. It can be said that the toy industry is an evergreen tree of China's foreign trade. From 2016 to 2021, China's toy exports achieved five consecutive years of growth. In the first eight months of 2022, China's toy exports totaled $31.68 billion, a year-on-year increase of 20.2%.

Liang Mei, President of China Toys and Infant and Child Products Association: From January to August 2022, toy exports to the United States increased by 27.2%, Mexico by 40%, Japan by 32.3%, and Malaysia and Vietnam by more than 58%. China's toy industry has formed the advantages of highly centralized supporting and cost-effective industrial chain through the development of industrial clusters.

In recent years, affected by the global epidemic, the toy industry has also encountered problems such as rising raw materials, poor logistics and transportation. But even in this context, China's toy industry still maintained a steady development. Behind this is the efforts of the entire toy industry chain in creating and upgrading.

The toy industry is a microcosm of China's foreign trade. Over the past decade, China's import and export volume of goods trade has reached new highs, increasing from 24.4 trillion yuan in 2012 to 39.1 trillion yuan in 2021, an increase of 14.7 trillion yuan, which is close to the total import and export value of 2009. In 2018, it broke through the 30 trillion yuan mark, followed by the 40 trillion yuan mark in 2021. The international market share also increased from 10.4% in 2012 to 13.5% in 2021 year, and the position of the world's largest trade country in goods has been consolidated. Since 2017, China has maintained its position as the largest country in the world's goods trade for five consecutive years. In the past ten years, the scale of China's trade in goods has risen continuously, which fully reflects that China is not only a world factory, but also a world market. While providing the global market with high-quality and affordable goods, it also provides countries with broader opportunities for China's market development.

Key concepts

autarky

opportunity cost

community indifference curve

marginal rate of substitution (MRS)

consumer equilibrium

gains from exchange

isoquant curve

isocost line

general equilibrium

elasticity of demand

consumer surplus

production possibility curve

marginal rate of transformation (MRT)

constant returns to scale

budget line

equilibrium-relative commodity price with trade

gains from specialization

marginal rate of technical substitution (MRTS)

producer equilibrium

partial equilibrium

producer surplus

offer curve

Summary

1. Production possibility curve or production possibility frontier is the combination of the maximum quantity of various commodities that can be produced by the economy under the given resources and technical conditions. The marginal rate of transformation (MRT) is another name for opportunity cost. The value of MRT is given by the slope of the production possibility curve.

2. A community indifference curve shows the various combinations of two commodities that yield equal satisfaction to the community or nation. Higher curves refer to greater satisfaction, lower curves to less satisfaction.

3. Consumer equilibrium is to study how a single consumer allocates his limited monetary income to the purchase of various goods to obtain the maximum utility. It can also be said that it is the equilibrium condition for a single consumer to achieve maximum utility under a given income.

4. In the absence of international trade, a nation is in equilibrium when it reaches the highest indifference curve possible given its production frontier. This occurs at the point where a community indifference curve is tangent to the nation's production frontier. The common slope of the two curves at the tangency point gives the internal equilibrium-relative commodity price in the nation and reflects the nation's comparative advantage.

5. A difference in relative commodity prices between two nations is a reflection of their comparative advantage and forms the basis for mutually beneficial trade. The nation with

the lower relative price for a commodity has a comparative advantage in that commodity and a comparative disadvantage in the other commodity, with respect to the second nation. Each nation should then specialize in the production of the commodity of its comparative advantage and exchange part of its output with the other nation for the commodity of its comparative disadvantage.

6. A nation's gains from trade can be broken down into two components: gains from exchange and gains from specialization.

7. A producer is in equilibrium when it maximizes output for a given cost outlay (i.e., when it reaches the highest isoquant possible with a given isocost). This occurs where an isoquant is tangent to an isocost.

8. Producer surplus refers to the additional income brought to producers due to the difference between the minimum supply price of production factors and products and the current market price.

9. Consumer surplus, also known as the net income of consumers, refers to the difference between the maximum total price that consumers are willing to pay and the total price that they actually pay when they buy a certain number of certain goods.

10. Offer curves (sometimes referred to as reciprocal demand curves) show how much of its import commodity the nation demands for it to be willing to supply various amounts of its export commodity.

Exercises

1. On one set of axes, sketch a community indifference curve tangent to the fairly flat section of a concave production frontier. On a second set of axes, sketch another (different) community indifference curve tangent to the fairly steep portion of another (different) concave production frontier.

   A. Draw in the line showing the equilibrium-relative commodity price in isolation in each nation.

   B. Which is the commodity of comparative advantage for each nation?

   C. Under what (unusual) condition would there be no such thing as comparative advantage or disadvantage between the two nations?

2. A. On the figures of Exercise 1, show, for each nation with trade, the direction (by an arrow on the production frontier) of specialization in production and the equilibrium point of production and consumption.

   B. How much does each nation gain in consumption compared with its autarky point?

3. On one set of axes, sketch Nation 1's supply of exports of commodity X so that the quantity supplied (QS) of X is $QS_X = 0$ at $P_X/P_Y = 1/4$, $QS_X = 40$ at $P_X/P_Y = 1/2$, $QS_X = 60$ at $P_X/P_Y = 1$, and $QS_X = 70$ at $P_X/P_Y = 1\%$. On the same set of axes, sketch Nation 2's demand for Nation 1's exports of commodity X so that the quantity demanded (QD) of X is $QD_X = 40$ at $P_X/P_Y = 1.2$, $QD_X = 60$ at $P_X/P_Y = 1$, and $QD_X = 120$ at $P_X/P_Y = 0.5$.

   A. Determine the equilibrium-relative commodity price of the exports of commodity X with trade.

   B. What would happen if P_X/P_Y were 1.5?

   C. What would happen if $P_X/P_Y = 0.5$?

4. If P_X/P_Y exceeds the equilibrium relative P_X/P_Y with trade _____.

   A. the nation exporting commodity X will want to export more of X than at equilibrium

   B. the nation importing commodity X will want to import less of X than at equilibrium

   C. P_X/P_Y will fall toward the equilibrium P_X/P_Y

   D. all of the above

5. The offer curve of a nation shows _____.

   A. the supply of a nation's imports

   B. the demand for a nation's exports

   C. the trade partner's demand for imports and supply of exports

   D. the nation's demand for imports and supply of exports

6. If a nation does not affect world prices by its trading, its offer curve _____.

   A. is a straight line

   B. bulges toward the axis measuring the import commodity

   C. intersects the straight-line segment of the world's offer curve

   D. intersects the positively-sloped portion of the world's offer curve

7. Sketch a figure similar to Figure 3.26, extend the P_F' price line and the offer curve of Nation 1 until they cross. (In extending it, let the offer curve of Nation 1 bent backward) and explain the forces that push P_F' towards PB in terms of commodity Y. And what does the backward-bending (negatively sloped) segment of Nation 1's offer curve indicate?

8. Which of the following statements is false?

   A. The gains from trade can be broken down into the gains from exchange and the gains from specialization

   B. gains from exchange result even without specialization

   C. gains from specialization result even without exchange

   D. none of the above

Chapter 4 Classical Trade Theory

Learning goals

After learning this chapter, you should be able to:

✓ understand the status of mercantilism.

✓ understand the trade theory of absolute advantage.

✓ understand the trade theory of comparative advantage.

✓ understand the relationship between opportunity costs and relative commodity prices.

✓ do general equilibrium analysis and partial equilibrium analysis for trade theories.

This chapter will review the history, combing classical economists about the division of labor and trade ideas, and thus we can understand how the international trade theory is produced and developed from the real economic life, and how the international trade theory model breaks through step by step the theoretical limitations and constantly improves and develops. Through the study of these international trade theories, we can understand why trade takes place among countries, how trade interests are generated, what criteria are for participating countries to participate in international division of labor and engage in international trade, and how trade interests are distributed among participating countries.

We begin with a brief discussion of the economic doctrines known as mercantilism that prevailed during the 17th and 18th centuries. We then go on to discuss the theory of absolute advantage, developed by Adam Smith. It remained, however, for David Ricardo, writing some 40 years after Smith, to truly explain the pattern of and the gains from trade with his law of comparative advantage. The law of comparative advantage is one of the most important laws of economics, with applicability to nations as well as to individuals.

4.1 Mercantilism

Mercantilism emerged and prevailed in Western Europe from the 15th century to the middle of the 17th century. It is an economic theory or economic system in the period of primitive accumulation of capital in Western Europe after the collapse of feudalism. It is an economic theory and policy system reflecting the interests of the bourgeoisie in the period of primitive accumulation of capital.

4.1.1　Early mercantilism

From the 5th to the 11th century, Western Europe was in a dark age. Not only the economy and culture of Western Europe were backward, but also relatively primitive. At that time, there was no unified national state or sovereign state in the sense of modern politics. Historians usually use lords, knights and castles to describe the social and political features of Western Europe before the 11th century. The castle is not only the military fortress of the lord but also their residence. These tall buildings are not only built in dangerous places, but also rise up on the flat land. In those most chaotic years, the lord's bedroom in the castle has his horses and weapons, ready to ride the horse to fight and attack. After the 11th century, the social and political situation in Western Europe gradually stabilized, the development of feudal countries entered a new stage, and countries gradually stepped into their own distinctive development tracks. Among them, Britain and France became stronger and stronger. From 1337 to 1453, a hundred year war broke out between Britain and France, and France won. After the Hundred Years' War, Britain broke out a civil war. The British and French kingship was constantly strengthened, and the country was gradually unified. Germany originated from the Eastern Frankish Kingdom, and later established the Roman Empire. After the demise of the Holy Roman Empire, Germany was divided into many countries, such as Austria. On the whole, during this period, Germany was always fragmented and its national strength was weak.

At the end of the 15th century, Western European society entered the period of disintegration of feudal society, and capitalist production relations began to sprout and grow. The great discovery of geography expanded the world market and gave great stimulus to industry, commerce and navigation. Industrial and commercial capital played a prominent role in promoting the unification of domestic markets and the formation of world markets, and promoting the development of industry, commerce and foreign trade. At the same time as industrial and commercial capital was strengthened, some Western European countries established enlightened and autocratic centralized states, and used state power to support the development of industrial and commercial capital. With the development of industrial and commercial capital and the implementation of national policies to support industrial and commercial capital, the requirements to explain these economic policies in theory have emerged, and the mercantilist theory has gradually formed.

From the 15th to the middle of the 16th century, early mercantilism was popular. The early mercantilism was called balance of money, also known as monetarism or bullionism. Early mercantilists regarded increasing domestic currency accumulation and preventing currency outflow as the guiding principles of foreign trade policy, and believed that the government should take administrative or legislative measures to directly control currency flow. They thought that all purchases would reduce the currency, and all sales would increase the currency. A country should try not to buy or buy less. Only in this way could a country accumulate more money and make the country rich. So in foreign trade, it was better to sell only and not to buy, in order to maintain a foreign trade surplus in every transaction, and gold and silver could flow into domestic market.

One of the main representatives was William Stafford (1554 − 1612) of England. William Stafford's masterpiece is *A Compendious Brief Examination of Certain Ordinary Complaints*, published in 1581. He pointed out in the book, "People must always pay attention. What we buy from others is not more than what we sell to them. Otherwise, we will fall into poverty, and they will become increasingly rich."

In 1615, Antoine de Montchretien, an early French mercantilist economist, used the term "political economy" for the first time to write and published his representative work *Political Economy for the King and Queen*, which strongly advocated the King's intervention in the management of the country's economic life.

4.1.2   Late mercantilism

From the middle of the 16th century to the second half of the 17th century, it was the late mercantilism stage. Like the early mercantilists, the late mercantilists still believed that money was the basic form of wealth, equating money with wealth and precious metals with money. They still insisted on developing foreign trade to import gold and silver coins as the primary way for a country to become rich and strong, and advocated that the state interfere in economic life, take restrictions, protection, incentives and other measures to promote the development of industry and trade, and increase the import of gold and silver coins. However, compared with the early mercantilists, the views of the late mercantilists on foreign trade issues have changed.

Late mercantilists had new ideas about increasing monetary accumulation. They believed that it was unwise to store up money for the purpose of accumulating wealth. They stressed that not only selling more could increase the accumulation of money, but also buying more. That is to say, a country can import goods from other countries and even increase its purchase of goods from other countries, but it should ensure that the total amount of goods purchased from other countries is less than the total amount of goods sold to other countries. That is, it should ensure that the total amount of output currency is less than the total amount of input currency, so as to exchange more currency.

Thomas Munn (1571–1641) is the representative of late British mercantilism and the main advocate of the British trade balance theory. In the 16th century, the early mercantilists' policy of prohibiting the export of gold and silver as currency was still dominant in Britain. In the early 17th century, they lashed out at the East India Company for exporting a large amount of gold and silver in foreign trade. In order to refute this accusation, in 1621, Thomas Munn published a book *On Trade between Britain and East India, and Answered All Kinds of Common Objections to This Trade*. He discussed that the East India Company exported gold and silver to buy goods in the East India region, and then sold them to other countries. The amount of gold and silver returned was far more than the amount shipped out. This shows that Munn has got rid of the old idea of banning the export of gold and silver. Thomas Munn's basic idea is to demand the abolition of the ban on currency export. He believes that the important thing is not to keep the currency, but to put the currency into profitable foreign trade. As long as the country strives for a surplus in foreign trade, it can bring more currency and make Britain rich.

In order to ensure the surplus of foreign trade, Thomas Munn proposed and demonstrated various measures that should be taken. He advocated expanding domestic commodity exports and reducing consumption of foreign commodities. To this end, he called for serious economy, reducing the import of luxury goods, expanding the cultivation of cash crops, and striving to be self-sufficient in food and clothing. He called for the elimination of various measures unfavorable to exports, such as stabilizing the value of the local currency and opposing fraud in currency quality and weight, promoting the development of local handicraft industry, exporting more manufactured products and reducing the export of raw materials, reducing or exempting taxes on export commodities, so that export commodities could enhance their competitiveness in the international market at low prices. He also stressed the role of protective tariffs, and advocated that export goods and goods imported and re-exported from foreign countries should be given tariff consideration, and imported goods to be consumed in the country should be subject to heavy taxes. He also noted the gains and losses of the so-called invisible import items in international trade, such as freight, insurance, tourism expenses, and so on. Munn also attached special importance to the development of the shipping industry and entrepot trade.

Another representative figure of late mercantilism is Jean Baptiste Colbert (1619 – 1683) of France, also an important political activist, finance minister and mercantilist practitioner in France. During his tenure as French finance minister, he carried out a whole set of mercantilist policies, known as Colbert doctrine, which made French mercantilism a model of mercantilism in other European countries. Colbert's mercantilist policy played a positive role in the development of France's industry and commerce. France was also called the most powerful country in the European continent during the Louis XIV Period, and its overseas expansion reached its peak for a time, thus becoming a model for other countries. Colbert encouraged the development of domestic industry. He abolished some domestic barriers, unified the tax rate, reformed the tax system, and changed the physical tax into the monetary tax. He improved transportation and facilitate domestic trade. He also implement a protective tariff policy to ban the import of foreign industrial products and encourage the import of raw materials. At the same time, the export of domestic agricultural products, especially grain, was prohibited. He established the navy, developed the shipping industry, and built a huge fleet and large merchant ships. He established trading companies between India and America to develop maritime trade, especially ocean trade.

Although Colbert could be called the most outstanding person who practiced this economic theory in the era of late mercantilism, most of his achievements were quickly squandered by Louis XIV. The king was constantly involved in large-scale wars, and the huge military expenditure dried up the government's financial resources, which eventually led to financial collapse. After Colbert's death, he was criticized a lot and his mercantilist policy was completely abandoned.

4.1.3 Evaluation

This book interprets mercantilism in the mid-15th to 17th century as " classical mercantilism", which means that the mercantilist economic theory produced before the emergence of classical economics is distinguished from the later new mercantilism.

The classical mercantilism generally attaches importance to money and regards the amount of money a country has as the standard to measure its wealth.

Mercantilists generally believe that it is impossible to increase national wealth through domestic trade alone. In domestic trade, the increase of one's wealth will inevitably lead to the decrease of another's wealth. Therefore, if a country wants to increase the total amount of money, it must carry out foreign trade. They also believe that foreign trade can not only convert domestic products into currency and flow into domestic market, but also be a source of profits. In foreign trade, a country should also follow certain principles: It can buy more and sell more, but it should ensure that income is greater than expenditure. That is, it should ensure that exports are greater than imports, maintain a foreign trade surplus, and make money flow into the country continuously.

In order to promote the expansion of foreign trade and the development of domestic industry, mercantilism put forward the idea of state intervention by using administrative means, tariff control and tax system. In the view of mercantilism, state intervention is to devote the whole country to promoting the prosperity and strength of the country. Internally, the country should establish unified market norms and commodity economic order, and reduce domestic trade taxes, reduce commodity prices, improve commodity quality, promote the development of commodity economy, and maintain the stability of commodity economy. Externally, the country should implement a protective tariff policy, strictly prohibit the import of domestically produced goods, restrict the consumption of foreign products in the country, and encourage the import of raw materials.

Since it is impossible for all trade-participating countries to make surpluses at the same time, and the total amount of gold and silver at any time is fixed, the profits of one country are always based on the losses of other countries. That is, international trade is a "zero sum game".

Mercantilism is developed on the basis of the realistic economic problem of seeking national prosperity and strength. In the process of development and evolution for more than two centuries, it not only inspires the emergence of political economy and classical economics in ideology, but also promotes the development of international trade in practice.

Firstly, mercantilism breaks through the narrow perspective of ancient and medieval scholars in analyzing economic issues, extends economic issues from traditional family and manor life to the whole country, brings economic issues back from the altar to reality, discusses the issue of national prosperity and strength from a macro perspective, and puts forward policy recommendations.

Secondly, mercantilism has promoted the development of the commodity economy. With the deepening of social division of labor, the workshop handicraft industry and manufacturing industry have continued to grow, promoting the establishment and development of the Western market economy, accelerating the collapse of the feudal system and the establishment of the capitalist system. National industrial development and commercial regulation have promoted the emergence of industrial capital. With the development of capitalist production relations, industrial capital has gradually replaced commercial capital to occupy the dominant position of production, and new classical economics has emerged.

Thirdly, mercantilism emphasizes the importance of international trade. First, the theory of trade surplus and the preliminary exploration of exchange rate put forward by them developed into the later balance of payments. Second, they changed their attitude towards businessmen. Mercantilists not only proposed to improve the status of businessmen, but also recognized the importance of businessmen to the country. They also allowed nobles to participate in commercial activities, and even allowed their descendants to intermarry with merchants, which closely linked the aristocratic lineage and commercial wealth. Third, the trading companies with monopoly privileges or other privileges proposed by them have become the forerunners of modern companies and influenced the establishment and development of European economic organizations through multilateral trade. Finally, the protective tariff and other trade policies they put forward still affect the establishment and implementation of national trade policies.

Fourthly, mercantilism has promoted the rise of Britain, France and other Western European nation states. Britain began to implement the mercantilist economic policy from the Tudor Dynasty, and vigorously developed industry, commerce and navigation. The development of maritime trade brought a large amount of commercial capital to Britain, which was in sharp contrast to the massive loss of gold and silver caused by Spain's failure to implement the mercantilist economic policy. The development of British Shipbuilding Industry and the improvement of navigation technology have made Britain gain obvious advantages at sea, laying a solid foundation for defeating the "invincible fleet" and establishing its hegemonic position. Through the implementation of mercantilist policies for several centuries, Britain and France occupied a dominant position in colonial expansion and foreign trade, promoted the accumulation of national commercial capital, and laid a solid economic foundation for the development of the later Industrial Revolution.

In view of the limitations of the times and the lack of in-depth understanding of the economy by mercantilist scholars, it is undeniable that mercantilism has some shortcomings.

Firstly, mercantilism believes that wealth comes from the circulation field, and the scope of commercial activities is the circulation field. It thinks about the circulation field, but it thinks little about the more important production field, and does not consider the value of goods and labor. And at that time, the development of the economic field was that circulation restricted production, not production restricted circulation, so they turned their attention more to the field of circulation. In addition, the reason why they attach importance to money and gold and silver is more as the form of wealth, and they fail to touch the true essence of wealth or money. Therefore, the theory of mercantilism has certain limitations.

Secondly, mercantilism regards international trade as a zero-sum game, which is obviously wrong. They believe that the total amount of currency is fixed. If a country wants to increase its currency, it must obtain it from other countries. The increase of one country's currency will inevitably lead to the decrease of other countries' currencies. Therefore, it is necessary to use various means, including protection of tariffs, colonial plunder, military war, etc., to obtain other countries' wealth. Therefore, it is necessary to think deeply about the importance of foreign trade.

 ### 4.1.4　New mercantilism

In 1776, when Adam Smith published his book, mercantilism was severely criticized. With the development of classical economics, the economic thought of laissez-faire was recognized by most economists. In addition, mercantilism was limited to the circulation field of commodity economy, and their ideas of money and wealth were abandoned. Mercantilism gradually declined in the long river of economic development. Western European countries represented by Britain gradually recognized the economic thought of free trade and laissez-faire of classical economics.

But, mercantilism had a new development after the Second World War, that is, new mercantilism. In the 1970s, in order to explain the trade protection policy and economic nation-state thought in American foreign trade, the term new mercantilism was proposed by several economists such as Paul Krugman. Because of its similarities with mercantilist trade theory, it was widely accepted by the economic community.

Since the 1920s, mercantilism has entered a new stage of new mercantilism. It can be found that the development of new mercantilism is constantly changing with the development of the American economy. Since John Maynard Keynes (1883 – 1946) proposed the economic policy of state intervention in the 1930s, the development of new mercantilism has been closely linked with the economic development of the United States. From the 1920s to the 1970s, it can be said that the economic thought of new mercantilism developed. At this time, although the economic thought had developed to a certain extent, influenced by the mainstream economics of Keynesianism, it was still Keynesian economics that played an important ideological guiding role in the economy. On the one hand, the new mercantilism of the United States attributes the cause of economic problems to the huge trade deficit, and proposes a trade policy of encouraging exports and restricting imports to reduce the trade deficit. On the contrary, the new mercantilism relies on the hegemonic status of the United States dollar to promote the appreciation of other countries' currencies and damage the economic development of other countries in order to reduce the trade deficit.

4.2　Absolute advantage trade theory

Under the above theory and policy recommendations of mercantilism, free trade never seems possible. However, Adam Smith, the founder of classical economics, strongly proved the possibility and inevitability of free trade in his book, thus establishing the classical school of trade theory.

4.2.1　Who

Adam Smith (1723—1790) is a famous British economist in the 18th century, also the pioneer of classical trade theory. In the history of economic thought, Smith is honored as the founder of the classical economic school. In 1776, Smith published a book named *An Inquiry into the Nature and Causes of the Wealth of Nations* (also called *The Wealth of Nations* for short), which had established the theoretical system of classical political economics. In this work, which Smith spent nearly a decade writing, he first attributed knowledge in all major areas of economic science into a unified and complete system, and the basic idea throughout it was the laissez-faire market economy idea. Smith's thought has had a major impact on the development of international trade and even the whole economics.

Adam Smith was born in the family of a customs officer in Kirkcaldy in County Fife of Scotland. Because his father died before he was born, Adam Smith lived with his mother all his life. For 60 years, Smith served his mother dutifully and never married. He entered the University of Glasgow at the age of 14, studied mathematics and philosophy, and became interested in economics. He transferred to Oxford College at the age of 17. After graduation, he went to Edinburgh University to teach rhetoric and literature in 1748. From 1751 to 1764, he returned to Glasgow University to teach. During this period, his ethics lecture was revised and published in 1759 under the name of *Theory of Moral Sentiments*, which won him a reputation. He resigned as a professor in 1764. As a private teacher, he traveled to Europe and met famous people such as François-Marie Arouet (also called Voltaire), who had a great influence on him. In 1767, he resigned and returned to his hometown to write *The Wealth of Nations*, which was published nine years later. In 1787, he became President of the University of Glasgow.

4.2.2　What

Smith started with the simple truth that for two nations to trade with each other voluntarily, both nations must gain. If one nation gained nothing or lost, it would simply refuse to trade. But how does this mutually beneficial trade take place, and from where do these gains from trade come?

According to Adam Smith, trade between two nations is based on absolute advantage. When one nation is more efficient than (or has an absolute advantage over) another in the production of one commodity but is less efficient than (or has an absolute disadvantage with respect to) the other nation in producing a second commodity, then both nations can gain by each specializing in the production of the commodity of its absolute advantage and exchanging part of its output with the other nation for the commodity of its absolute disadvantage. By this process, resources are utilized in the most efficient way, and the output of both commodities will rise. This increase in the output of both commodities measures the gains from specialization in production available to be divided between the two nations through trade.

For example, because of climatic conditions, Canada is efficient in growing wheat but inefficient in growing bananas (hot houses would have to be used). On the contrary, Nicaragua is efficient in growing bananas but inefficient in growing wheat. Thus, Canada has an absolute advantage over Nicaragua in the cultivation of wheat but an absolute disadvantage in the cultivation of bananas. The opposite is true for Nicaragua.

Under these circumstances, both nations would benefit if each specialized in the production of the commodity of its absolute advantage and then traded with the other nation. Canada would specialize in the production of wheat (i.e., produce more than needed domestically) and exchange some of it for (surplus) bananas grown in Nicaragua. As a result, both more wheat and more bananas would be grown and consumed, and both Canada and Nicaragua would gain.

In this respect, a nation behaves no differently from an individual who does not attempt to produce all the commodities he or she needs. Rather, the individual produces only that commodity that he or she can produce most efficiently and then exchanges part of the output for the other commodities she or he needs or wants. In this way, total output and the welfare of all individuals are maximized.

Thus, while the mercantilists believed that one nation could gain only at the expense of another nation and advocated strict government control of all economic activity and trade, Adam Smith (and the other classical economists who followed him) believed that all nations would gain from free trade and strongly advocated a policy of laissez-faire (i.e., as little government interference with the economic system as possible). Free trade would cause world resources to be utilized most efficiently and would maximize world welfare. There were only a few exceptions to this policy of laissez-faire and free trade. One of these was the protection of industries important for national defense.

In view of this belief, it seems paradoxical that today most nations impose many restrictions on the free flow of international trade. Trade restrictions are invariably rationalized in terms of national welfare. In reality, trade restrictions are advocated by the few industries and their workers who are hurt by imports. As such, trade restrictions benefit the few at the expense of the many (who will have to pay higher prices for competing domestic goods).

Smith believes that the differences in labor productivity among countries and the reasons for the resulting international division of labor are natural. What products a country is best at producing, and it has absolute advantages in which products, are not only caused by historical conditions, but also by a country's geographical environment, soil, climate and other natural conditions. Smith's views are further developed in later theories of international trade.

4.2.3　Model assumptions

In order to better explain Adam Smith's absolute advantage trade theory, this book constructs a theoretical model to analyze the trade pattern and trade gains under the guidance of this theory.

As with all other economic analyses, when studying international trade theories, economists often assume many variables constant, and simplify as much as possible the other conditions that do not directly affect the analysis.

The assumptions of the absolute advantage trade theory are as follows:

①There are two countries (Country 1 and Country 2), two commodities (commodity X and commodity Y).

②The two countries have different production technologies for the same products, but within each country, all enterprises use the same technology to produce the same products. Moreover, the technological levels of both countries remain unchanged.

③In each country, labor is the only factor input. The labor resources of each country are fixed and homogeneous at a given time.

④Labor market is always in the state of full employment.

⑤Labor factors can flow between different domestic sectors, but not between countries.

⑥Returns to scale remain unchanged.

⑦All markets are perfectly competitive. No producer or consumer has enough power to exert influence on the market. They are all price recipients. Moreover, the price of products produced in various countries is equal to the average production cost of products, and there is no economic profit.

⑧There is free trade among countries, and there is no government intervention or regulation on trade.

⑨Transportation and other transaction costs are zero.

⑩The trade between the two countries is balanced, so there is no need to consider the flow of money between countries.

4.2.4 Model illustration

Now, a specific example is used to explain the absolute advantage trade model. Suppose that the existing two countries, China and the United States, both produce cotton and wheat, but with different technical levels. Labor is the only input factor invested, and the workforce in both countries is 100. Labor productivity varies between the two countries due to different production technical levels, and the amount of output varies. Table 4.1 shows the production possibilities in both countries.

Table 4.1   Production possibilities

	China	United States
cotton (10,000 meters)	100	80
wheat (tons)	50	100

From the perspective of labor productivity (E), China can produce 10,000 meters of cotton per person per year, while the United States can only 8,000 meters per person per year, so China has the absolute advantage of producing cotton. The United States can produce 1 ton of wheat per year, but China can only produce 0.5 tons per person per year, so the United States has the absolute advantage of producing wheat, as shown in Table 4.2.

Table 4.2   Labor productivity

	China	United States
cotton (10,000 meters)	1 = 100 units/100 labor	0.8 = 80 units/100 labor
wheat (tons)	0.5 = 50 units/100 labor	1 = 100 units/100 labor

From the perspective of production cost (C), it only needs 1 labor force per 10,000 meters of cotton in China, but 1.25 labor force in the United States. Therefore, with $C_{China} <$ C_{US}, China has the absolute advantage of producing cotton. On the contrary, 2 labor per ton of wheat needs to be invested in China, and only 1 in the United States, namely $C_{China} > C_{US}$, so the United States has an absolute advantage in wheat production, as shown in Table 4.3.

Table 4.3　Production cost

	China	United States
cotton (10,000 meters)	1 = 100 labor/100 units	1.25 = 100 labor/80 units
wheat (tons)	2 = 100 labor/50 units	1 = 100 labor/100 units

The results between the two methods are consistent, namely that China has an absolute advantage in cotton and the United States has an absolute advantage in wheat. According to the theory of absolute advantage, China should solely produce and export cotton and import wheat. And the United States should export wheat and import cotton. This is also called complete division of labor.

In a closed economy, the largest amount of products that China and the United States can consume is their respective cotton and wheat yields. Assuming that both countries allocate their resources to the production of both products, China's production (consumption) is 50 units of cotton and 25 units of wheat, while the United States is 28 units of cotton and 65 units of wheat, as shown in Table 4.4.

Table 4.4　Gains of trade

		China		United States		World	
		cotton	wheat	cotton	wheat	cotton	wheat
Before trade	production	50	25	28	65	78	90
	exchange rate	1 : 0.5		1 : 1.25			
	consumption	50	25	28	65	78	90
After trade	production	100	0	0	100	100	100
	exchange rate	1 : 1					
	consumption	70	30	30	70	100	100
Comparison	production	+50	−25	−28	+35	+22	+10
	consumption	+20	+5	+2	+5	+22	+10

According to the data in above tables, the production possibility curves of China and the United States can be obtained, as shown in Figure 4.1. Demand in the two countries is represented by indifference curves. Please note that since labor is the only factor of production and homogeneous, in this case, the opportunity cost is unchanged, and the production possibility curve is displaced by a straight line.

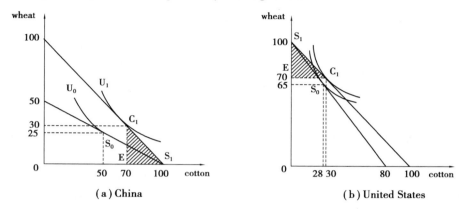

(a) China   (b) United States

Figure 4.1   General equilibrium

After specialized production, China puts all its resources (labor) to cotton production at 100 units, and the United States puts all its resources (labor) to wheat production at 100 units. Both production points move from S_0 when no trade to S_1. Suppose that China keeps 70 units of cotton for consumption by itself, and takes out the remaining 30 units to exchange for wheat with the United States, while the United States keeps 70 units of wheat for its own consumption, and exchanges the remaining 30 units of wheat with China for cotton. In this way, 30 units of cotton are exchanged for 30 units of wheat in the international market. As a result of the trade, China has 70 units of cotton (self-produced) and 30 units of wheat (imported), 20 units and 5 units more than self-sufficient. And the United States has 30 units of cotton (imported) and 70 units of wheat (self-produced), 2 units and 5 units more than self-sufficient. Consumption has increased in both countries, reaching levels impossible when self-sufficient. That is, the consumption point moves from S_0 to C_1. This is the trade gain or the trade benefit.

The difference between the production point (S_1) and the consumption point (C_1) is the triangle of international trade volume. The "trade triangle" is C_1ES_1, where ES_1 means the number of exports, and C_1E means the number of imports.

As can be seen from Figure 4.1, the production capacity (expressed by the production possibility curve) of both countries has not changed after the specialized production, but the consumption level has improved, and both countries have gained benefits from the international division of labor and international trade, reaching a higher level of social welfare than that before the trade (from U_0 to U_1).

It should be noted that in the general equilibrium analysis, the level of the social indifference curve is welfare rather than the absolute consumption of products. If China has a particular preference for cotton, its post-trade consumption level could also be 80 units of cotton cloth and 20 units of wheat. At this point, the consumption of cotton increases and the wheat consumption decreases compared with before the trade, but the overall level of social welfare is still increased. Therefore, the increase in the consumption of both products after the trade can be used to illustrate the trade gains of the whole country, but the trade gains does not necessarily need to be proved by increase in consumption of both products.

Unlike general equilibrium analysis, the partial equilibrium analysis only discusses a certain product market rather than the economy as a whole. Partial equilibrium analysis helps to understand the price, production, consumption and consumption of a specific product market and the interests of the producers and consumers of this product, and also helps to understand how the equilibrium price of goods is determined and changed.

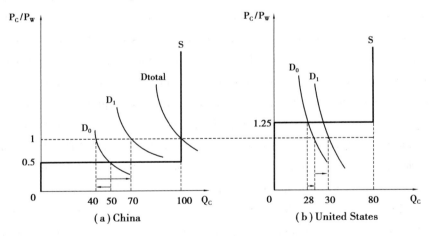

Figure 4.2   Partial equilibrium

In the cotton market, as shown in Figure 4.2, the exchange ratio between Chinese cotton and US wheat is $1:1$, while in practice that ratio (namely the international price) is constantly changing. Its level depends on the supply and demand of the two products in the international market. It is always certain that China cannot exchange 1 unit of cotton for less than 0.5 units of wheat, and for the United States, importing 1 unit of Chinese cotton will pay no more than 1.25 units of wheat, or it is unprofitable. Therefore, the relative price of cotton (wheat/cotton exchange ratio) in free trade should be between 0.5 and 1.25, which is what both countries can profit from the trade.

In China, the relative price (compared with wheat) of cotton is 0.5, so, if the relative price of cotton cloth is less than 0.5, China will not produce the cotton. If the relative price of cotton equals 0.5, China may or may not produce, the output ranging from 0 to 100 (maximum output). If the relative price of cotton is above 0.5, China will use all resources to produce cotton, but the supply will not exceed its production capacity (100). So the supply curve of Chinese cotton is vertical at 100. Similar situations happen in the United States. If the relative price of US cotton is below 1.25, the United States will not produce cotton. If the relative price of cotton is equal to 1.25, the United States may or may not produce, the output ranging from 0 to 80 (maximum output), and if the relative price is above 1.25, the supply curve is vertical at 80.

The actual amount of production is determined by demand (expressed in the "D" line). According to the hypothesis, the production of cotton is 50 units and 28 units respectively in the two countries. Because the relative price of Chinese cotton is lower than that of the United States, once trade occurs, the relative price of cotton cloth between the two countries will converge. That is, the relative price of Chinese cotton cloth will rise, while the United States decreases, thus resulting in the production of Chinese cotton cloth reaching 100, while the United States dropping to 0. At this time, China becomes the only producer of cotton needed by the world. China will face the total demand for cotton in both countries. The international price of cotton is determined by China's supply and the total demand of both countries. In this case, this final international equilibrium price is assumed to be 1. It should be noted that here the aggregate demand for cotton in both countries does not equal the demand for cotton cloth under closed conditions (with "D_0" line represents) simply added up, but the sum of the demand for cotton cloth (with "D_1" line represents) between the two countries in terms of free trade.

How will the free trade affect cotton consumption in the two countries? Firstly, the demand for cotton will be affected by price changes. According to the law of demand, the demand for cotton decreases in countries where cotton prices rise, and the demand for cotton cloth increases in countries where cotton prices lower down. This effect is called the price effect. The price effect is shown that the demand slides up and down along the original demand curve. Secondly, demand for cotton cloth is also affected by changes in income generated through trade. As a result of their participation in trade, countries have not only increased their income directly through exports, but also saved money on the consumption of the same amount of cheap importing products. International trade increases national total revenues, as measured in kind or at their original prices. Since here cotton is a normal product (revenue demand elasticity is positive) , as revenue increases, demand increases, and the demand curve moves to the right. This effect is called the income effect.

Therefore, when China exports cotton, the relative price of domestic cotton rises. Through the price effect, people will reduce the consumption of cotton and the consumption will move to the upper left along the original demand curve (assuming that the consumption drops to 40). At the same time, as China solely produces cotton and can exchange cotton for more wheat than in closed conditions, the increased national income measured in kind shifts the demand curve for cotton out (from D_0 to D_1), and the increase in total demand may even exceed the decline in consumption due to the price effect. As shown in Figure 4.2, the price effect of Chinese cotton demand is a decrease of 10 (from 50 to 40), while the income effect is an increase of 30 (from 40 to 70), with a net increase of 20. It can be seen that whether China's final demand for cotton increases or decreases depends. For the United States, the situation is relatively clear. Because the price effect and income effect are consistent. The cotton price drops and demand increases, and with the same amount of wheat now exchange for more cotton to increase the income of American labor force measured in kind, the demand curve of cotton moving outward (from D_0 to D_1), increasing the total demand for cotton at the same price. It is uncertain how much the final increase of the US cotton consumption is, but it is certain that the final consumption is more than before importing, unless cotton is an inferior good.

If we don't know the production capacity and only know the labor productivity, we can also infer the mode of trade and the gains from trade. Table 4.5 shows that 1 hour of labor time produces 6 bushels of wheat in the United States but only 1 in the United Kingdom. On the contrary, 1 hour of labor time produces 5 yards of cloth in the United Kingdom but only 4 in the United States. Thus, the United States is more efficient than, or has an absolute advantage over, the United Kingdom in the production of wheat, whereas the United Kingdom is more efficient than, or has an absolute advantage over, the United States in the production of cloth. With trade, the United States would specialize in the production of wheat and exchange part of it for British cloth. The opposite is true for the United Kingdom.

Table 4.5 Labor productivity in absolute advantage

	United States	United Kingdom
wheat (bushels/hour)	6	1
cloth (yards/hour)	4	5

If the United States exchanges 6 bushels of wheat (6W) for 6 yards of British cloth (6C), the United States gains 2C or saves 1/2 hour or 30 minutes of labor time (since the United States can only exchange 6W for 4C domestically). Similarly, the 6W that the United Kingdom receives from the United States is equivalent to or would require 6 hours of labor time to produce in the United Kingdom. These same 6 hours can produce 30C in the United Kingdom (6 hours times 5 yards of cloth per hour). By being able to exchange 6C (requiring a little over 1 hour to produce in the United Kingdom) for 6W with the United States, the United Kingdom gains 24C, or saves almost 5 labor hours.

The fact that the United Kingdom gains much more than the United States is not important at this time and we will discuss it later. What is important is that both nations can gain from specialization in production and trade.

The absolute advantage trade theory reveals the law that international division of labor and specialized production can make more effective use of resources and thus improve labor productivity. It is the first time to demonstrate the idea that both sides of trade can benefit from international trade.

4.3 Comparative advantage trade theory

Absolute advantage, however, can explain only a very small part of world trade today, such as some of the trade between developed and developing countries. Most of the world trade, especially trade among developed countries, cannot be explained by absolute advantage. It remains for David Ricardo, with the law of comparative advantage, to truly explain the basis for and the gains from trade. Indeed, absolute advantage will be seen to be only a special case of the more general theory of comparative advantage.

4.3.1　Who

David Ricardo (1772−1823) is an economist in the period of the British Industrial Revolution and a master of classical political economy. He inherited and developed the labor value theory founded by Adam Smith, and took it as the theoretical basis for establishing the comparative advantage theory.

David Ricardo was born in London, in the family of a rich security broker. From the age of 14, he followed his father in trading activities and became rich through speculation. However, Ricardo fell in love with a girl with a religious belief different from his family. His father resolutely disagreed with the marriage. The young and vigorous Ricardo fell out with his old father, and got married with the girl. At the age of 21, his father drove Ricardo out of his home. Ricardo had to operate independently. With his 7 years' experience in the security-trading industry, as well as the help of his friends, Ricardo's career was soon on the right track. In just a few years, he had already made a fortune. At the age of 25, he became a large asset owner with millions of pounds. At first, he was enthusiastic about natural science, but after reading Adam Smith's book *On the Nature and Causes of National Wealth* in 1799 (when he was 27 years old), he became very interested in political economy, which started his lifelong research career. In his 14 year short academic career, he left behind a large number of books, articles, notes, letters and speeches for future generations. Among them, the book *On the Principles of Political Economy and Taxation* published in 1817 is the most famous. This is an epoch-making economic work, which has developed the British classical political economy to a new highest level. In this book, Ricardo discussed the problems of value, land rent, distribution and international trade, all of which were necessary for the economic and social development at that time. Starting from the development of social productive forces, Ricardo focused on the issue of distribution and believed that distribution was the center of political and economic research. He was elected to the House of Lords in 1819, but died in 1823 at the age of 51 suddenly due to the infection of ears.

4.3.2 What

As an important figure in classical political economy, David Ricardo, like Adam Smith, advocated free trade, believing that everyone would naturally benefit the whole society while pursuing his own interests. Based on Smith's trade theory of absolute advantage, Ricardo proposed the trade theory of comparative advantage.

The theory holds that the basis of international trade is not limited to absolute differences in labor productivity. As long as there are relative differences in labor productivity among countries, there will be relative differences in production costs and product prices, so that countries can have comparative advantages in different products and make international division of labor and international trade possible. Therefore, each country should focus on the production and export of products with "comparative advantages" and give up the production of and import products with "comparative disadvantages", by following the principle—"Of two interests choose the more, while of two evils choose the less".

4.3.3 Model illustration

In addition to emphasizing the relative differences in labor productivity rather than the absolute differences between the two countries, the assumptions of the comparative advantage trade model are basically the same as the absolute advantage trade model.

In the comparative advantage trade model, the production and trade patterns are determined by the relative differences in the labor productivity and the differences in the resulting relative production costs. Countries should specialize in producing and export products with comparative advantage and import products with comparative disadvantage.

Now we use the similar example of the United States and China to explain the comparative advantage trade model. Table 4.6 shows the production possibilities in both countries.

Table 4.6 Production possibilities

	China	**United States**
cotton (10,000 meters)	100	120
wheat (tons)	50	100

How to judge which goods a country has comparative advantage in? It can be judged by three methods: relative labor productivity, relative production cost and opportunity cost.

Relative labor productivity (RE) is the ratio of labor productivity of different products, or the ratio of per capita output of two different products, as expressed by the formula:

$$RE_{1A} = \frac{E_{1A}}{E_{1B}} = \frac{Q_A/L}{Q_B/L}$$

If the relative labor productivity of Country 1 producing product A is higher than that of Country 2 producing the same product, namely, $RE_{1A} > RE_{2A}$, then Country 1 has a comparative advantage in the production of this product A. Conversely, it has a comparative disadvantage.

Table 4.7 Comparative labor productivity

	China	**United States**
cotton (/wheat)	2= 1/0.5 √	1.2= 1.2/1
wheat (/cotton)	0.5= 0.5/1	0.83 =1/1.2√

According to the formula, the relative labor productivity of China's cotton is 2 units, while this in the United States is 1.2. Because of 2 > 1.2, the relative labor productivity of Chinese cotton is higher than that of the United States, so China has a comparative advantage in the production of cotton. The same method shows that the United States has a comparative advantage in wheat production, as shown in Table 4.7.

Relative production cost (RC) refers to the ratio of factor input of unit product to that of another product, as expressed by the formula:

$$RC_{1A} = \frac{C_{1A}}{C_{1B}} = \frac{L/Q_A}{L/Q_B}$$

If the relative cost of Country 1 to produce product A is lower than the relative cost of Country 2 to produce the same product A, namely, $RC_{1A} < RC_{2A}$, then Country 1 has a comparative advantage in the production of this product A.

The calculation shows that the relative cost of Chinese cotton is 0.5, lower than that of the United States, so it has a comparative advantage in cotton production, while the United States has a comparative advantage in wheat production, as shown in Table 4.8.

Table 4.8 Comparative cost

	China	United States
cotton (/wheat)	0.5 = 1/2 √	0.83 = 0.83/1
wheat(/cotton)	2 = 2/1	1.2 = 1/0.83 √

Opportunity cost (OC) means the quantity of product B that must be abandoned in order to produce more of product A. The opportunity cost of product A is:

$$OC_{1A} = \frac{\Delta Q_{1B}}{\Delta Q_{1A}}$$

If the opportunity cost of Country 1 to produce product A is lower than the relative cost of Country 2 to produce the same product A, namely, $OC_{1A} < OC_{2A}$, then Country 1 has a comparative advantage in the production of this product A.

Table 4.9 Opportunity cost

	China	United States
cotton (/wheat)	0.5 √	0.83
wheat (/cotton)	2	1.2 √

If China wants to produce 1 unit of cotton, it needs to input 1 labor, and if China wants to produce 1 unit of wheat, it needs to input 2 labors, based on the production possibility. That means in China, to increase 1 unit of cotton has to sacrifice 0.5 units of wheat. There the opportunity cost of cotton in China is 0.5. Similarly we can obtain the opportunity costs of other products. As shown in Table 4.9, the opportunity cost of wheat in the United States is lower, so it has a comparative advantage in wheat, while China has a lower opportunity cost in cotton, so it has a comparative advantage in cotton.

From the calculation results of the above 3 different methods, we can know that the three methods lead to the same conclusion. At the same time, it can also be found that a country has an absolute advantage in the production of a certain product, but not necessarily a comparative advantage, such as American cotton. Moreover, a country has no absolute advantage in the production of certain products, but may have a comparative advantage, such as Chinese cotton. In this case, according to Ricardo's comparative advantage theory, China should specifically produce and export cotton and import wheat, while the United States should specifically produce and export wheat and import cotton.

Table 4.10   Gains of trade

		China		United States		World	
		cotton	wheat	cotton	wheat	cotton	wheat
Before trade	production	50	25	60	50	78	90
	exchange rate	1 : 0.5 (2 : 1)		1 : 0.833 (6 : 5)			
	consumption	50	25	60	50	78	90
After trade	production	100	0	0	100	100	100
	exchange rate	3 : 2 (1 : 0.66)					
	consumption	40	40	60	60	100	100
Comparison	production	+50	−25	−60	+50	−10	+25
	consumption	−10	+15	+0	+10	−10	+25

In a closed economy, the largest amount of products that China and the United States can consume is their respective cotton and wheat yields. Assuming that both countries allocate their resources to the production of both products, China's production (consumption) is 50 units of cotton and 25 units of wheat, while the United States is 60 units of cotton and 50 units of wheat, as shown in Table 4.10.

It can be seen from Table 4.10 that none of the two countries would suffer from free international trade. Only the gains distribution between the two countries depends.

We can make the general equilibrium analysis based on the above tables, as Figure 4.3 shows.

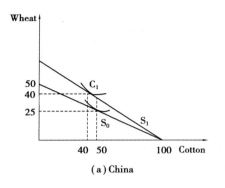
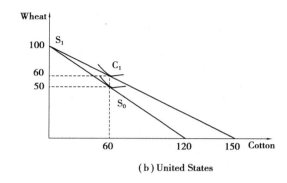

(a) China   (b) United States

Figure 4.3   General equilibrium of comparative advantage

After specialized production, China puts all resources (labor) into cotton production at 100 units, and the United States puts all resources (labor) to wheat production at 100 units. Both production points move from S_0 without trade to S_1 with trade. Assuming that the international trade price (wheat to cotton exchange ratio) is 2/3 (between 1/2 and 5/6). It also assumes that China keeps 40 units of cotton for itself and exchanges the remaining 60 units for wheat with the United States. The United States keeps 60 units of wheat for itself and trades the remaining 40 units of wheat for just 60 units of cotton from China. As a result of trade, China has 40 units of cotton (its own production) and 40 units of wheat (imported). The United States has 60 units of cotton (imported) and 60 units of wheat (its own production). Consumption in both countries has increased overall, reaching levels impossible when self-sufficient. That is, the consumption point moves from S_0 to C_1.

It is obvious that the consumption levels of the two countries that participated in international trade have increased, although the production capacities (expressed by the production possibility curve) do not change. That is, both countries benefit from the international trade, reaching a higher level of social welfare than before the trade.

Like Figure 4.2, the partial equilibrium analysis can be obtained by supply curve and demand curve of the two countries.

We can also prove the comparative advantage trade theory by the example in Table 4.5, but with a little change in the numbers, as Table 4.11 shows. The only difference from Table 4.5 is that 1 hour labor in the United Kingdom can produce 2 units of cloth, instead of 5. This leads to the result that the United States has absolute advantage in both products. However, the RE of the UK cloth is 2 and the RE of US cloth is 4/6, meaning that RE of the UK cloth is higher and the United Kingdom has comparative advantage in cloth.

Table 4.11　Labor productivity in absolute advantage

	United States	United Kingdom
wheat（bushels/hour）	6	1
cloth（yards/hour）	4	2

To start with, we know that the United States would be indifferent to trade if it received only 4C from the United Kingdom in exchange for 6W, since the United States can produce exactly 4C domestically by utilizing the resources released in giving up 6W（see Table 4.11）. And the United States would certainly not trade if it received less than 4C for 6W. Similarly, the United Kingdom would be indifferent to trade if it had to give up 2C for each 1W it received from the United States, and it certainly would not trade if it had to give up more than 2C for 1W.

To show that both nations can gain, suppose the United States could exchange 6W for 6C with the United Kingdom. The United States would then gain 2C（or save 1/2 hour of labor time）since the United States could only exchange 6W for 4C domestically. To see that the United Kingdom would also gain, note that the 6W that the United Kingdom receives from the United States would require 6 hours to produce in the United Kingdom. The United Kingdom could instead use these 6 hours to produce 12C and give up only 6C for 6W from the United States. Thus, the United Kingdom would gain 6C or save 3 hours of labor time. Once again, the fact that the United Kingdom gains more from trade than the United States is not important at this point. What is important is that both nations can gain from trade even if one of them（in this case the United Kingdom）is less efficient than the other in the production of both commodities.

We can convince ourselves of this by considering a simple example from everyday life. Suppose a lawyer can type twice as fast as his secretary. The lawyer then has an absolute advantage over his secretary in both the practice of law and typing. However, since the secretary cannot practice law without a law degree, the lawyer has a greater absolute advantage or a comparative advantage in law, and the secretary has a comparative advantage in typing. According to the law of comparative advantage, the lawyer should spend all of his time practicing law and let his secretary do the typing. For example, if the lawyer earns $100 per hour practicing law and must pay his secretary $10 per hour to do the typing, he would actually lose $80 for each hour that he typed. The reason for this is that he would save $20（since he can type twice as fast as his secretary）but forgo earning $10 in the practice of law.

Returning to the case of the United States and the United Kingdom, we see that both nations would gain by exchanging 6W for 6C. However, this is not the only rate of exchange at which mutually beneficial trade can take place. Since the United States could exchange 6W for 4C domestically (in the sense that both require 1 hour to produce), the United States would gain if it could exchange 6W for more than 4C from the United Kingdom. On the contrary, in the United Kingdom, 6W = 12C (in the sense that both require 6 hours to produce). Anything less than 12C that the United Kingdom must give up to obtain 6W from the United States represents a gain from trade for the United Kingdom. To summarize, the United States gains to the extent that it can exchange 6W for more than 4C from the United Kingdom. The United Kingdom gains to the extent that it can give up less than 12C for 6W from the United States. Thus, the range for mutually advantageous trade is:

$$4C < 6W < 12C$$

The spread between 12C and 4C (i.e., 8C) represents the total gains from trade available to be shared by the two nations by trading 6W. For example, we have seen that when 6W are exchanged for 6C, the United States gains 2C and the United Kingdom 6C, making a total of 8C. The closer the rate of exchange is to 4C = 6W (the domestic, or internal, rate in the United States—see Table 4.11), the smaller is the share of the gain going to the United States and the larger is the share of the gain going to the United Kingdom. On the contrary, the closer the rate of exchange is to 6W = 12C (the domestic, or internal, rate in the United Kingdom), the greater is the gain of the United States relative to that of the United Kingdom.

For example, if the United States exchanged 6W for 8C with the United Kingdom, both nations would gain 4C, for a total gain of 8C. If the United States could exchange 6W for 10C, it would gain 6C and the United Kingdom only 2C. (Of course, the gains from trade are proportionately greater when more than 6W are traded.) In general, all we want to do is to prove that mutually beneficial trade can take place even if one nation is less efficient than the other in the production of both commodities.

So far the gains from specialization in production and trade have been measured in terms of cloth. However, the gains from trade can also be measured in terms of wheat, or both.

We can also further analyze trade income by drawing their production possibility curves and indifference lines based on the examples of the United Kingdom and the United States, assuming their respective production possibilities.

In the absence of trade, the United States might choose to produce and consume combination A (90W and 60C) on its production possibility frontier (see Figure 4.4), and the United Kingdom might choose combination A′ (40W and 40C).

With trade possible, the United States would specialize in the production of wheat (the commodity of its comparative advantage) and produce at point B (180W and 0C) on its production possibility frontier. Similarly, the United Kingdom would specialize in the production of cloth and produce at B′ (0W and 120C). If the United States then exchanges 70W for 70C with the United Kingdom, it ends up consuming at point E (110W and 70C), and the United Kingdom ends up consuming at E′ (70W and 50C). Thus, the United States gains 20W and 10C from trade (compare point E with point A), and the United Kingdom gains 30W and 10C (compare point A′ with point E′).

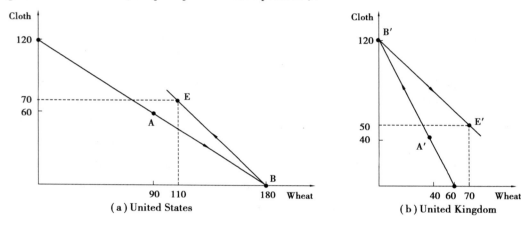

Figure 4.4　Gains from trade

The increased consumption of both wheat and cloth in both nations is made possible by the increased output that results as each nation specializes in the production of the commodity of its comparative advantage. That is, in the absence of trade, the United States produces 90W and the United Kingdom 40W, for a total of 130W. With specialization in production and trade, 180W are produced (all in the United States). Similarly, in the absence of trade, the United States produces 60C and the United Kingdom 40C, for a total of 100C. With specialization in production and trade, 120C are produced (all in the United Kingdom).

It is this increase in output of 50W and 20C resulting from specialization in production that is shared by the United States and the United Kingdom and represents their gains from trade. Recall that in the absence of trade, the United States would not specialize in the production of wheat because it also wanted to consume some cloth. Similarly, the United Kingdom would not specialize in the production of cloth in the absence of trade because it also wanted to consume some wheat.

The comparative advantage trade model has put forward the concept of relative cost, enriched and developed the trade theory of absolute advantage, and pointed out the direction for the later development and deepening of trade theory. However, there are still too many assumptions, especially "constant opportunity cost" and "complete division of labor", making this model out of touch with reality. And it fails to consider the dynamic change of a nation's advantage.

4.4　Empirical tests of the Ricardian model

We now examine the results of empirical tests of the Ricardian trade model. We will see that if we allow for different labor productivities in various industries in different nations, the Ricardian trade model does a reasonably good job at explaining the pattern of trade.

The first such empirical test of the Ricardian trade model was conducted by MacDougall in 1951 and 1952, using labor productivity and export data for 25 industries in the United States and the United Kingdom for the year 1937.

Since wages were twice as high in the United States as in the United Kingdom, MacDougall argued that costs of production would be lower in the United States in those industries where American labor was more than twice as productive as British labor. These would be the industries in which the United States had a comparative advantage with respect to the United Kingdom and in which it would undersell the United Kingdom in third markets (i.e., in the rest of the world). On the contrary, the United Kingdom would have a comparative advantage and undersell the United States in those industries where the productivity of British labor was more than one-half the productivity of American labor.

In his test, MacDougall excluded trade between the United States and the United Kingdom because tariffs varied widely from industry to industry, tending to offset the differences in labor productivity between the two nations. At the same time, both nations faced generally equal tariffs in third markets. The exclusion of trade between the United States and the United Kingdom did not bias the test because their exports to each other constituted less than 5 percent of their total exports.

Figure 4.5 summarizes MacDougall's results. The vertical axis measures the ratio of output per US worker to output per the UK worker. The higher this ratio, the greater the relative productivity of US labor. The horizontal axis measures the ratio of the United States to the United Kingdom exports to third markets. The higher this ratio, the larger are US exports in relation to UK exports to the rest of the world. Note that the scales are logarithmic

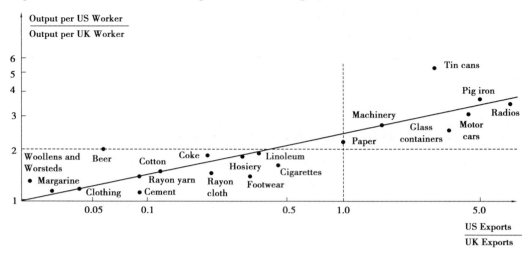

(so that equal distances refer to equal percentage changes) rather than arithmetic (where equal distances would measure equal absolute changes).

Figure 4.5   Relative labor productivities and comparative advantage between the United States and the United Kingdom

The points in the figure exhibit a clear positive relationship (shown by the solid line) between labor productivity and exports. That is, those industries where the productivity of labor is relatively higher in the United States than in the United Kingdom are the industries with the higher ratios of US to UK exports. This was true for the 20 industries shown in the figure (out of the total of 25 industries studied by MacDougall). The positive relationship between labor productivity and exports for the United States and the United Kingdom was confirmed by subsequent studies by Balassa using 1950 data and Stern using 1950 and 1959 data.

One possible question remained. Why did the United States not capture the entire export market from the United Kingdom (rather than only a rising share of exports) in those industries where it enjoyed a cost advantage (i.e., where the ratio of the productivity of US labor to UK labor was greater than 2)? MacDougall answered that this was due mainly to product differentiation. That is, the output of the same industry in the United States and the United Kingdom is not homogeneous. An American car is not identical to a British car. Even if the American car were cheaper, some consumers in the rest of the world could still prefer the British car. Thus, the United Kingdom continues to export some cars even at a higher price. However, as the price difference grows, the United Kingdom's share of car exports can be expected to decline. The same is true for most other products. Similarly, the United States continues to export to third markets some commodities in which it has a cost disadvantage with respect to the United Kingdom.

Additional and more recent confirmation of the Ricardian trade model is provided by Golub, Golub and Hseih, Costinot, Donaldson, Komunjer, and Kerr. All of these tests confirm that the actual pattern of trade seems to be based on the difference in labor productivities in different industries between nations. Production costs other than labor costs, demand considerations, political ties, and various obstructions to the flow of international trade did not break the link between relative labor productivity and export shares.

Even though the simple Ricardian trade model has been empirically verified to a large extent, it has a serious shortcoming in that it assumes rather than explains comparative advantage. That is, Ricardo and classical economists in general provided no explanation for the difference in labor productivity and comparative advantage between nations, and they could not say much about the effect of international trade on the earnings of factors of production. By providing answers to both of these important questions, the Heckscher-Ohlin model (H-O model) and the specific-factor model discussed later, as well as the trade model based on economies of scale and product differentiation discussed later, theoretically improve and extend the basic Ricardian model.

4.5 Reciprocal demand theory

Since David Ricardo did not explain how to determine the international commodity exchange rate and how the trade benefits would be distributed, nor did he consider the important influence of demand factors on international trade, John Stuart Mill (1806 – 1873) put forward the reciprocal demand theory to make an important supplement to the theory of comparative advantage.

John Stuart Mill, a famous British philosopher, psychologist and economist, an influential classical liberal thinker in the 19th century. He was born in London, and joined the East India Company in 1823, and then took the official career as his post until the East India Company was dissolved in 1856. This official career allowed him to spend a lot of time in ideological work during his life.

His reciprocal demand theory states that the exchange rate between the two countries is determined by the intensity of mutual demand between the two countries. If the demand of Country A for the export commodities of Country B is stronger than that of Country B for the export commodities of Country A, Country A will have to make some concessions in negotiation, and the international exchange rate will be closer to the domestic exchange rate of Country A. The closer the international exchange rate is to the domestic exchange rate when Country A is self-sufficient, the less Country A gains from trade.

This can be proved in Table 4.4, Table 4.10 and Figure 4.4.

On the basis of Mill's theory, British economist Alfred Marshall (1842 – 1924) put forward the offer curve to prove how supply and demand determine the international trade ratio by geometric method. Mill and Marshall's theories together constitute the theory of reciprocal demand, which discusses how the terms of trade, that is, the international exchange rate formed by the exchange of products between the two countries in international trade, can be determined and achieve equilibrium.

China-perspective case study

The export of energy storage batteries in China has increased dramatically due to high demand and low cost

Nowadays, lithium battery has been regarded as the first choice of modern energy storage equipment worldwide due to its high charging and discharging power. Previously, Europe, the United States, Australia and other countries have issued policies to vigorously promote the promotion and application of photovoltaic energy storage system. In particular, household photovoltaic energy storage has become a common energy supply road in Germany, the United States and other places to ensure daily power supply and save electricity consumption. Especially, the Russia-Ukraine campaign has intensified the European energy crisis. The prices of natural gas and coal fossil energy in Europe have risen significantly. The price of electricity in international countries has soared. The cost of energy consumption has increased sharply. In addition, the market is facing the pressure of power failure. The demand for energy storage products has increased greatly. As a result, China's lithium battery exports have also ushered in an explosive increase.

China has always been a big producer of lithium batteries. With the addition of overseas orders, the production plan has also been expanding, which further boost China's lithium battery export plan.

China's lithium-ion battery industry sustained rapid expansion in the first 10 months of 2022, official data showed. The total output of lithium-ion batteries exceeded 580 gigawatt-hours (GWh) in the January-October period, data from the Ministry of Industry and

Information Technology showed. Specifically, the output of lithium-ion batteries used for consumer products surpassed 84 GWh. The installed capacity of power batteries for new energy vehicles (NEVs) came in at about 224 GWh in the first 10 months. Exports of lithium-ion battery products soared 87 percent year-on-year, according to the ministry.

Behind the addition of export planning, there are breakthroughs in technology. With the synergy of technological innovation, planning economy, manufacturing experience and other factors, China's lithium battery industry is further promoted to increase planning and rapidly reduce costs. The cost of energy storage battery also brings export advantages to enterprises. Take Paineng Technology, a household energy storage representative enterprise, as an example. The data shows that the unit price of its energy storage battery system has continued to decline, from 2.03 yuan/Wh in 2017 to 1.37 yuan/Wh in 2021.

Key concepts

mercantilism	zero sum game	absolute advantage
labor productivity	production cost	gains of trade
comparative advantage	free trade	basis of international trade
trade patterns	constant opportunity cost	empirical tests
reciprocal demand theory	complete division of labor	

Summary

1. The early mercantilism was called balance of money, also known as monetarism or bullionism. Early mercantilists regarded increasing domestic currency accumulation and preventing currency outflow as the guiding principles of foreign trade policy, and they suggested trying not to buy or buy less. Only in this way could a country accumulate more money and make the country rich.

2. Late mercantilists had new ideas about increasing monetary accumulation. They believed that it was unwise to store up money for the purpose of accumulating wealth. They stressed that a country could import goods from other countries and even increase its purchase of goods from other countries, but it should ensure that the total amount of goods purchased from other countries was less than the total amount of goods sold to other countries.

3. According to Adam Smith, trade between two nations is based on absolute advantage. When one nation is more efficient than (or has an absolute advantage over) another in

the production of one commodity but is less efficient than (or has an absolute disadvantage with respect to) the other nation in producing a second commodity, then both nations can gain by each specializing in the production of the commodity of its absolute advantage and exchanging part of its output with the other nation for the commodity of its absolute disadvantage.

4. According to David Ricardo, the basis of international trade is not limited to absolute differences in labor productivity. As long as there are relative differences in labor productivity among countries, there will be relative differences in production costs and product prices, so that countries can have comparative advantages in different products and make international division of labor and international trade possible. Therefore, each country should focus on the production and export of products with "comparative advantages" and give up the production of and import products with "comparative disadvantages", by following the principle—"Of two interests choose the more, while of two evils choose the less".

5. The assumptions of the absolute and comparative advantage trade theories are important to support views of Adam Smith and David Ricardo. However, these assumptions, especially "constant opportunity cost" and "complete division of labor", making this model out of touch with reality. And it fails to consider the dynamic change of a nation's advantage.

6. The Ricardian trade model has been empirically verified to a large extent. But Ricardo and classical economists in general provided no explanation for the difference in labor productivity and comparative advantage between nations, and they could not say much about the effect of international trade on the earnings of factors of production.

7. John Stuart Mill put forward the reciprocal demand theory to make an important supplement to the theory of comparative advantage. His reciprocal demand theory states that the exchange rate between the two countries is determined by the intensity of mutual demand between the two countries. If the demand of Country A for the export commodities of Country B is stronger than that of Country B for the export commodities of Country A, Country A will have to make some concessions in negotiation, and the international exchange rate will be closer to the domestic exchange rate of Country A. The closer the international exchange rate is to the domestic exchange rate when Country A is self-sufficient, the less Country A gains from trade.

Exercises

1. Table 4.12 shows bushels of wheat and yards of cloth that the United States and the United Kingdom can produce with one hour of labor time under four different hypothetical situations. In each case, identify the commodity in which the United States and the United Kingdom have an absolute advantage or disadvantage.

Table 4.12   Labor productivity in the United States and the United Kingdom

	Case A		Case B		Case C		Case D	
	United States	United Kingdom	United States	United Kingdom	United States	United Kingdom	United States	United Kingdom
wheat (bushels/hour)	4	1	4	1	4	1	4	2
cloth (yards/hour)	1	2	3	2	2	2	2	1

2. With respect to Table 4.12, indicate in each case the commodity in which each nation has a comparative advantage or disadvantage.

3. With respect to Table 4.12, indicate in each case whether or not trade is possible and the basis for trade.

4. Suppose that in Case B in Table 4.12, the United States exchanges 4W for 4C with the United Kingdom.

   A. How much does the United States gain in terms of cloth?

   B. How much does the United Kingdom gain in terms of cloth?

   C. What is the range for mutually beneficial trade?

   D. How much would each nation gain if they exchanged 4W for 6C instead?

5. Assume that the data in Case B in Table 4.12 refer to millions of bushels of wheat and millions of yards of cloth.

   A. Plot on graph paper the production frontiers of the United States and the United Kingdom.

   B. What is the relative price of wheat (i.e., P_W/P_C) in the United States and in the United Kingdom in autarky (no trade)?

   C. What is the relative price of cloth (i.e., P_C/P_W) in the United States and in the United Kingdom in autarky?

6. Using the US and UK production frontiers from Exercise 5, assume that the no-trade or autarky point is 3W and 3/4C (in million units) in the United States and 1/2W and 1C in the United Kingdom. Also assume that with the opening of trade the United States exchanges 1W for 1C with the United Kingdom. Show graphically for the United States and the United Kingdom the autarky (or no-trade) point of production and consumption, the point of production and consumption with trade, and the gains from trade.

7. Draw a figure similar to Figure 4.4 showing that the United Kingdom is a small country, half the size shown in the right panel of Figure 4.4, and trades 20C for 30W with the United States at $P_W/P_C = 2/3$.

Chapter 5 // Neo-classical Trade Theory

The classical international trade theory, both Adam Smith's absolute advantage trade theory and David Ricardo's comparative advantage trade theory, explained the basis and pattern of the international trade, measured the international trade gains, which made an extremely important contribution. Many important contemporary theories and policies still benefit from the inspiration of classical international trade theory.

However, the classical international trade theory did not explain the reasons for this comparative advantage in depth, nor did it analyze the impact of international trade on factor prices of trade-participating countries. This chapter will explore these two new aspects and expand the international trade theories further.

5.1 Background of neo-classical trade theory

The basis of classical international trade theory is classical economics. As an important part of classical economic theory, classical trade theory is also based on the labor theory of value—labor is the only factor that creates value and causes the difference in production costs. Therefore, in the analysis of the classical school, the production technology is assumed to be unchanged, and there is only one factor of production (labor) input. With two or more factors invested, many of its analytical processes and conclusions are no longer valid. However, since the middle and late 19th century, capital has become an increasingly important factor of production. Product production is no longer determined by a single factor, but affected by multiple input factors at the same time.

Therefore, the relevant economic theory of studying the input-output relationship has also been developed. At the end of the 19th century and the beginning of the 20th century, the neo-classical economics represented by Léon Walras (1834−1910) and Alfred Marshall (1842−1924) gradually formed, and the neo-classical international trade theory of analyzing international trade under the framework of neo-classical economics also emerged.

Besides, in the 1870s, the world economic cycle began to shift from the second long wave of steam power and railway era to the third long wave of electricity and steel era. In the period of technological change, most British enterprises did not change their original production mode, and still stuck to the former paradigm of traditional industries such as textile and iron smelting. The United States, and Germany, for example, these latecomers, have not only accelerated the upgrading of their technological systems by developing emerging industries such as electricity, chemical industry and steel, but also increased institutional innovation to adapt to the development of new technologies. For example, the establishment of research universities and vocational education systems has increased the supply of engineers and skilled workers in emerging industries. Enterprises began to establish internal R&D institutions, such as Bayer and BASF in Germany, General Electric and DuPont in the United States, and took the lead in establishing their own R&D departments. Other enterprises followed suit and quickly spread in other emerging industries. These two important organizational system innovations have promoted the development of new technologies and new industries, and ultimately promoted the leapfrog economic development of the United States and Germany. As a result, these latecomers like Germany, France, the United States and Japan have developed rapidly, catching up with the United Kingdom. There are many exchanges among these developed countries, and the technology gap is small. The argument that technological differences lead to international trade, as stated in classical international trade theories, is no longer tenable.

5.2   Heckscher-Ohlin theory

At the end of the 19th century and the beginning of the 20th century, neo-classical economics gradually formed, and the neo-classical trade theory that analyzed international trade under the framework of neo-classical economics also came into being. The core of neo-classical trade theory is the Heckscher-Ohlin theory (H-O theory), also called the factor endowment theory, which is jointly constructed by the two famous economists: Heckscher and Ohlin.

5.2.1   Who

Eli F Heckscher (1879−1959), Swedish economist, was born in a Jewish family in Stockholm. Since 1897, Heckscher studied history and economics at Uppsala University, and obtained a doctor's degree in 1907. After graduation, he became a professor of economics and statistics in Stockholm University. Because of his outstanding talent in scientific research, the school appointed him as the director of the newly established Institute of Economic History. He succeeded in making Economic History a postgraduate course in Swedish universities.

Heckscher's thesis *Effect of Foreign Trade on Distribution of Income* was published in 1919, as the origin of the modern H-O theory in international trade. This book focused on the relationship between factor endowment and commodity trade patterns of various countries, and used the general equilibrium analysis method. Heckscher believed that the equalization of absolute factor prices was an inevitable result of international trade. This thesis was of pioneering significance. Later, this theory was further developed by his student Bertil Gotthard Ohlin.

Bertil Gotthard Ohlin (1899−1979), Swedish economist and politician, was born in Sweden. At the age of 16, Ohlin finished high school and was admitted to Lund University in Sweden in 1915. There he began to study economics, statistics and mathematics. It took him only two years to complete the courses of Lund University and obtain a bachelor's degree. During the First World War, he was enlisted for military service, and then he went to Stockholm University to study as a graduate student. Later, Ohlin went to Cambridge University in the United Kingdom for short-term study, and then went to Harvard University in the United States for further study for one year. Studying abroad has increased his knowledge, broadened his horizons and enriched his thoughts. After returning to Stockholm University, he immediately finished his doctoral thesis. He received his doctorate in 1924 in

Stockholm University. In 1925, he became a professor of economics at Copenhagen University in Denmark. In 1930, he was recruited back to Stockholm University, to replace his teacher, Eli F Heckscher, as a professor of economics. He has held this position for 35 years.

In 1933, Ohlin further enriched, modified and improved his trade theoretical system, and completed and published the famous work *Interregional and International Trade*. At this time, the H-O theory system was finally formed. In the book, Ohlin gave up the classical labor value theory and analyzed the flow of domestic and international factors of production, especially their relationship with the flow of goods.

In 1938, Ohlin was elected as a member of parliament. Ohlin was not only an economist, but also a famous political activist in Sweden. In 1944, he was appointed as the chairman of the Liberal Party, the main opposition party in Sweden, and he also acted as the trade minister in the coalition government. He served as the chairman of the Liberal Party for 23 years.

In 1977, Bertil Gotthard Ohlin, together with James Edward Meade (1907−1995) of Cambridge University, won the Nobel Prize in Economics for his pioneering research on international trade theory and international capital movement theory.

5.2.2 What

The H-O theory holds that a nation will export the commodity whose production requires the intensive use of the nation's relatively abundant and cheap factor and import the commodity whose production requires the intensive use of the nation's relatively scarce and expensive factor. In short, the relatively labor-rich nation exports the relatively labor-intensive (L-intensive) commodity and imports the relatively capital-intensive (K-intensive) commodity.

In terms of our previous discussion, this means that Nation 1 exports commodity X because commodity X is the L-intensive commodity and L is the relatively abundant and cheap factor in Nation 1. Conversely, Nation 2 exports commodity Y because commodity Y is the K-intensive commodity and K is the relatively abundant and cheap factor in Nation 2 (i.e., r/w is lower in Nation 2 than in Nation 1).

Of all the possible reasons for differences in relative commodity prices and comparative advantage among nations, the H-O theory isolates the difference in relative factor abundance, or factor endowments, among nations as the basic cause or determinant of comparative advantage and international trade. For this reason, the H-O model is often referred to as the factor-endowment theory. That is, each nation specializes in the production and export of the commodity intensive in its relatively abundant and cheap factor and imports the commodity intensive in its relatively scarce and expensive factor.

Thus, the H-O theory explains comparative advantage rather than assuming it (as was the case for classical economists). In other words, the H-O theory postulates that the difference in relative factor abundance and prices is the cause of the pre-trade difference in relative commodity prices between two nations. This difference in relative factor and relative commodity prices is then translated into a difference in absolute factor and commodity prices between the two nations. It is this difference in absolute commodity prices in the two nations that is the immediate cause of trade.

The framework of the H-O theory can be visualized and summarized with the use of Figure 5.1. Starting at the lower right-hand corner of the diagram, we see that tastes and the distribution in the ownership of factors of production (i.e., the distribution of income) together determine the demand for commodities. The demand for commodities determines the derived demand for the factors required to produce them. The demand for factors of production, together with the supply of the factors, determines the price of factors of production under perfect competition. The price of factors of production, together with technology, determines the price of final commodities. The difference in relative commodity prices between nations determines comparative advantage and the pattern of trade (i.e., which nation exports which commodity). Figure 5.1 shows clearly how all economic forces jointly determine the price of final commodities.

However, out of all these forces working together, the H-O theory isolates the difference in the physical availability or supply of factors of production among nations (in the face of equal tastes and technology) to explain the difference in relative commodity prices and trade among nations. Specifically, Ohlin assumed equal tastes (and income distribution) among nations. This gave rise to similar demands for final commodities and factors of production in different nations. Thus, it is the difference in the supply of the various factors of production in different nations that is the cause of different relative factor prices in different nations. Finally, the same technology but different factor prices lead to different relative commodity prices and trade among nations. Thus, the difference in the relative supply of factors leading to the difference in relative factor prices and commodity prices is shown by the dotted arrows in Figure 5.1.

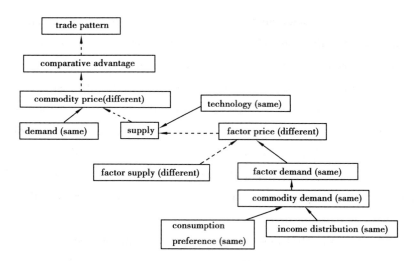

Figure 5.1   Framework of H-O theory

5.2.3   Assupmtions

The H-O theory is based on a number of simplifying assumptions (some made only implicitly by Heckscher and Ohlin). Rather than note these assumptions along the way as they are needed in the analysis, it is both logical and convenient to present them together and explain their meaning at this point. This will not only allow us to view the theory to be presented in a better perspective but will also make the presentation smoother and more direct. To make the theory more realistic, we will relax these assumptions in the next chapter and examine the effect that such relaxation has on the conclusions reached in this chapter.

①There are two nations (Nation 1 and Nation 2), two commodities (commodity X and commodity Y), and two factors of production (labor and capital).

②Both nations use the same technology in production.

③Commodity X is L-intensive, and commodity Y is K-intensive in both nations.

④Both commodities are produced under constant returns to scale in both nations.

⑤There is incomplete specialization in production in both nations.

⑥Tastes are equal in both nations.

⑦There is perfect competition in both commodities and factor markets in both nations.

⑧There is perfect factor mobility within each nation but no international factor mobility.

⑨All resources are fully employed in both nations.

⑩There are no transport costs, tariffs, or other obstructions to the free flow of international trade.

⑪International trade between the two nations is balanced.

Assumption 1 is made in order to be able to illustrate the theory with a two-dimensional figure. This assumption is made with the knowledge (discussed in the next chapter) that its relaxation (so as to deal with the more realistic case of more than two nations, more than two commodities, and more than two factors) will leave the conclusions of the theory basically unchanged.

Assumption 2 means that both nations have access to and use the same general production techniques. Thus, if factor prices were the same in both nations, producers in both nations would use exactly the same amount of labor and capital in the production of each commodity. Since factor prices usually differ, producers in each nation will use more of the relatively cheaper factor in the nation to minimize their costs of production.

Assumption 3 means that commodity X requires relatively more labor to produce than commodity Y in both nations. In a more technical and precise way, this means that the labor-capital ratio (L/K) is higher for commodity X than for commodity Y in both nations at the same relative factor prices. This is equivalent to saying that the capital-labor ratio (K/L) is lower for X than for Y. But it does not mean that the K/L ratio for X is the same in Nation 1 and Nation 2, only that K/L is lower for X than for Y in both nations.

Assumption 4 means that increasing the amount of labor and capital used in the production of any commodity will increase output of that commodity in the same proportion. For example, if Nation 1 increases by 10 percent both the amount of labor and the amount of capital that it uses in the production of commodity X, its output of commodity X will also increase by 10 percent. If it doubles the amount of both labor and capital used, its output of X will also double. The same is true for commodity Y and in Nation 2.

Assumption 5 means that even with free trade, both nations continue to produce both commodities. This implies that neither of the two nations is "very small".

Assumption 6 means that demand preferences, as reflected in the shape and location of indifference curves, are identical in both nations. Thus, when relative commodity prices are equal in the two nations (as, for example, with free trade), both nations will consume X and Y in the same proportion.

Assumption 7 means that producers, consumers, and traders of commodity X and commodity Y in both nations are each too small to affect the price of these commodities. The same is true for each user and supplier of labor time and capital. Perfect competition also means that, in the long run, commodity prices equal their costs of production, leaving no (economic) profit after all costs (including implicit costs) are taken into account. Finally, perfect competition means that all producers, consumers, and owners of factors of production have perfect knowledge of commodity prices and factor earnings in all parts of the nation and in all industries.

Assumption 8 means that labor and capital are free to move, and indeed do move quickly, from areas and industries of lower earnings to areas and industries of higher earnings until earnings for the same type of labor and capital are the same in all areas, uses, and industries of the nation. At the same time, there is zero international factor mobility (i.e., no mobility of factors among nations), so that international differences in factor earnings would persist indefinitely in the absence of international trade.

Assumption 9 means that there are no unemployed resources or factors of production in either nation.

Assumption 10 means that specialization in production proceeds until relative (and absolute) commodity prices are the same in both nations with trade. If we allowed for transport costs and tariffs, specialization would proceed only until relative (and absolute) commodity prices differed by no more than the costs of transportation and the tariff on each unit of the commodity traded.

Assumption 11 means that the total value of each nation's exports equals the total value of the nation's imports.

5.2.4 Geometric derivation of H-O theory

Factor intensity and factor abundance are the two key concepts of factor endowment theory. Therefore, it is important to understand the two terms clearly and accurately.

In a world of two commodities (X and Y) and two factors (labor and capital), we say that commodity Y is K-intensive if the capital-labor ratio (K/L) used in the production of Y is greater than K/L used in the production of X.

For example, if two units of capital (2K) and two units of labor (2L) are required to produce one unit of commodity Y, the capital-labor ratio is one. That is, 2/2 in the production of Y. If at the same time 1K and 4L are required to produce one unit of X, K/L = 1/4 for commodity X. Since K/L = 1 for Y and K/L = 1/4 for X, we say that Y is K-intensive and X is L-intensive.

Note that it is not the absolute amount of capital and labor used in the production of commodities X and Y that is important in measuring the capital and labor intensity of the two commodities, but the amount of capital per unit of labor (i.e., K/L). For example, suppose that 3K and 12L (instead of 1K and 4L) are required to produce 1X, while to produce 1Y requires 2K and 2L (as indicated earlier). Even though to produce 1X requires

3K, while to produce 1Y requires only 2K, commodity Y would still be the K-intensive commodity because K/L is higher for Y than for X. That is, K/L = 2/2 for Y, but K/L = 3/12 = 1/4 for X.

If we plotted capital (K) along the vertical axis of a graph and labor (L) along the horizontal axis, and production took place along a straight-line ray from the origin, the slope of the line would measure the capital-labor ratio (K/L) in the production of the commodity. This is shown in Figure 5.2.

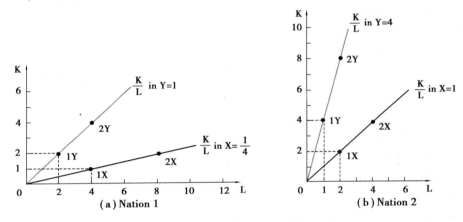

Figure 5.2   Factor intensities for commodities X and Y in Nation 1 and Nation 2

Figure 5.2 shows that Nation 1 can produce 1Y with 2K and 2L. With 4K and 4L, Nation 1 can produce 2Y because of constant returns to scale (see assumptions). Thus, K/L = 2/2 = 4/4 = 1 for Y. This is given by the slope of 1 for the ray from the origin for commodity Y in Nation 1 (see Figure 5.2). On the contrary, 1K and 4L are required to produce 1X, and 2K and 8L to produce 2X, in Nation 1. Thus, K/L = 1/4 for X in Nation 1. This is given by the slope of 1/4 for the ray from the origin for commodity X in Nation 1. Since K/L, or the slope of the ray from the origin, is higher for commodity Y than for commodity X, we say that commodity Y is K-intensive and commodity X is L-intensive in Nation 1.

In Nation 2, K/L (or the slope of the ray) is 4 for Y and 1 for X. Therefore, Y is the K-intensive commodity, and X is the L-intensive commodity in Nation 2. This is illustrated by the fact that the ray from the origin for commodity Y is steeper (i.e., has a greater slope) than the ray for commodity X in both nations.

Even though commodity Y is K-intensive in relation to commodity X in both nations, Nation 2 uses a higher K/L in producing both Y and X than Nation 1. For Y, K/L = 4 in Nation 2, but K/L = 1 in Nation 1. For X, K/L = 1 in Nation 2, but K/L = 1/4 in Nation 1. The obvious question is: Why does Nation 2 use more K-intensive production techniques in both commodities than Nation 1? The answer is that capital must be relatively cheaper in Nation 2 than in Nation 1, so that producers in Nation 2 use relatively more capital in the production of both commodities to minimize their costs of production. But why is capital relatively cheaper in Nation 2? To answer this question, we must define factor abundance and examine its relationship to factor prices.

Before doing this, however, we must settle one other related point of crucial importance. This refers to what happens if, for whatever reason, the relative price of capital falls. Producers would substitute capital for labor in the production of both commodities to minimize their costs of production. As a result, both commodities would become more K-intensive. However, only if K/L in the production of commodity Y exceeds K/L in the production of commodity X at all possible relative factor prices can we say unequivocally that commodity Y is the K-intensive commodity. This is basically an empirical question and will be explored in Section 5.6. For now, we will assume that this is true (i.e., that commodity Y remains the K-intensive commodity at all possible relative factor prices).

To summarize, we say that commodity Y is unequivocally the K-intensive commodity if K/L is higher for commodity Y than for commodity X at all possible relative factor prices. Nation 2 uses a higher K/L in the production of both commodities because the relative price of capital is lower in Nation 2 than in Nation 1. If the relative price of capital declines, producers will substitute K for L in the production of both commodities to minimize their costs of production. Thus, K/L will rise for both commodities, but Y continues to be the K-intensive commodity.

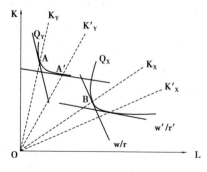

Figure 5.3   Factor intensity in a nation

The points on the rays in Figure 5.2 represent the production points where the manufacturer uses different factor combinations. In fact, these points are also the tangent points of the manufacturer's isoquant curve and isocost line. As shown in Figure 5.3. Please note that in a nation at a certain time, all cost isolines are parallel, due to the same w/r ratio.

There are two ways to define factor abundance. One way is in terms of physical units (i.e., in terms of the overall amount of capital and labor available to each nation). Another way to define factor abundance is in terms of relative factor prices (i.e., in terms of the rental price of capital and the price of labor time in each nation).

According to the definition in terms of physical units, Nation 2 is K-abundant if the ratio of the total amount of capital to the total amount of labor (T_K/T_L) available in Nation 2 is greater than that in Nation 1 (i.e., if T_K/T_L for Nation 2 exceeds T_K/T_L for Nation 1). Note that it is not the absolute amount of capital and labor available in each nation that is important but the ratio of the total amount of capital to the total amount of labor. Thus, Nation 2 can have less capital than Nation 1 and still be the K-abundant

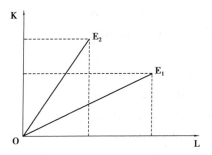

Figure 5.4 Factor abundance

nation if T_K/T_L in Nation 2 exceeds T_K/T_L in Nation 1. As shown in Figure 5.4 that Nation 2 is K-abundant and Nation 1 is L-abundant, for point E_2 is higher than E_1.

According to the definition in terms of factor prices, Nation 2 is K-abundant if the ratio of the rental price of capital to the price of labor time (P_K/P_L) is lower in Nation 2 than in Nation 1 (i.e., if P_K/P_L in Nation 2 is smaller than P_K/P_L in Nation 1). Since the rental price of capital is usually taken to be the interest rate (r) while the price of labor time is the wage rate (w), $P_K/P_L = r/w$. Once again, it is not the absolute level of that determines whether or not a nation is the K-abundant nation, but r/w. For example, r may be higher in Nation 2 than in Nation 1, but Nation 2 will still be the K-abundant nation if r/w is lower there than in Nation 1.

The relationship between the two definitions of factor abundance is clear. The definition of factor abundance in terms of physical units considers only the supply of factors. The definition in terms of relative factor prices considers both demand and supply (since we know from principles of economics that the price of a commodity or factor is determined by both demand and supply considerations under perfect competition). Also from principles of economics, we know that the demand for a factor of production is a derived demand-derived from the demand for the final commodity that requires the factor in its production.

Since we have assumed that tastes, or demand preferences, are the same in both nations, the two definitions of factor abundance give the same conclusions in our case. That is, with T_K/T_L larger in Nation 2 than in Nation 1 in the face of equal demand conditions (and technology), P_K/P_L will be smaller in Nation 2. Thus, Nation 2 is the K-abundant nation in terms of both definitions.

This is not always the case. For example, it is conceivable that the demand for commodity Y (the K-intensive commodity), and therefore the demand for capital, could be so much higher in Nation 2 than in Nation 1 that the relative price of capital would be higher in Nation 2 than in Nation 1 (despite the relatively greater supply of capital in

Nation 2). In that case, Nation 2 would be considered K-abundant according to the definition in physical terms and L-abundant according to the definition in terms of relative factor prices.

In such situations, it is the definition in terms of relative factor prices that should be used. That is, a nation is K-abundant if the relative price of capital is lower in it than in the other nation. In our case, there is no such contradiction between the two definitions. Nation 2 is K-abundant and Nation 1 is L-abundant in terms of both definitions. We will assume this to be the case throughout the rest of the chapter, unless otherwise explicitly indicated.

When the production technology conditions of the two countries are the same, the difference in factor endowment between the countries will eventually affect the production capacity of the two countries, thus causing the difference in the supply capacity. This difference can be intuitively judged by examining the skewness of the production possibility curves between the two countries.

As illustrated in the left panel of Figure 5.5, we can judge that Country A is K-abundant and Country B to be L-abundant. We can also judge that commodity X is K-intensive and Y L-intensive. And for Country A, when all factors of production are used in X department, the number of X produced is equal to the output level X_A represented by the isoquant curve of X. When all factors of production are used in Y department, the number of Y produced is equal to Y_A represented by the isoquant curve of Y. Both isoquant curves pass through point E_A. According to the left panel of Figure 5.5, the two end points of the production possibility curve in Country A are marked in the right panel of Figure 5.5, and connected with a convex curve, which can help to obtain the production possibility of Country A. The production possibility curve for Country B can be obtained using the same method.

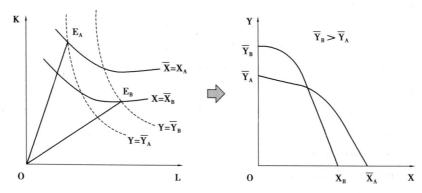

Figure 5.5   Factor endowment and production possibility curve

In the left panel of Figure 5.5, the isoquant curve of X passing point E_A is above the isoquant curve of X passing point E_B, namely $\overline{X}_A > \overline{X}_B$, and the isoquant curve of Y passing point E_A is below the isoquant curve of Y passing through point E_B, namely $\overline{Y}_A < \overline{Y}_B$. In the right panel of Figure 5.5, thus, the intersection of the production possibility curve and the X-axis of Country B is on the left of the intersection of the production possibility curve and the X-axis of Country A. The intersection point of the production possibility curve of Country A and the Y-axis is located below the intersection point of the production possibility curve of Country B and the Y-axis. That is, the production possibility curve of Country A is more skewed along the X-axis than that of Country B.

It can be concluded that the shape of a country's production possibility curve is related to its factor abundance. Under the condition of the same production technology, the difference of production possibility curve between the two countries A and B is completely caused by the difference of factor endowment between the two countries. The production possibility curve of Country A is biased to the X-axis, which means that under the same relative price of goods, the relative supply capacity of Country A on X commodities is stronger than that of Country B, while Country B is stronger than that of Country A on Y commodities. The H-O theory can be stated that K-abundant countries have strong relative supply capacity in K-intensive products, while L-abundant countries have strong relative supply capacity in L-intensive products.

▶ 5.2.5   General equilibrium

The general equilibrium of H-O theory is illustrated in Figure 5.6. The left panel of the figure shows the production frontiers of Nation 1 and Nation 2. As indicated above, Nation 1's production frontier is skewed along the X-axis because commodity X is the L-intensive commodity, Nation 1 is the L-abundant nation, and both nations use the same technology. Furthermore, since the two nations have equal tastes, they face the same indifference map. Indifference curve Ⅰ (which is common for both nations) is tangent to Nation 1's production frontier at point A and to Nation 2's production frontier at A'. Indifference curve Ⅰ is the highest indifference curve that Nation 1 and Nation 2 can reach in isolation, and points A and A' represent their equilibrium points of production and consumption in the absence of trade. Note that although we assume that the two nations have identical tastes (indifference map), the two nations need not be on the same indifference curve in isolation and end up on the same indifference map with trade. We only did so in order to simplify the figure.

The tangency of indifference curve Ⅰ at points A and A' defines the no-trade, or autarky, equilibrium-relative commodity prices of P_A in Nation 1 and P'_A in Nation 2 (see Figure 5.6). Since $P_A < P'_A$, Nation 1 has a comparative advantage in commodity X, and Nation 2 has a comparative advantage in commodity Y.

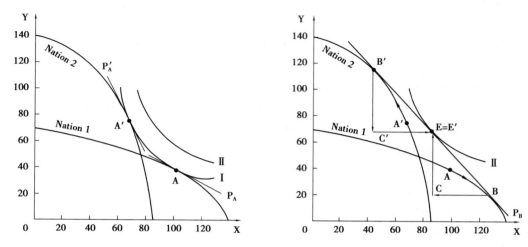

Figure 5.6   H-O model

The right panel of Figure 5.6 shows that with trade Nation 1 specializes in the production of commodity X and Nation 2 specializes in the production of commodity Y (see the direction of the arrows on the production frontiers of the two nations). Specialization in production proceeds until Nation 1 has reached point B and Nation 2 has reached point B′, where the transformation curves of the two nations are tangent to the common relative price line P_B. Nation 1 will then export commodity X in exchange for commodity Y and consume at point E on indifference curve II (see trade triangle BCE). On the contrary, Nation 2 will export Y for X and consume at point E′, which coincides with point E (see trade triangle B′C′E′).

Note that Nation 1's exports of commodity X equal Nation 2's imports of commodity X (i.e., BC = C′E′). Similarly, Nation 2's exports of commodity Y equal Nation 1's imports of commodity Y (i.e., B′C′ = CE). At $P_X/P_Y > P_B$, Nation 1 wants to export more of commodity X than Nation 2 wants to import at this high relative price of X, and P_X/P_Y falls toward P_B. On the contrary, at $P_X/P_Y < P_B$, Nation 1 wants to export less of commodity X than Nation 2 wants to import at this low relative price of X, and P_X/P_Y rises toward P_B. This tendency of P_X/P_Y could also be explained in terms of commodity Y.

Also to be noted is that point E involves more of Y but less of X than point A. Nevertheless, Nation 1 gains from trade because point E is on higher indifference curve II. Similarly, even though point E′ involves more X but less Y than point A, Nation 2 is also better off because point E′ is on higher indifference curve II. This pattern of specialization in production and trade and consumption will remain the same until there is a change in the underlying demand or supply conditions in commodity and factor markets in either or both nations.

It is now instructive briefly to compare Figure 5.6 with Figure 4.4. In Figure 4.4, the difference in the production frontiers of the two nations is reinforced by their difference in tastes, thus making the autarky-relative commodity prices in the two nations differ even more than in Figure 5.6. On the contrary, the tastes of the two nations could be different in such a way as to make mutually beneficial trade impossible. This would occur if the different indifference curves in the two nations were tangent to their respective and different production frontiers in such a way as to result in equal autarky-relative commodity prices in the two nations.

Note also that the H-O theory does not require identical tastes (i.e., equal indifference curves) in the two nations. It only requires that if tastes differ, they do not differ sufficiently to neutralize the tendency of different factor endowments and production possibility curves from leading to different relative commodity prices and comparative advantage in the two nations. Thus, in a sense, Figure 4.4 can be regarded as a more general illustration of the H-O model than Figure 5.6.

❯ 5.2.6　Partial equilibrium

According to the production possibility curve and social indifference curve, we can deduce the supply curve and demand curve of products, as well as the equilibrium price of the market.

In Figure 5.7, lines S and D represent the supply and demand of the exporting commodity in Country A respectively. Before the trade, the equilibrium price of this commodity in the exporting country was 0.5, which is lower than the price of the same commodity in another Country B, so it has a comparative advantage and export motivation. After the export, the international price rises to 1. The manufacturers in this country expand production of this product, while consumers reduce demand due to the rising price, resulting in surplus production. This surplus is the export.

In this case, as the price of product rises, the surplus of producers increases, and the area increased is a+b, while the surplus of consumers decreases, and the area decreased is a, so the net increase of the total social welfare of this Country A is (a+b)−a=b. Trade benefits the producers of the export industry, and harms its consumers.

In Figure 5.8, lines S and D represent the supply and demand of the importing commodity in Country A respectively. Before the trade, the equilibrium price of this commodity in the exporting country was 2, which is higher than the price of the same commodity in another Country B, so it does not have a comparative advantage and prefers to import this product. After the import, the international price cuts to 1. The manufacturers in this country lower production of this product, while consumers increase demand due to the cutting price, resulting in production shortage. This shortage is the import.

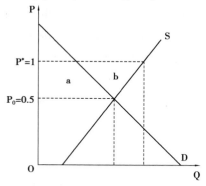

Figure 5.7 Partial equilibrium of the exporting commodity

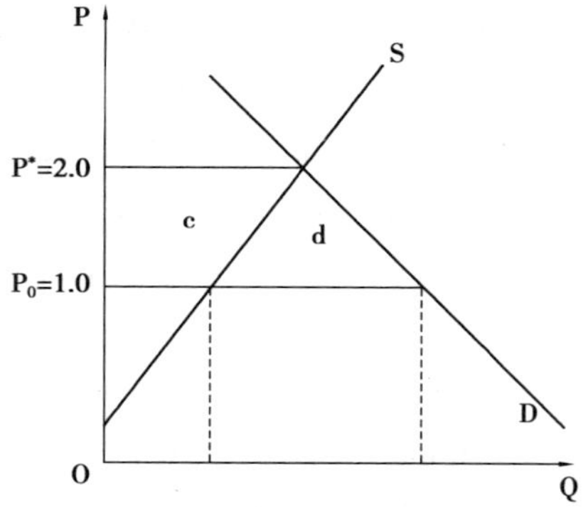

Figure 5.8 Partial equilibrium of the importing commodity

In this case, as the price of product cuts, the surplus of producers decreases, and the area decreased is c, while the surplus of consumers increases, and the area increased is c+ d, so the net increase of the total social welfare of this country is (c+d)-c = d. Trade makes producers in import competitive industries suffer and consumers benefit.

For Country A, the change in the welfare of the whole country must be positive, which is b+d. In other words, free trade can increase welfare of the whole country, although some industry may suffer.

5.2.7 Evaluation of H-O theory

The H-O theory develops the comparative advantage theory and explains the terms of trade. The comparative advantage theory points out that the relative cost difference is the cause of international trade, while the H-O model points out that the difference of factor endowment is the cause of the relative cost difference.

Specifically, compared with the classical trade theory, the development of the neo-classical trade theory with the H-O theory as the core is mainly reflected in the following two aspects: ①Analyze the production cost of products in the framework of two or more production factors. ②Analyze the mutual influence of international trade and the change of production factors in the general equilibrium framework. International trade not only affects the market price of products on both sides, but also causes changes in the factor market prices of various countries. The change of product price and factor price will not only affect the production and consumption of a country, but also cause the redistribution of income among various factors. The flow of factors between domestic sectors or changes in the proportion of factor reserves will in turn affect production and trade patterns.

However, the H-O theory also has some restrictions. Firstly, it is still based on a series of hypothetical conditions far from reality, and cannot explain more trade phenomena. Secondly, strictly following the theory may worsen the terms of trade of developing countries.

Suppose a country (especially a developing country) produces and exports primary products and L-intensive products in full accordance with its comparative advantages. In international trade with developed countries who mainly export capital and technology-intensive products, although it can gain benefits, its industrial structure cannot be upgraded and it maintains low economic competitiveness, thus falling into the "comparative advantage trap".

5.3   Factor-price equalization theorem

After the emergence of the H-O model, many economists have conducted further research on its basis, and obtained many new inferences and research results. And Paul A. Samuelson is the most representative one. In 1948, the American economist Paul A. Samuelson proposed the factor-price equalization theorem based on the H-O model. This section will mainly introduce this theorem and explain its implications, based on which, the impact of international trade on the income distribution of each trade-participating country is examined.

Paul A. Samuelson (1915 – 2009) is a famous American economist and professor of economics at Massachusetts Institute of Technology. He received his bachelor's degree from the University of Chicago in 1935, master's degree from the University of Chicago in 1936, and doctor's degree from Harvard University in 1941. While studying at Harvard, he studied economics under the guidance of lots of famous economic masters, such as Joseph Alois Schumpeter, Wassily Leontief, Gottfried Von Haberler and Alvin Hansen who is known as "Keynes of America". Samuelson was born in a family of economists. He became the first winner of the John Bates Clark Medal in 1947. He was the first American to win the Nobel Prize in Economics in 1970. He is the last economic generalist and has made pioneering contributions to almost all fields of economics.

The factor-price equalization theorem can also be called H-O-S theorem due to the contribution from Samuelson, states that although the production factors cannot flow freely among countries, the free flow of goods between countries can replace the free flow of factors of production, and ultimately make the factor prices among countries tend to be equal. In short, wages and other factor returns will be the same after the occurance of specialization and trade. The international trade causes a redistribution of income from the relatively expensive (scarce) factor to the relatively cheap (abundant) factor.

In section 5.2, we have already known that in the absence of trade, the relative price of commodity X is lower in Nation 1 than in Nation 2 because the relative price of labor, or the wage rate, is lower in Nation 1. As Nation 1 specializes in the production of commodity X (the L-intensive commodity) and reduces its production of commodity Y (the K-intensive commodity), the relative demand for labor rises, causing wages (w) to rise, while the relative demand for capital falls, causing the interest rate (r) to fall. The exact opposite occurs in Nation 2. That is, as Nation 2 specializes in the production of Y and reduces its production of X with trade, its demand for L falls, causing w to fall, while its demand for K rises, causing r to rise.

To summarize, international trade causes w to rise in Nation 1 (the low-wage nation) and to fall in Nation 2 (the high-wage nation). Thus, international trade reduces the pre-trade difference in w between the two nations. Similarly, international trade causes r to fall in Nation 1 (the K-expensive nation) and to rise in Nation 2 (the K-cheap nation), thus reducing the pre-trade difference in r between the two nations. This proves that international trade tends to reduce the pre-trade difference in w and r between the two nations.

We can go further and demonstrate that international trade not only tends to reduce the international difference in the returns to homogeneous factors, but would in fact bring about complete equalization in relative factor prices when all of the assumptions made hold. This is so because as long as relative factor prices differ, relative commodity prices differ and trade continues to expand. But the expansion of trade reduces the difference in factor prices between nations. Thus, international trade keeps expanding until relative commodity prices are completely equalized, which means that relative factor prices have also become equal in the two nations.

We can show graphically that relative factor prices are equalized by trade in the two nations (if all the assumptions of H-O model hold). In Figure 5.9, the relative price of labor (w/r) is measured along the horizontal axis, and the relative price of commodity X (P_X/P_Y) is measured along the vertical axis. Since each nation operates under perfect competition and uses the same technology, there is a one-to-one relationship between w/r and P_X/P_Y. That is, each w/r ratio is associated with a specific P_X/P_Y ratio.

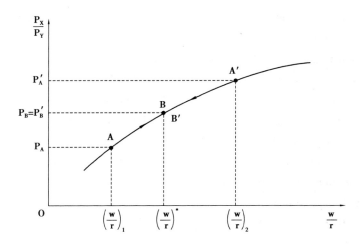

Figure 5.9   Relative factor-price equalization

Before trade, Nation 1 is at point A, with $w/r = (w/r)_1$ and $P_X/P_Y = P_A$, while Nation 2 is at point A', with $w/r = (w/r)_2$ and $P_X/P_Y = P'_A$. With w/r lower in Nation 1 than in Nation 2 in the absence of trade, P_A is lower than P'_A so that Nation 1 has a comparative advantage in commodity X.

As Nation 1 (the relatively L-abundant nation) specializes in the production of commodity X (the L-intensive commodity) and reduces the production of commodity Y, the demand for labor increases relative to the demand for capital and w/r rises in Nation 1. This causes P_X/P_Y to rise in Nation 1. On the contrary, as Nation 2 (the K-abundant nation) specializes in the production of commodity Y (the K-intensive commodity), its relative demand for capital increases and r/w rises (i.e., w/r falls). This causes P_Y/P_X to rise (i.e., P_X/P_Y to fall) in Nation 2. The process will continue until point B = B', at which $P_B = P'_B$ and $w/r = (w/r)^*$ in both nations (see Figure 5.9). Note that $P_B = P'_B$ only if w/r is identical in the two nations, since both nations operate under perfect competition and use the same technology (by assumption). Note also that $P_B = P'_B$ lies between P_A and P'_A, and $(w/r)^*$ lies between $(w/r)_1$ and $(w/r)_2$. To summarize, P_X/P_Y will become equal as a result of trade, and this will occur only when w/r has also become equal in the two nations (as long as both nations continue to produce both commodities).

The preceding paragraph shows the process by which relative, not absolute, factor prices are equalized. Equalization of absolute factor prices means that free international trade also equalizes the real wages for the same type of labor in the two nations and the real rate of interest for the same type of capital in the two nations. However, given that trade equalizes relative factor prices, that perfect competition exists in all commodity and factor markets, and that both nations use the same technology and face constant returns to scale in the production of both commodities, it follows that trade also equalizes the absolute returns to homogeneous factors.

Suppose that Countries 1 and 2 produce two commodities A and B. And technology is the same between the two countries. When $(P_A/P_B)_1 = (P_A/P_B)_2$, and $(w/r)_1 = (w/r)_2$, we have $(K/L)_{1A} = (K/L)_{2A}$, $(K/L)_{1B} = (K/L)_{2B}$ based on assumptions in H-O model. Since constant returns to scale for X and Y in both nations, if the $P_K/P_L(w/r)$ of the two countries is the same, the K/L of the two countries is the same. The MP_K of the two countries will be equal, and the MP_L of the two countries will be equal. Under the condition of perfect competition, equilibrium condition is that the factor's value of marginal product (VMP) equals the price of factor:

$$VMP = \frac{dTR(L)}{dL} = \frac{d[Q(L) \cdot P]}{dL} = MP \cdot P$$

$$\frac{dC(L)}{dL} = \frac{d(w \cdot L)}{dL} = w$$

$$w = VMP = MP \times P$$

Therefore, for labor in Country 1 we have:

$$P_{1A} \times MP_{L1A} = w_{1A}, \quad P_{1B} \times MP_{L1B} = w_{1B}$$

And for labor in Country 2 we have:

$$P_{2A} \times MP_{L2A} = w_{2A}, \quad P_{2B} \times MP_{L2B} = w_{2B}$$

Since $MP_{L1A} = MP_{L2A}$, $MP_{L1B} = MP_{L2B}$, we have:

$$\frac{w_{1A}}{P_{1A}} = \frac{w_{2A}}{P_{2A}}, \quad \frac{w_{1B}}{P_{1B}} = \frac{w_{2B}}{P_{2B}}$$

For commodity A, the w/P of Country 1 is equal to the w/P of Country 2. That is, the real price of labor between the two countries are the same.

Note that trade acts as a substitute for the international mobility of factors of production in its effect on factor prices. With perfect mobility (i.e., with complete information and no legal restrictions or transport costs), labor would migrate from the low-wage nation to the high-wage nation until wages in the two nations became equal. Similarly, capital would move from the low-interest to the high-interest nation until the rate of interest was equalized in the two nations. While trade operates on the demand for factors, factor mobility operates on the supply of factors. In either case, the result is complete equalization in the absolute returns of homogeneous factors. With some (rather than perfect) international mobility of factors, a smaller volume of trade would be required to bring about equality in factor returns between the two nations.

In the long run, a country's capital and labor are fully liquid. As the inference of factor endowment theory, the theorem of factor-price equalization shows the influence of international trade on factor price through the international flow of commodities. The significance of the factor-price equalization theorem lies in two aspects: First, it proves that international trade, as the replacement of the international flow of factors, can indirectly realize the optimal allocation of factors in the world. Second, it shows how international trade affects the income distribution pattern of trading countries.

Generally speaking, the equality of the factor prices depends on the free flow of the factors. However, according to the theorem of factor-price equalization, even if the factors of production cannot flow freely between countries, the free trade of goods can eventually make the returns of the factors the same. This conclusion is very shocking. Looking at the reality of all countries in the world, we cannot fully deny this principle or fully affirm this conclusion. On the one hand, international trade has caused great changes in the prices of a country's essential factors, such as the fact that China's more than 20 years of reform and opening-up has narrowed the income gap between Chinese workers and the United States in some industries. On the contrary, there are also huge differences in factor prices between countries. For the same factors of production, such as workers with the same skills, their incomes vary greatly in different countries. In some areas and countries, the gap still tends to widen.

How to view this inconsistency between the theory and the reality? In terms of the theory itself, its economic logic is clear and tight. So what is the problem? As with all economic theories, factor-price equalization theorem is also based on a set of assumptions that tend to make the real world more simplified. A review of the underlying assumptions of the theorem shows that many do not exist in reality. Firstly, international trade is not completely free. The existence of various interest groups, and the conflict of economic interests between countries have created many trade obstacles, leaving the price of similar goods in countries not be the same. Secondly, the factors of production cannot realize free movement. The prices of factors cannot be the same. Finally, the production technology is not fixed. Workers' wages in developed countries enjoy continuous growth for their continuous innovation of production technology. Thus, despite increasingly free international trade, wages still fall widely apart between workers in developed and developing countries.

But it is too simple to deny the significance of the theorem. If technological progress is excluded, trade is indeed narrowing the factor price gap of individual industries. From a dynamic point of view, the factor price gap expands due to the development of science and technology in developed countries, but it is also reduced through trade. Without international trade, the gap in factor prices between countries could be even greater. The factor-price equalization theorem is still of great significance.

5.4 Stolper-Samuelson theorem

How does the international trade influence the income distribution inside a participating country in a long run? In 1941, the article "Protectionism and Real Wage" jointly written by Wolfgang Stolper and Paul Samuelson, first proposed the impact of tariffs on the price of domestic factors of production or domestic income distribution. It is called the Stolper-Samuelson theorem, which proves that protectionism will increase the actual price of a country's relatively scarce factors.

If the relative price of product A (K-intensive) in a country rises, all factors will be willing to move to the A sector. The expansion of A sector requires more K and less L. And product B is L-intensive and can only release less K and more L. Thus the supply of K exceeds the demand, and supply of L exceeds the demand, leading to surplus of L and shortage of K. The price of L decreases and the price of K increases. Manufacturers will prefer to use more L and less K to reduce their cost. Based on the decreasing law of marginal product of factors, the marginal product of L ($MP_L = w/P$) decreases, the marginal product of K ($MP_K = r/P$) increases. Therefore, if the relative price of product A (K-intensive) rises, the actual price of capital increases, too.

That is, an increase in the relative price of a certain commodity will lead to an increase in the actual price or income of the factors intensively used by the commodity, while the actual price or income of another factor of production will decrease.

In free trade, export makes the exporting commodity price rise, and the factor intensively used by the export commodity is the abundant and cheap factor of the country. So, free trade will increase the real price of the relatively abundant factor in a country, and reduce the real price of the relatively scarce factor.

Although free international trade will improve the overall welfare level of a country, but this improvement cannot be equally shared by all people.

Since in developed nations (e.g. the United States, Germany, Japan, France, Britain, Italy, Canada), capital is the relatively abundant factor, international trade tends to reduce the real income of labor and increase the real income of owners of capital. This is why labor unions in developed nations generally favor trade restrictions. In less developed nations (e.g., India, Egypt, Mexico), however, labor is the relatively abundant factor, and international trade will increase the real income of labor and reduce the real income of owners of capital.

Since, according to the H-O theory, international trade causes real wages and the real income of labor to fall in a K-abundant and labor-scarce nation such as the United States, shouldn't the US government restrict trade? The answer is almost invariably no. The reason is that the loss that trade causes to labor (particularly unskilled labor) is less than the gain received by owners of capital. With an appropriate redistribution policy of taxes on owners of capital and subsidies to labor, both broad classes of factors of production can benefit from international trade. Such a redistribution policy can take not only the form of retraining labor displaced by imports but also the form of tax relief for labor and provision of some social services.

Case 5.1   Has international trade increased US wage inequalities?

Has international trade increased wage inequalities between skilled and unskilled workers in the United States and other industrial countries during the past two decades? The answer is yes, but it is probably not a major cause. First, some facts. Between 1979 and 1993, average real wages declined by more than 20 percent for US high school graduates but rose by 20 percent for college graduates, resulting in a large increase in skilled-unskilled workers' real wage inequalities. According to another study, the real wage differential between college and high school graduates in the United States increased by 63 percent between 1973 and 1996. The question is how much did international trade contribute to this increase?

Here, there are wide disagreements. Some economists argue that the growth of manufactured exports from newly industrializing economies was the major cause of the increased wage inequalities in the United States and unemployment in Western Europe between 1980 and 2000. Other economists, however, point out that industrial countries' nonpetroleum imports from low-wage countries are only about 3 percent of their GDP and, hence, it could not possibly have been the major cause of the large fall in the real wages of unskilled workers in the United States and large increase in unemployment (because of more rigid wages) in Western Europe. They acknowledge that international trade certainly contributed to the unskilled workers' problems in industrial countries, but that it played only a minor role (i.e., it may have been responsible for no more than 10-15 percent) in the increase in US unskilled-skilled real wage inequalities. Most of the increase in unskilled-skilled real wage inequalities was probably due to technological changes, such as automation and the computerization of many jobs, which sharply reduced the demand for unskilled workers in the United States and Europe.

The weight of evidence seems to be with this latter view—international trade seems to have had only a small direct impact (about 10 percent) on the demand and wages of unskilled labor in industrial nations until the mid-1990s. Most of the increase in wage inequality was due to other factors. Some economists believe, however, that since the mid-1990s the importance of international trade as a cause of skilled-unskilled wage inequalities has increased. Edwards and Lawrence point out that to the extent that international trade leads advanced countries to export increasingly skill-intensive products and to increasingly outsource low skill-intensive parts and components, they stimulate more technological change, which then leads indirectly to greater skilled-unskilled wage inequalities in the United States and in other advanced economies. Ebenstein et al. find that the effect of these forces on wage inequalities in the United States is much greater than previously thought and perhaps comparable to that of technological change.

5.5 Specific-factors model

The effect of international trade on the distribution of income discussed in the previous section is based on the assumption that factors are perfectly mobile among the nation's industries or sectors. Although this is likely to be true in the long run, it may not be true in the short run, when some factors (say, capital) may be immobile or specific to some industry or sector. In this case, the conclusions of the H-O model on the effect of international trade on distribution need to be modified as explained by the specific-factors model.

In order to examine the specific-factors model, suppose that a nation that is relatively L-abundant produces two commodities: commodity X, which is L-intensive, and commodity Y, which is K-intensive. Both commodities are produced with labor and capital, but labor is mobile between the two industries, while capital is specific to each industry. That is, the capital used in the production of X (say, food) cannot be used in the production of Y (say, cloth), and vice versa.

With the opening of trade, as shown in Figure 5.10, the nation will specialize in the production of and will export commodity X (the L-intensive commodity) and import commodity Y (the specific K-intensive commodity). This will increase the relative price of X (i.e., P_X/P_Y) and the demand and nominal wage rate of labor in the nation. To simplify, suppose P_X rises and P_Y remains constant. As P_X rises, the production of X will be enlarged and the demand for labor will increase as well. The VMP_{LX} line will move upward to VMP'_{LX}. So labor price of X rises from w_0 to w_2, while that of Y is still w_0. Since labor can move freely, some labor will move from the production of Y to the production of X for higher wages. So industry Y will have to pay the higher wage rate for labor, until the labor price of the two sectors become the same. The labor prices of X and Y again converged to a new equilibrium, point E_1, where both sectors will have to pay w_1 for the employed labors. So we can see that after trade, the nominal wage will increase ($w_1 > w_0$), but the increase is less than the increase of X commodity price($w_1 < w_2$).

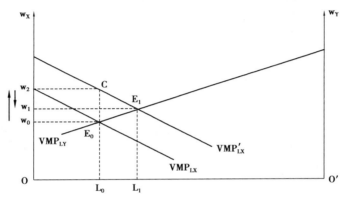

Figure 5.10 Specific-factors model

The effect of this on the real wage rate of labor in the nation is ambiguous. The real wage rate of labor is $\frac{w_X}{P_X} = MP_{LX}$ if labor owner spends all his income on the consumption of X. The increase of P_X leads to the increase of L in X production, MP_{LX} will decrease due to the law of diminishing marginal returns of factors, real price of labor w_X/P_X down. And if labor owner spends all his income on the consumption of Y, the real wage rate of labor is $\frac{w_Y}{P_Y} = MP_{LY}$. The increase of P_X leads to more L in X production and less L in Y production, and MP_{LY} will increase, real price of labor w_Y/P_Y up. Therefore, the real wage will fall for those workers who consume mainly commodity X and will increase for those workers who consume mainly commodity Y.

The result for specific capital is not ambiguous. When the interest rate of capital is earned from sector X, the real price of capital (interest rate) is $\frac{r_X}{P_X} = MP_{KX}$ if capital owner spends all his income on the consumption of X. The increase of P_X leads to more L and less K in X production, MP_{KX} will increase, real price of labor r_X/P_X up. So the nominal price of capital r_X is also increased. The real price of capital (interest rate) is $\dfrac{r_X}{P_Y} \neq MP_{KX}$ if capital owner spends all his income on the consumption of Y. Since r_X is up, P_Y constant, real price of labor w_Y/P_Y will increase.

When the interest rate of capital is earned from sector Y, the real price of capital (interest rate) is $\dfrac{r_X}{P_Y} = MP_{KY}$ if capital owner spends all his income on the consumption of Y. The increase of P_X leads to more L and less K in X production, and less L and more K in Y production, MP_{KY} will decrease, real price of labor r_Y/P_Y down. So the nominal price of capital r_Y is also decreased. The real price of capital (interest rate) is $\dfrac{r_Y}{P_X} \neq MP_{KX}$ if capital owner spends all his income on the consumption of X. The nominal price of capital r_Y is down, P_X is up, as analyzed above, so the real price of labor r_Y/P_X drops.

The conclusion reached by the specific-factors model is that trade has an ambiguous effect on the nation's mobile factors, benefits the immobile factors specific to the nation's export commodities or sectors, and harms the immobile factors specific to the nation's import-competing commodities or sectors.

5.6 Empirical tests of H-O model

This section presents and evaluates the results of empirical tests of the H-O model. A model must be successfully tested empirically before it is accepted as a theory. If a model is contradicted by empirical evidence, it must be rejected and the alternative model drawn up.

The first empirical test of the H-O model was conducted by Wassily Leontief in 1951 using US data for the year 1947. Since the United States was the most K-abundant nation in the world, Leontief expected to find that it exported K-intensive commodities and imported L-intensive commodities.

Wassily Leontief (1906 – 1999) was born in Petersburg in the summer of 1906. In 1921, he was admitted to the University of Petersburg and majored in sociology. In 1925, he obtained a master's degree in sociology. After graduation, he was retained as a teaching assistant by the university. Influenced by his father, he became very interested in economic issues and began to explore them. He was responsible for heavy teaching work while reading books on economic theory. In 1927, he came to Germany, Marx's hometown, and entered the doctoral class of Berlin University for further study. In 1928, he obtained his doctorate in economics from Berlin University. In 1931, he immigrated to the United States, first worked in the National Bureau of Economic Research, and then taught in Harvard University a few months later, for 40 years. In 1973, Leontief was highly praised by the Western economic circles and won the Nobel Prize in Economics for his development of the input-output analysis method and its great role in the economic field.

For this test, Leontief utilized the input-output table of the US economy to calculate the amount of labor and capital in a "representative bundle" of $1 million worth of US exports and import substitutes for the year 1947. (The input-output table is a table showing the origin and destination of each product in the economy. Leontief himself had contributed importantly to the development of this new technique of analysis and received the Nobel Prize in 1973 for his contributions.)

To be noted is that Leontief estimated K/L for US import substitutes rather than for imports. Import substitutes are commodities, such as automobiles, that the United States produces at home but also imports from abroad (because of incomplete specialization in production). Leontief was forced to use US data on import substitutes because foreign production data on actual US imports were not available. However, Leontief correctly reasoned that even though US import substitutes would be more K-intensive than actual imports (because K was relatively cheaper in the United States than abroad), they should still be less K-intensive than US exports if the H-O model held true. Of course, the use of US data on import substitutes, instead of foreign data on actual US imports, also eliminated from the calculation commodities, such as coffee and bananas, not produced at all in the United States.

The results of Leontief's test were startling. US import substitutes were about 30 percent more K-intensive than US exports. That is, the United States seemed to export L-intensive commodities and import K-intensive commodities. This was the opposite of what the H-O model predicted, and it became known as the Leontief paradox.

Case 5.2　Capital and labor requirements in US trade

Table 5.1 gives the capital and labor requirements per million dollars of US exports and import substitutes, as well as the capital/worker-year for imports relative to exports. For example, dividing the capital/worker-year of $18,180 for US import substitutes by the capital/worker-year of $14,010 for exports using 1947 data (see the third row of the table), Leontief obtained the capital/worker-year for imports relative to exports of 1.30. Since the United States is a relatively K-abundant nation and US import substitutes are more K-intensive than US exports, we have a paradox. Using 1951 trade data, the K/L ratio for imports/exports fell to 1.06, and, excluding natural resource industries, the ratio fell to 0.88 (thus eliminating the paradox). Using 1958 input requirements and 1962 trade data, Baldwin obtained the K/L ratio for imports/exports of 1.27. When natural resource industries were excluded, the ratio fell to 1.04, and when human capital was included, it fell to 0.92 (once again, eliminating the paradox).

Table 5.1 Capital and labor requirements per million dollars of US exports and import substitutes

Leontief (1947 input requirements, 1947 trade):			
	Exports	**Import substitutes**	**Imports/exports**
Capital	$2,550,780	$3,091,339	
Labor (worker-years)	182	170	
Capital/worker-year	$14,010	$18,180	1.30
Leontief (1947 input requirements, 1951 trade):			
	Exports	**Import substitutes**	**Imports/exports**
Capital	$2,256,800	$2,303,400	
Labor (worker-years)	174	168	
Capital/worker-year	$12,977	$13,726	1.06
Capital/worker-year, excluding natural resources			0.88
Baldwin (1958 input requirements, 1962 trade):			
	Exports	**Import substitutes**	**Imports/exports**
Capital	$1,876,000	$2,132,000	
Labor (worker-years)	131	119	
Capital/worker-year	$14,200	$18,000	1.27
Capital/worker-year, excluding natural resources			1.04
Capital/worker-year, excluding natural resources and including human capital			0.92

The explanations for the Leontief paradox are as follows:

(1) Higher labor productivity in the United States

In the same study, Leontief tried to rationalize his results rather than reject the H-O model. He argued that what we had here was an optical illusion. Since in 1947 US labor was about three times as productive as foreign labor, the United States was really an L-abundant nation if we multiplied the US labor force by 3 and compared this figure to the availability of capital in the nation. Therefore, it was only appropriate that US exports should be L-intensive in relation to US import substitutes. This explanation is not acceptable, and Leontief himself subsequently withdrew it. The reason is that while US labor was definitely more productive than foreign labor (though the multiple of 3 used by Leontief was largely arbitrary), so was US capital. Therefore, both US labor and US capital should be multiplied by a similar multiple, leaving the relative abundance of capital in the United States more or less unaffected.

(2) US tastes were biased in favor of K-intensive commodities

Similarly invalid is another explanation that postulated that US tastes were biased so strongly in favor of K-intensive commodities as to result in higher relative prices for these commodities in the United States. Therefore, the United States would export relatively L-intensive commodities. The reason this explanation is not acceptable is that tastes are known to be similar across nations. A study by Houthakker in 1957 on household consumption patterns in many countries found that the income elasticity of demand for food, clothing, housing, and other classes of goods was remarkably similar across nations. As a result, this explanation of the Leontief paradox based on a difference in tastes is also unacceptable.

If this really happens, it can be called a demand reversal. When a country has a comparative advantage in the production of a certain product, but its people have a special preference for this product in consumption, the relative price of this product will rise, thus changing the import and export direction originally determined according to the H-O model.

(3) Two-factor model neglecting natural resources

A more general source of bias is that Leontief used a two-factor model (L and K), thus abstracting from other factors such as natural resources (soil, climate, mineral deposits, forests, etc.). However, a commodity might be intensive in natural resources so that classifying it as either K- or L-intensive (with a two-factor model) would clearly be inappropriate. Furthermore, many production processes using natural resources—such as coal mining, steel production, and farming—also require large amounts of physical capital.

The US dependence on imports of many natural resources, therefore, might help explain the large capital intensity of US import-competing industries.

(4) US policy's function

US tariff policy was another source of bias in the Leontief study. A tariff is nothing else than a tax on imports. As such, it reduces imports and stimulates the domestic production of import substitutes. In a 1956 study, Kravis found that the most heavily protected industries in the United States were the L-intensive industries. This biased the pattern of trade and reduced the labor intensity of US import substitutes, thus contributing to the existence of the Leontief paradox.

(5) Human capital and knowledge capital

Perhaps the most important source of bias was the fact that Leontief included in his measure of capital only physical capital (such as machinery, other equipment, buildings, and so on) and completely ignored human capital. Human capital refers to the education, job training, and health embodied in workers, which increase their productivity. The implication is that since US labor embodies more human capital than foreign labor, adding the human capital component to physical capital would make US exports more K-intensive relative to US import substitutes. (In fairness to Leontief, it must be said that the analysis of human capital became fully developed and fashionable only following the work of Schultz in 1961 and Becker in 1964.)

Somewhat related to human capital is the influence of R&D on US exports. The "knowledge" capital resulting from R&D leads to an increase in the value of output derived from a given stock of material and human resources. Even casual observation shows that most US exports are R&D and skill-intensive. Thus, human and knowledge capital are important considerations in determining the pattern of US trade. These were not considered by Leontief in his study.

The most important of the numerous empirical studies following a human capital approach were undertaken by Kravis, Keesing, Kenen, and Baldwin. In two studies published in 1956, Kravis found that wages in US export industries in both 1947 and 1951 were about 15 percent higher than wages in US import-competing industries. Kravis correctly argued that the higher wages in US export industries were a reflection of the greater productivity and human capital embodied in US exports than in US import substitutes.

In a 1966 study, Keesing found that US exports were more skill-intensive than the exports of nine other industrial nations for the year 1957. This reflected the fact that the United States had the most highly trained labor force, embodying more human capital than other nations.

It remained for Kenen, in a 1965 study, to actually estimate the human capital embodied in US exports and import-competing goods, add these estimates to the physical capital requirements, and then re-compute K/L for US exports and US import substitutes. Using 1947 data and without excluding products with an important natural resource content (as in the original Leontief study), Kenen succeeded in eliminating the Leontief paradox.

In a 1971 study, Baldwin updated Leontief's study by using the 1958 US input-output table and US trade data for 1962. Baldwin found that excluding natural resource industries was not sufficient to eliminate the paradox unless human capital was included.

(6) Factor-intensity reversal

Factor-intensity reversal refers to the situation where a given commodity is the L-intensive commodity in the L-abundant nation and the K-intensive commodity in the K-abundant nation. For example, factor-intensity reversal is present if commodity X is the L-intensive commodity in Nation 1 (the low-wage nation), and, at the same time, it is the K-intensive commodity in Nation 2 (the high-wage nation).

To determine when and why factor-intensity reversal occurs, we use the concept of the elasticity of substitution of factors in production. The elasticity of substitution measures the degree or ease with which one factor can be substituted for another in production as the relative price of the factor declines. For example, suppose that the elasticity of substitution of L for K is much greater in the production of commodity X than in the production of commodity Y. This means that it is much easier to substitute L for K (or vice versa) in the production of commodity X than in the production of commodity Y.

$$\text{elasticity} = \frac{\Delta(K/L)/(K/L)}{\Delta(w/r)/(w/r)}$$

Factor-intensity reversal is more likely to occur if the difference in the elasticity of substitution of L for K is greater in the production of the two commodities. With a large elasticity of substitution of L for K in the production of commodity X, Nation 1 will produce commodity X with L-intensive techniques because its wages are low. On the contrary, Nation 2 will produce commodity X with K-intensive techniques because its wages are high. If at the same time the elasticity of substitution of L for K is very low in the production of commodity Y, the two nations will be forced to use similar techniques in producing commodity Y even though their relative factor prices may differ greatly. As a result, commodity X will be the L-intensive commodity in Nation 1 and the K-intensive commodity in Nation 2, and we have a case of factor-intensity reversal.

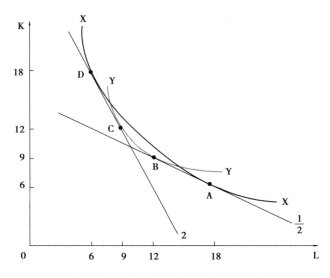

Figure 5.11   Factor-intensity reversal

Figure 5.11 shows a single isoquant for commodity X and a single isoquant for commodity Y. We know that with a homogeneous production function of degree one, a single isoquant completely describes the entire production function of each commodity. Furthermore, since both nations are assumed to use the same technology, we can use the single X- and Y-isoquants to refer to both nations.

Figure 5.11 shows that at $w/r = 1/2$, commodity X is produced at point A, where the X-isoquant is tangent to the isocost line with slope (w/r) equal to $1/2$ and $K/L = 6/18 = 1/3$. Commodity Y is produced at point B, where the Y-isoquant is tangent to the same isocost line with slope (w/r) equal to $1/2$ and $K/L = 9/12 = 3/4$. Thus, at $w/r = 1/2$, K/L is higher for commodity Y, so that commodity X is the relatively L-intensive commodity.

On the contrary, at $w/r = 2$, commodity Y is produced at point C, where the Y-isoquant is tangent to the isocost line with slope (w/r) equal to 2 and $K/L = 12/9 = 4/3$, commodity X is produced at point D, where the X-isoquant is tangent to the same isocost line with slope (w/r) equal to 2 and $K/L = 18/6 = 3$. Thus, at $w/r = 2$, commodity X is the relatively K-intensive commodity.

As a result, commodity X is L-intensive at $w/r = 1/2$ and K-intensive at $w/r = 2$ with respect to commodity Y, and we say that factor-intensity reversal is present.

With factor-intensity reversal, both the H-O theorem and the factor-price equalization theorem must be rejected. To see this, suppose that Nation 1 is the relatively L-abundant nation with $w/r = 1/2$, while Nation 2 is the relatively K-abundant nation with $w/r = 2$. With $w/r = 1/2$, Nation 1 should specialize in the production of and export commodity X because

Nation 1 is the L-abundant nation and commodity X is the L-intensive commodity there. With $w/r = 2$, Nation 2 should specialize in the production of and export commodity X because Nation 2 is the K-abundant nation and commodity X is the K-intensive commodity there. Since both nations cannot export to each other the same homogeneous commodity (i.e., commodity X), the H-O theorem no longer predicts the pattern of trade.

When the H-O model does not hold, the factor-price equalization theorem also fails. To see this, note that as Nation 1 (the low-wage nation) specializes in the production of commodity X (the L-intensive commodity), the demand for labor rises, and w/r and w rise in Nation 1. With Nation 1 specializing in and exporting commodity X to Nation 2, Nation 2 must specialize in and export commodity Y to Nation 1 (since the two nations could not possibly export the same homogeneous commodity to each other). However, since commodity Y is the L-intensive commodity in Nation 2, the demand for labor rises, and w/r and w rise in Nation 2 (the high-wage nation), too. Thus, wages rise both in Nation 1 (the low-wage nation) and in Nation 2 (the high-wage nation).

If wages rise faster in Nation 1 than in Nation 2, the difference in wages between the two nations declines, as predicted by the factor-price equalization theorem. If wages rise more slowly in Nation 1 than in Nation 2, the wage difference increases. If wages rise by the same amount in both nations, the wage difference remains unchanged. Since there is no a priori way to determine the effect of international trade on the difference in factor prices in each case, we must reject the factor-price equalization theorem.

From Figure 5.11, we can see that factor-intensity reversal arises because the X-isoquant has a much smaller curvature than the Y-isoquant and the X- and Y-isoquants cross twice within the two relative factor price lines. When the two isoquants have similar curvature, they will only cross once and there is no factor-intensity reversal.

That factor-intensity reversal does occur in the real world is beyond doubt. The question is how prevalent it is. If factor reversal is very prevalent, the entire H-O theory must be rejected. If it occurs but rarely, we can retail the H-O model and treat factor reversal as an exception. The frequency of factor reversal in the real world is an empirical question.

The first empirical research on this topic was a study conducted by Minhas in 1962, in which he found factor reversal to be fairly prevalent, occurring in about one-third of the cases that he studied. Howeret, by correcting an important source of bias in the Minhas study, Leontief showed in 1964 that factor reversal occurred in only about 8 percent of the cases studied, and that if two industries with an important natural resource content were excluded, factor reversal occurred in only 1 percent of the cases.

A study by Ball, published in 1966 and testing another aspect of Minhas's results, confirmed Leontief's conclusion that factor-intensity reversal seems to be a rather rare occurrence in the real world. As a result, the assumption that one commodity is L-intensive and the other commodity is K-intensive at all relative factor prices generally holds, so that the H-O model can be retained.

——— *China-perspective case study* ———

The export competitiveness of L-intensive manufacturing industry is declining, and China's trade structure is facing huge changes

In the past 40 years, the opening-up of China mainly relied on the manufacturing industry's participation in the global industrial chain, which led to the expansion of the manufacturing industry, technology upgrading and competitiveness improvement. The development of service trade was relatively lagging behind.

At present, the export competitiveness of China's L-intensive manufacturing industry has declined, and the export of human K-intensive service industry needs to accelerate growth. Energy resources are long-term constraints, and the transformation of exports to a low-carbon structure requires service exports to play an important role. The people's living standards have been improved, and the import of high-level service trade can meet the people's desire for a better life. The transformation and upgrading of manufacturing industry has been comprehensively promoted, and high-level producer service trade can play an important role. This is a very clear requirement of the four central points of the new growth pattern, and also a weak point and pain point for future growth. Service trade must play a strong role.

Promoting China's digital service trade and promoting the development of service trade will play an important role in building a new development pattern. High level employment, transformation of trade structure, meeting people's aspirations for a better life and promoting the transformation and upgrading of manufacturing industry will all play an important role in these four aspects. China's industrial base, market size and enterprise competitiveness have all created a good foundation for the development of service trade, especially digital service trade. Digital producer services in particular have good conditions for development. We need to accelerate the development of service trade and help build a new development pattern.

Key concepts

same technology	Heckscher-Ohlin (H-O) theory
labor-intensive commodity	capital-intensive commodity
factor abundance	labor-capital ratio (L/K)
factor-proportions theory	capital-labor ratio (K/L)
factor-price equalization theorem	constant returns to scale
specific-factors model	perfect competition
input-output table	internal factor mobility
import substitutes	international factor mobility
Leontief paradox	human capital
relative factor prices	factor-intensity reversal
derived demand	elasticity of substitution

Summary

1. The H-O theory holds that a nation will export the commodity whose production requires the intensive use of the nation's relatively abundant and cheap factor and import the commodity whose production requires the intensive use of the nation's relatively scarce and expensive factor. In short, the relatively labor-rich nation exports the relatively L-intensive commodity and imports the relatively K-intensive commodity.

2. Factor intensity and factor abundance are the two key concepts of factor endowment theory (H-O theory).

3. Under the condition of the same production technology, the difference of production possibility curve between Country A and B is completely caused by the difference of factor endowment between the two countries. The production possibility curve of Country A is biased to the X-axis, which means that under the same relative price of goods, the relative supply capacity of Country A on X is stronger than that of Country B, while Country B is stronger than that of Country A on Y.

4. H-O theory does not require identical tastes (i.e., equal indifference curves) in the two nations. It only requires that if tastes differ, they do not differ sufficiently to neutralize the tendency of different factor endowments and production possibility curves from leading to different relative commodity prices and comparative advantage in the two nations.

5. Suppose a country (especially a developing country) produces and exports primary products and L-intensive products in full accordance with its comparative advantages. In international trade with developed countries who mainly export technology and K-intensive products, although it can gain benefits, its industrial structure cannot be upgraded and it maintains low economic competitiveness, thus falling into the "comparative advantage trap".

6. The factor-price equalization theorem can also be called H-O-S theorem due to the contribution from Samuelson, states that although the production factors cannot flow freely among countries, the free flow of goods between countries can replace the free flow of factors of production, and ultimately make the factor prices among countries tend to be equal.

7. Stolper-Samuelson theorem states that an increase in the relative price of a certain commodity will lead to an increase in the actual price or income of the factors intensively used by the commodity, while the actual price or income of another factor of production will decrease. In free trade, export makes the exporting commodity price rise, and the factor intensively used by the export commodity is the abundant and cheap factor of the country. So, free trade will increase the real price of the relatively abundant factor in a country, and reduce the real price of the relatively scarce factor.

8. The specific-factors model states that trade has an ambiguous effect on the nation's mobile factors, benefits the immobile factors specific to the nation's export commodities or sectors, and harms the immobile factors specific to the nation's import-competing commodities or sectors.

9. The first empirical test of the H-O model was conducted by Wassily Leontief in 1951, which proved that the United States seemed to export L-intensive commodities and import K-intensive commodities. This was the opposite of what the H-O model predicted, and it became known as the Leontief paradox.

Exercises

1. Draw two sets of axes, one for Nation 1 and the other for Nation 2, measuring labor along the horizontal axis and capital along the vertical axis.

   A. Show by straight lines through the origin that K/L is higher for commodity Y than for commodity X in both nations in the absence of trade and that K/L is higher in Nation 2 than in Nation 1 for both commodities.

   B. What happens to the slope of the lines measuring K/L of each commodity in Nation 2 if r/w rises in Nation 2 as a result of international trade?

C. What happens to the slope of the lines measuring K/L in Nation 1 if r/w falls in Nation 1 as a result of international trade?

D. Given the results of parts A and C, does international trade increase or reduce the difference in the K/L in the production of each commodity in the two nations as compared with the pre-trade situation?

2. Please show graphically that even with a small difference in tastes in the two nations, Nation 1 and Nation 2 would continue to act according to the H-O model.

3. Please show graphically that sufficiently different tastes in the two nations could conceivably neutralize the difference in their factor endowments and lead to equal relative commodity prices in the two nations in the absence of trade.

4. If you have traveled to poor developing countries, you will have noticed that people there consume very different goods and services than consumers in developed countries. Does this mean that tastes in developing countries are very different from those in the developed countries? Explain.

5. Starting from the pre-trade equilibrium point in Figure 5.6, assume that tastes in Nation 1 change in favor of the commodity of its comparative disadvantage (i.e., in favor of commodity Y).

A. What is the effect of this change in tastes on P_X/P_Y in Nation 1? How did you reach such a conclusion?

B. What is the effect of this change in tastes on r/w in Nation 1?

C. What is the effect of this change in tastes on the volume of trade and on the trade partner?

Chapter 6 | New Trade Theory

Learning goals

After learning this chapter, you should be able to:

✓ explain how international trade can result from economies of scale.

✓ explain how product differentiation leads to intra-industry trade.

✓ understand the technological gap and product life cycle models of trade.

✓ understand how demand affects trade.

✓ understand the relationship between transport costs and environmental standards in international trade.

The above two chapters show that international trade occurs due to the comparative cost advantages and disadvantages between countries, and the difference in comparative costs can arise from both the difference in production technology (classical trade theory) and the difference in factor endowment (neo-classical trade theory). But these theories cannot better explain the large amount of trade between industrialized countries with similar technical levels and factor endowments.

Since the 1960s, some new international trade theories have been proposed to try to explain the above phenomena. Because these theories change the assumptions of the traditional trade theory, and the analysis framework is also different, so they are called the new international trade theory. This chapter mainly introduces the new trade theory created by Paul Krugman based on economies of scale and imperfect competitive market structure. In addition, the reasons for international trade are also discussed from the perspective of demand.

In the beginning of the 21st century, the trade model with the framework of imperfect competitive market has had a new development, which is called the new trade theory, but will not be introduced in this book, for it is usually for advanced study and still remains a bit controversial.

6.1　Background of new trade theory

After the Second World War, especially since the late 1950s, due to the great influence of the third scientific and technological revolution (i.e., the new technological revolution) and the rapid development of multinational corporations, the international division of labor has been greatly promoted in the world. At the same time, the various characteristics of economic globalization have been continuously strengthened, and the multilateral trading system represented by the General Agreement on Tariffs and Trade (GATT) and the World Trade Organization (WTO) has gradually taken shape and been continuously improved and developed. In the face of the major changes in international trade practice, the traditional international trade theory has encountered a challenge. That is, many new phenomena in international trade are not only unable to be explained by traditional trade theories, but are even contrary to traditional trade theories.

For example, before the 1950s most of the trade occurred between developed and developing countries (called "North-South trade"), but after the 1950s, the pattern of world trade has changed to the main trade between developed countries (called "North-North trade"). In addition, the trade between industrialized countries became mainly intra-industrial trade. Many countries not only export manufactured products, also import a large number of similar manufactured products, these manufactured goods trade between developed countries cannot be explained by the traditional trade theories. Besides, industrial leading position is transferred between different countries, and thus the comparative advantage is no longer maintained in the same country as time changes.

At the same time, with the development of economics, new theories have emerged, such as industrial organization theory, competitive market theory, game theory and new institutional economic theories, etc., which pay more attention to the market structure of imperfect competition.

6.2　Development of new trade theory

In the first half of the 20th century, the theory of factor endowment, expressed in the form of neo-classical model, occupied an absolute dominant position in international trade theory. In the 1950s, Leontief's empirical test results made people doubt the theory of factor endowment. In the 1960s, S B Linder and Raymond Vernon proposed a new trade basis different from comparative advantage from different perspectives, but the theory of factor endowment was not really challenged. It was not until the late 1970s that the development of international trade theory really made a major breakthrough.

In the late 1970s and early 1980s, a group of economists represented by American economist Paul Krugman put forward the so-called "new trade theory". According to the new trade theory, besides resource differences, economies of scale are another independent determinant of the causes of international trade and the sources of international trade gains. As Krugman pointed out, "Even in the absence of differences in preferences, technology and resource endowments, and economies of scale can guide countries to carry out specialized division of labor and trade." The new trade theory introduces the assumption of economies of scale, thus breaking the two basic assumptions of comparative advantage trade theory about constant returns to scale and perfect competition, making the focus of research shift from differences between countries to market structure and manufacturer behavior. If the comparative advantage trade theories are the "perfect competition theoretical model of international trade", the new trade theory can be called the "imperfect competition theoretical model of international trade".

As the imperfect competition theory has not yet formed a unified analysis model, the new trade theory has not reached the perfect level in the form of expression as the comparative advantage trade theory. However, this does not prevent the great application value of this theory from being recognized. So far, after more than 50 years of development, the new trade theory has become an important part of international economics or international trade textbooks.

The emergence of new trade theory is inseparable from the development of industrial organization theory which provides a solid theoretical foundation. In fact, Adam Smith had already put forward the idea of economies of scale in his famous judgment on how to expand the size of the trade market and thus improve labor productivity. However, with the rise of the neo-classical school, economies of scale have been excluded because it opposes the completely competitive market structure theory. Although economists such as Antoine Augustin Cournot (1801－1877) and E H Chamberlin (1899－1967) have made great innovations and contributions to imperfect competition analysis, imperfect competition analysis has been drifted away from mainstream economics for a long time. The industrial organization theory emerging in the 1940s can be regarded as a subsequent development of the market structure theory in microeconomics. It takes the imperfect competitive market structure as the investigation object, and mainly analyzes the causal relationship between the market structure, manufacturer behavior and market performance. In the mid-1970s, the introduction of game theory research method made a major breakthrough in the analysis and research of manufacturer behavior under the imperfect competitive market structure (mainly oligopoly market). In 1978, Krugman proposed to promote the monopoly competition model, taking into account differential products and (internal) economies of scale, to the conditions of an open economy, thus proving for the first time that economies of scale are another cause of international trade, and that differential products determine the trade model as intra-industrial trade. Krugman was the first economist to analyze modern international trade and build up theoretical models with both economies of scale and imperfect competition.

New international trade theory is produced and developed on the basis of the traditional trade theory. The emergence of the new trade theory does not mean that it replaces the traditional comparative advantage trade theory. In fact, they have the following differences. First, they explain different phenomena of trade. The traditional trade theory is to explain trade between developed and developing countries, and the new trade theory will explain trade between developed countries. Second, the traditional trade theory is based on the theory of constant returns to scale and complete competition, and the new trade theory is based on imperfect competition. Therefore, the two are not alternative relations, but complementary relations. They jointly enrich and develop the system of international trade theory.

We can examine the assumptions set in traditional trade theories to clarify their differences. The trade cannot happen if the following assumptions hold: ①The production technology is the same in both countries. ②The two countries have the same relative factor endowments. ③Consumption preferences are the same in both countries. ④Constant returns to scale remain unchanged. ⑤The commodity markets and factor markets of both countries are perfectly competitive.

Traditional international trade models typically use two countries, two products (or sectors), and two elements, namely, the 2-2-2 model. Under the premise of perfect competition, the relative price difference under closed conditions is the basis of international trade, and the relative price difference determines the products (or departments) of a country with comparative advantages and comparative disadvantage. Differences in supply and demand between countries are the root cause of the relative price differences. After trade, the international equilibrium price is determined jointly by the supply and demand of the two countries. The international equilibrium price is between the relative prices under the closed conditions of the two countries, and international trade is good for all parties involved in trade. It can be seen that if any one of the five conditions are removed, the basis of trade will be created. Therefore, under the premise of constant returns to scale, and in a fully competitive market, countries with the same technology, factor endowment and consumption preferences will have the same relative price under closed conditions, so there is no incentive to trade. And if countries differ in these, or at least one, comparative advantage arises, triggering international trade.

If the assumption 1 is removed and other conditions remain unchanged, the production technology of the same kind of goods between the two countries will no longer be the same, and the shape of the production possibility curve will also be different. Since the shape of the social indifference curve is still the same, the relative prices of the two countries under closed conditions must be different. The foundation of trade was created. Therefore, in this case, the difference in production technology is an important reason for international trade. This is the core content of classical trade theory.

If the assumption 2 is removed and other conditions remain unchanged, then the shape of the production possibility curve of the two countries will be different, and the relative price difference will occur. Therefore, the difference in relative factor endowments has become another important reason for international trade. This is the core content of H-O model.

The difference in production technology or relative factor endowment reflects the difference in supply between the two countries. In the history of the development of international trade theory, the trade theory that explains the causes of international trade from the supply side, that is, from the differences in production technology and factor endowments, has long occupied a major position. Of course, if the supply conditions of the two countries are identical, but assumption 3 is removed, that is, the difference in demand can also lead to international trade.

When removing assumptions 4 or 5, it should be noted that some new problems will be encountered. Under the conditions of increasing returns to scale or imperfect competition, the relative price difference is no longer the only basis for international trade. In this case, even if there is no relative price difference between the two countries, international trade can still occur, because economies of scale will lead to full specialization of international division of labor. Different countries can choose to produce different varieties of goods and then exchange them. In addition, in the case of imperfect competition, the analytical methods and models of traditional international trade theory based on perfect competition are no longer applicable.

Therefore, the theory of international trade actually includes two different theoretical systems: the theory of perfect competition in international trade and the theory of imperfect competition in international trade, that is, the traditional theory of international trade and the new theory of international trade.

6.3　Intra-industry trade

The traditional trade is mainly the inter-industry trade. That is, the trade between countries is mainly the trade of products produced in different industries. In the contemporary international trade, the trade between developed countries, the internal trade of multinational companies and the intra-industry trade are three prominent and interrelated phenomena. Since the Second World War, many countries have exported industrial products and imported a large number of similar industrial products. The traditional mode of "exporting industrial products—importing primary products" in industrial countries has gradually changed, and lots of trade, including export and import, happens inside the same industry. For example, the United States exports a large number of cars every year, but it also imports a large number of cars from Japan, Germany, South Korea and so on. This trade mode that both imports and exports are the same products is called "intra-industry trade".

Similar products here generally refer to the products having at least the same top three digits in the Standard International Trade Classification (SITC), that is, the products with at least the same category, the same chapter, and the same group. The intra-industry trade mode reflects that, even if the two countries have exactly the same capital/labor ratio, their manufacturers will produce similar but different products.

Intra-industry trade arises in order to take advantage of important economies of scale in production. That is, international competition forces each firm or plant in industrial countries to produce only one, or at most a few varieties and styles of the same product rather than many different varieties and styles. This is crucial in keeping unit costs low. With few varieties and styles, more specialized and faster machinery can be developed for a continuous operation and a longer production run. The nation then imports other varieties and styles from other nations. Intra-industry trade benefits consumers because of the wider range of choices (i.e., the greater variety of differentiated products) available at the lower prices made possible by economies of scale in production.

The importance of intra-industry trade became apparent when tariffs and other obstructions to the flow of trade among members of the EU, or Common Market, were removed in 1958. Balassa found that the volume of trade surged, but most of the increase involved the exchange of differentiated products within each broad industrial classification. That is, German cars were exchanged for French and Italian cars, French washing machines were exchanged for German washing machines, Italian typewriters for German and French typewriters, and so on.

Even before the formation of the EU, plant size in most industries was about the same in Europe and the United States. However, unit costs were much higher in Europe, primarily because European plants produced many more varieties and styles of a product than did their American counterparts. As tariffs were reduced and finally eliminated and trade expanded within the EU, each plant could specialize in the production of only a few varieties and styles of a product, and unit costs fell sharply as a result.

The level of intra-industry trade can be measured by the index of intra-industry trade (IIT):

$$IIT = 1 - \frac{|X - M|}{X + M}$$

X and M represent, respectively, the value of exports and imports of a particular industry or commodity group and the vertical bars in the numerator of equation denote the absolute value. The value of IIT ranges from 0 to 1, or from 0 to 100 as a percentage. IIT = 0 when a country only exports or only imports the good in question (i.e., there is no intra-industry trade). On the contrary, if the exports and imports of a good are equal, IIT = 1 (i.e., intra-industry trade is maximum).

Grubel and Lloyd calculated the IIT for various industries in 10 industrial countries for the year 1967. They found that the weighted average of IIT for the 10 industrial countries ranged from 0.30 for mineral fuels, lubricants, and related industries to 0.60 for chemicals, for an overall or combined weighted average of IIT for all industries in all 10 countries of 0.48. This means that in 1967, nearly half of all the trade among these 10 industrial countries involved the exchange of differentiated products of the same industry. The IIT is also called Grubel-Lloyd Index due to their contribution. The value of IIT has also risen over time. It was 0.36 in 1959, 0.42 in 1964, and 0.48 in 1967.

Table 6.1 presents some more recent estimates of intra-industry trade for the leading industrial and developing countries.

Table 6.1　Manufacturing intra-industry trade as a percentage of total manufacturing trade

Country	1988−1991	1996−2000	Country	1988−1991	1996−2000
France	75.9	77.5	Denmark	61.6	64.8
Canada	73.5	76.2	Italy	61.6	64.7
Austria	71.8	74.2	Poland	56.4	62.6
United Kingdom	70.1	73.7	Portugal	52.4	61.3
Mexico	62.5	73.4	South Korea	41.4	57.5
Hungary	54.9	72.1	Ireland	58.6	54.6
Switzerland	69.8	72.0	Finland	53.8	53.9
Germany	67.1	72.0	Japan	37.6	47.6
Belgium/Luxembourg	77.6	71.4	New Zealand	37.2	40.6
Spain	68.2	71.2	Turkey	36.7	40.0
Netherlands	69.2	68.9	Norway	40.0	37.1
United States	63.5	68.5	Greece	42.8	36.9
Sweden	64.2	66.6	Australia	28.6	29.8

Table 6.1 presents data on the share of intra-industry trade in manufactured products of industrial countries in 1988−1991 and 1996−2000. The table shows that in 1996−2000, France had the highest level of intra-industry trade (77.5), followed by Canada (76.2) and Austria (74.2). For the other G7 countries, the United Kingdom had an index of 73.7, Germany 72.0, the United States 68.5, Italy 64.7, and Japan 47.6. The highest indices were for European countries (except for Canada, Mexico, and the United States) and the lowest were for Pacific and developing countries (except for Norway and Greece). The highest percentage growth in the index between the two periods was for Hungary, South Korea, Mexico, and Japan. For some countries (such as Belgium/Luxembourg, Greece, and Ireland), the index actually declined.

There is a serious shortcoming in using the IIT to measure the degree of intra-industry trade, however. This results from the fact that we get very different values for IIT, depending on how broadly we define the industry or product group. Specifically, the more broadly we define an industry, the greater will be the value of IIT. The reason for this is that the more broadly an industry is defined, the more likely it is that a country will export some varieties of differentiated products and import others (see Table 6.2). Thus, the IIT must be used with caution. It can, nevertheless, be very useful in measuring differences in intra-industry trade in different industries in a nation.

Table 6.2   IIT for some G20 coutries

Country	SITC-3 Digit	SITC-5 Digit	Country	SITC-3 Digit	SITC-5 Digit
France	0.600	0.424	Brazil	0.373	0.137
Canada	0.599	0.421	India	0.318	0.127
Germany	0.570	0.419	Argentina	0.313	0.156
United Kingdom	0.525	0.362	China	0.305	0.182
United States	0.503	0.317	South Africa	0.294	0.092
Italy	0.497	0.344	Indonesia	0.291	0.117
Mexico	0.478	0.334	Turkey	0.217	0.130
Thailand	0.449	0.252	Russia	0.146	0.047
Korea	0.412	0.240	Saudi Arabia	0.070	0.011
Japan	0.398	0.238	*Unweighted Average*	0.387	0.229

Table 6.2 gives intra-industry trade indexes for the G20 (the largest and most important advanced and emerging market economies plus the EU as a whole) in 2006 at the SITC 3-digit and 5-digit levels. An index of 0 indicates no intra-industry trade, whereas an index of 1 indicates that the exports and imports of the country are equal in each product category. We would expect that for each country, the intra-industry trade index at the 3-digit level be greater than that at the 5-digit level (i. e., the greater the degree of aggregation—transportation equipment, which includes automotive products, trains, and air-planes as compared simply to automobiles—the higher the intra-industry trade index). From the table, we can see that the index for developed countries is generally higher than for the other G20 countries.

6.4　Economies of scale and international trade

The traditional international trade theories are mainly used to explain the inter-industry trade. For the above-mentioned new trade phenomenon, intra-industry trade, new theories are needed. Since the 1960s, many economists began to explore how to explain the new trade phenomenon. One of the most representative belongs to Paul Krugman's international trade theory based on economies of scale.

6.4.1　Who

Paul R Krugman (1953—) was born in New York in 1953. After graduating from John F. Kennedy High School, he came to the famous Massachusetts Institute of Technology to study economics. In 1977, he received a doctor's degree from Massachusetts Institute of Technology, and later successively taught at Yale, Massachusetts Institute of Technology and Stanford University. From 1982 to 1983, he served as a member of the Council of Economic Advisers of the President. In 1988, he published the book *The Age of Reduced Expectations*. His research fields include international trade, international finance, currency crisis and exchange rate change theory. In 1991, Krugman won the Clark Prize of the American Economic Society, which was regarded as an important indicator of the Nobel Prize. He published the book *Popular Internationalism* in 1996, which accurately predicted the Asian financial crisis. Later, he became famous as a famous economic prophet. In 2000, he worked as a professor of economics at the School of Public and International Affairs of Princeton University. In 2008, he was awarded the Nobel Prize in Economics for his achievements in "analysis of trade patterns and location of economic activity".

Krugman is currently the distinguished professor of economics of City University of New York (CUNY) Graduate Center. The new trade theory proposed by Krugman is a major innovation in international trade theory.

Krugman is also a star writer. He has kept writing for many years. Krugman has published 20 books and more than 200 papers in professional journals. The latest publication, "Arguing with Zombies: Economics, Policies, and the Fight for a Better Future", has selected several columns on the complexity of policy issues published by him in the *New York Times*. He is the "Top 10 Most Influential Thinkers in 2013" and "Top 50 Most Influential Financial Figures in the World in 2011" rated by Bloomberg. In addition, he has been selected as the "Top 100 Global Thinkers" in Foreign Policy for four consecutive years (2009—2012).

6.4.2   What is economies of scale?

The traditional trade theories assume constant returns to scale. That is, if all inputs are doubled, the output doubles as well. In the pre-industrial era of primary product production, this assumption is basically close to reality. However, in the modern society, especially in the industrial production, the production of many products has the characteristics of increasing returns to scale. That is, if the scale of production is expanded, each unit input of production factors will have more output. If other conditions remain unchanged, when the scale is expanded, the increasing returns to scale will lead to economies of scale, because the additional products generated by the increasing returns to scale reduce the average cost, making the average cost decrease with the expansion of scale.

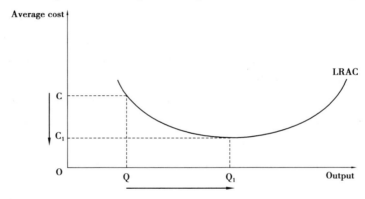

Figure 6.1   Economies of scale

When an enterprise expands its scale from Q to Q_1, the increase of its total output is greater than the increase of its total cost. That is, the long-term average total cost decreases from C to C_1. As shown in Figure 6.1, we can say that this enterprise is at the stage of economies of scale.

Economies of scale usually have two types. One is the internal economies of scale, meaning that the average cost of an enterprise decreases as its own production scale expands. The internal economies of scale always appear in enterprises with certain monopoly power. The other is external economies of scale, meaning that when the output of the whole industry (due to the increase of the number of enterprises) expands, the long-term average cost of the industry decreases, and the average cost of each enterprise in the industry also decreases. The external economies of scale mainly come from the increase and concentration of enterprises in an industry, which can lead to a decreased costs of enterprises in information collection, product sales and other aspects. External economies of scale generally appear in highly competitive and homogeneous product industries. For example, in the United States, there are many computer companies, each not very large, but all together, forming external economies of scale. Beijing's "Zhongguancun computer city", Guangzhou's "Tianhe computer city" and Zhejiang's "button city", "small commodity market", all have the characteristics of external economies of scale.

6.4.3 How is economies of scale related to trade?

With economies of scale, mutually beneficial trade can occur even if nations are identical in every way. Economies of scale will guide manufacturers in various countries to produce some goods instead of all goods alone, so as to obtain the benefits from economies of scale: The cost is lower than the price.

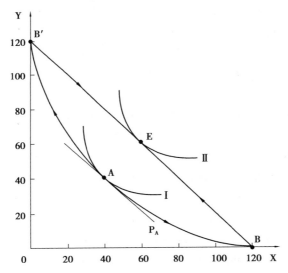

Figure 6.2   Trade based on economies of scale

Figure 6.2 shows how mutually beneficial trade can be based on increasing returns to scale which can lead to economies of scale. In the case of increasing returns to scale, the opportunity cost of product production is not increasing, but decreasing, so the production possibility curve is no longer concave to the origin, but convex to the origin, or inward-bending, as shown in Figure 6.2.

If the two nations are assumed to be identical in every respect, we can use a single production frontier and a single indifference map to refer to both nations. With identical production frontiers and indifference maps, the no-trade equilibrium-relative commodity prices in the two nations are also identical. In Figure 6.2, this is $P_X/P_Y = P_A$ in both nations and is given by the slope of the common tangent to the production frontier and indifference curve I at point A.

With trade, Nation 1 could specialize completely in the production of commodity X and produce at point B. Nation 2 would then specialize completely in the production of commodity Y and produce at point B'. By exchanging 60X for 60Y with each other, each nation would end up consuming at point E on indifference curve II, thus gaining 20X and 20Y. These gains from trade arise from economies of scale in the production of only one commodity in each nation. In the absence of trade, the two nations would not specialize in the production of only one commodity because each nation wants to consume both commodities.

Note that the no-trade equilibrium point A is unstable in the sense that if, for whatever reason, Nation 1 moves to the right of point A along its production frontier, the relative price of X (the slope of the production frontier) will fall and will continue to fall until Nation 1 becomes completely specialized in the production of commodity X. Similarly, if Nation 2 moves to the left of point A along its production frontier, P_X/P_Y will rise (so that its inverse, P_Y/P_X, falls) until Nation 2 becomes completely specialized in the production of commodity Y.

Several additional aspects of the preceding analysis and Figure 6.2 must be clarified. First of all, it is a matter of complete indifference which of the two nations specializes in the production of commodity X or commodity Y. In the real world, this may result from historical accident. Second, it should be clear, at least intuitively, that the two nations need not be identical in every respect for mutually beneficial trade to result from increasing returns to scale. Third, if economies of scale persist over a sufficiently long range of outputs, one or a few firms in the nation will capture the entire market for a given product, leading to monopoly (a single producer of a commodity for which there is no close substitute) or oligopoly (a few producers of a homogeneous or differentiated product).

(1) Internal economies of scale and trade

The enterprises with internal economies of scale are in monopolistic competition, which is characterized by large scale of enterprises, different products produced, and the demand curve inclines downward to the right.

Before trade, the enterprise only faces the domestic demand curve D_1. According to the principle of profit maximization, $MR_1 = MC$, and the manufacturer's optimal production is Q_1. Due to economies of scale, AC curve is inclined downward to the right. In equilibrium, AC curve is tangent to the demand curve D_1, the product price is equal to its average cost ($P_1 = AC_1$), and the super-normal profit is zero, as shown in Figure 6.3.

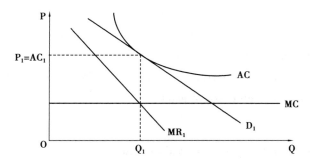

Figure 6.3　Before trade situation

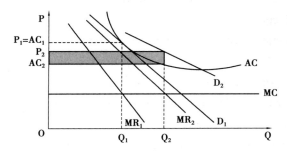

Figure 6.4　After trade situation for a short time

In trade, in Figure 6.4, in a short time, as there is foreign demand, the demand curve moves outward from D_1 to D_2, MR1 moves outward to MR_2, Q_1 increases to Q_2, AC_1 decreases to AC_2. The average cost decreases faster than the product price (P_1 to P_2), leading to super-normal profit. Note that the product price P_2 may be lower than P_1 and the consumer surplus increases. However, P_2 may also be higher than P_1, causing domestic consumption to decline and consumers to suffer.

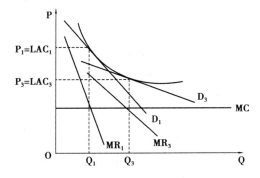

Figure 6.5　After trade situation for a long time

But in the long run, attracted by super-normal profit, new domestic manufacturers enter, the demand of original domestic manufacturers decreases from D_2 to D_3, and the super-normal profit disappears. Q_1 increases to Q_3, AC_1 decreases to AC_3, and P_1 decreases to P_3. The consumers' welfare is increased. So enterprises with internal economies of scale, even if two nations are identical in every way, are still possible to gain competitive advantage in the international market by participating in international trade, expanding production scale with lower unit cost of goods.

Case 6.1   Offshoring of the multinational corporations and economies of scale

Today, more and more products manufactured by international corporations have parts and components made in many different nations. The reason is to minimize production costs. For example, the motors of some Ford Fiestas are produced in the United Kingdom, the transmissions in France, the clutches in Spain, and the parts are assembled in Germany for sales throughout Europe. Similarly, Japanese and German cameras are often assembled in Singapore to take advantage of cheaper labor there.

Foreign sourcing of inputs is often not a matter of choice to earn higher profits but simply a requirement to remain competitive. Firms that do not look abroad for cheaper inputs face loss of competitiveness in world markets and even in the domestic market. US firms now spend more than $100 billion on outsourcing, and by doing so, they cut costs by 10-15 percent. Outsourcing now accounts for more than one-third of total manufacturing costs by Japanese firms, and this saves them more than 20 percent of production costs.

Firms must constantly explore sources of cheaper inputs and overseas production in order to remain competitive in our rapidly shrinking world. Indeed, this process can be regarded as manufacturing's new international economies of scale in today's global economy. Just as companies were forced to rationalize operations within each country in the 1980s, they now face the challenge of integrating their operations for their entire system of manufacturing around the world in order to take advantage of these new international economies of scale.

In fact, global firms are not just outsourcing and offshoring (i.e., themselves producing abroad) many parts and components that go into their products, but they are reaching the point where a great deal of their production is actually dispersed over many parts of the world (a process known as fragmentation) as part of a global supply or value chain. This became very evident when the tsunami that hit Japan in March 2011 not only caused thousands of deaths and major damage to the nation's infrastructures (including the melt-down of three nuclear reactors) but also disrupted the global supply or value chain of many products, especially that of automobiles.

In such a world of production fragmentation and global supply or value chains, multinational corporations are focusing more and more on their core competencies (such as R&D in advanced countries) that are indispensable to the company's competitive position over subsequent product generations—and outsourcing and producing abroad (offshoring) all the other parts and components in which outside suppliers have a distinctive production advantage (such as those requiring low-skilled labor in the least developed nations). In a sense, nations increasingly trade as much or more in inputs or factors of production embodied in their exports as in those products and services themselves.

(2) External economies of scale and trade

With external economies of scale, mutually beneficial trade can occur even if nations are identical in every way.

Suppose that China's shoe industry is completely competitive, as shown in Figure 6.6, and D_1 is the domestic demand curve. S_1 is the short-term supply curve of the industry before trade. MC_1 and AC_1 are the marginal cost and average cost curves of a single enterprise before trade respectively. The downward inclination of LAC indicates that the industry has external economies of scale.

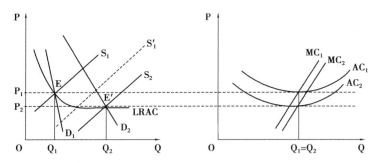

Figure 6.6   An example: external economies of scale

The initial equilibrium point E is at the intersection of S_1 and D_1. Since P_1 has no price advantage, trade will not occur. With industry scale expansion, more enterprises enter this industry, and the supply curve shifts to S_1'. Due to the external economies of scale of the industry, the MC_1 and AC_1 of enterprises will drop, and more enterprises will enter (or the original enterprises will expand their scale), the industry S_1' will continue to move to S_2, and the price will drop. The expansion of the industry and the decline of the average cost make the industry have a competitive advantage in the international market, so the enterprise has the initiative to export shoes. International trade is generated, D_1 increases to D_2, and the final price decreases from P_1 to $P_2 = AC$.

So enterprises with external economies of scale, even if two nations are identical in every way, are still possible to gain competitive advantage in the international market by its industry participating in international trade, expanding production scale with lower unit cost of goods.

(3) Economies of scale and trade pattern

There is no fixed pattern for a specific country to produce a specific product. The trade pattern can be produced naturally (through competition) or through agreement. The pattern of intra-industry trade based on economies of scale is unpredictable.

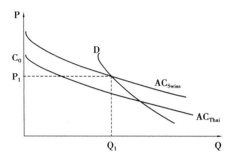

Figure 6.7 Trade pattern

As shown in Figure 6.7, D represents total world demand of watches. The Swiss watchmaking industry was first established and is now sold at the price P_1, which is less than the initial cost C_0 of manufacturers in Thailand. Therefore, even if Thailand has a potential lower cost, due to historical reasons, the mode of specialized production of watches in Swiss will continue.

The pursuit of economies of scale by countries/enterprises will enhance the exclusiveness of products in one industry or within the industry. The countries/enterprises that enter first can gradually expand their production scale to form cost advantages of unit products, thus forming price advantages.

This is caused by first-move advantage or pioneer advantage, which was first appeared in the early 1980s to describe the significant relationship between companies' preemptive entry into new markets and success.

(4) Policy implications

In the real contemporary world, imperfect competition and economies of scale are the most abundant and widespread phenomena. In many industrial fields, trade is controlled by a limited number of enterprises, which are quite powerful enough to control market prices. A government that implements a trade intervention policy of slight subsidies can enable domestic manufacturers to obtain a greater share of monopoly profits in the world competition.

6.5　Trade based on dynamic technological differences

When examining the causes of international trade, the factor endowment theory assumes that two countries use the same technology in their production and have the same production function of the same product. Traditional trade theory basically does not regard technology as an independent factor of production, but believes that although technology can improve the productivity of labor, capital and land, it can only play this role through other factors of production. Therefore, technology is often regarded as a premise or condition in the analysis of production functions.

But there is a gap in the technologies used by countries, and the gap is dynamic. Especially with the rise and development of the third scientific and technological revolution after the Second World War, science and technology affect the development of a country's economy with unprecedented power, determining whether a country's products have competitive advantages. At this time, trade economists find that if technology is analyzed as an independent factor of production, some phenomena in international trade would be able to be more clearly understood and explained. Moreover, their research confirms that technology does have the basic conditions of a factor of production. That is, technology is produced through investment in science and technology research, and it is not very different from the capital formed through savings and investment. At the same time, the new technology can be profitable, priced and sold like other factors of production through royalties. They also find that one of the important phenomena of contemporary international trade is the changing leading or dominant position of major exporters in the world market. So, how to explain the causes and trade patterns of international trade based on technological changes?

According to the technological gap model sketched by Michael V Posner in 1961, a great deal of the trade among industrialized countries is based on the introduction of new products and new production processes. These give the innovating firm and nation a temporary monopoly in the world market. Such a temporary monopoly is often based on patents and copyrights, which are granted to stimulate the flow of inventions.

As the most technologically advanced nation, the United States exports a large number of new high-technology products. However, as foreign producers acquire new technology, they eventually are able to conquer markets abroad, and even the US market for the product, because of their lower labor costs. In the meantime, US producers may have introduced still newer products and production processes and may be able to export these products based on the new technological gap established. A shortcoming of this model, however, is that it does not explain the size of technological gaps and does not explore the reason that technological gaps arise or exactly how they are eliminated over time.

A generalization and extension of the technological gap model is the product life cycle model, which was fully developed by Raymond Vernon in 1966. According to this model, when a new product is introduced, it usually requires highly skilled labor to produce. As the product matures and acquires mass acceptance, it becomes standardized; it can then be produced by mass production techniques and less skilled labor. Therefore, comparative advantage in the product shifts from the advanced nation that originally introduced it to less advanced nations, where labor is relatively cheaper. This may be accompanied by foreign direct investments from the innovating nation to nations with cheaper labor.

Vernon also pointed out that high-income and labor-saving products are most likely to be introduced in rich nations because the opportunities for doing so are greatest there, the development of these new products requires proximity to markets so as to benefit from consumer feedback in modifying the product, and there is a need to provide service. While the technological gap model emphasizes the time lag in the imitation process, the product life cycle model stresses the standardization process. According to these models, the most highly industrialized economies are expected to export non-standardized products embodying new and more advanced technologies and import products embodying old or less advanced technologies.

A classic example of the product life cycle model is provided by the experience of US and Japanese radio manufacturers since the Second World War. Immediately after the war, US firms dominated the international market for radios, based on vacuum tubes developed in the United States. However, within a few years, Japan was able to capture a large share of the market by catching up US technology and utilizing cheaper labor. The United States recaptured technological leadership with the development of transistors. But, once again, in a few short years, Japan imitated the technology and was able to undersell the United States. Subsequently, the United States re-acquired its ability to compete successfully with Japan by introducing printed circuits. It remains to be seen whether this latest technology will finally result in radios being L- or K-intensive and whether the United States will be able to stay in the market—or whether both the United States and Japan will eventually be displaced by still cheaper producers in nations such as South Korea and Singapore.

In a 1967 study, Gruber, Mehta, and Vernon found a strong correlation between expenditures on R&D and export performance. The authors took expenditures on R&D as a proxy for the temporary comparative advantage that firms and nations acquire in new products and new production processes. As such, these results tend to support both the technological gap model and the closely related product life cycle model. For example, the technological lead of the United States based on R&D has now almost disappeared with respect to Europe, and Japan and has sharply narrowed with respect to some of the most advanced emerging markets such as China.

Note that trade in these models is originally based on new technology developed by the relatively abundant factors in industrialized nations (such as highly skilled labor and expenditures on R&D). Subsequently, through imitation and product standardization, less developed nations gain a comparative advantage based on their relatively cheaper labor. As such, trade can be said to be based on changes in relative factor abundance (technology) among nations over time. Therefore, the technological gap and product life cycle models can be regarded as extensions of the basic H-O model into a technologically dynamic world, rather than as alternative trade models. In short, the product life cycle model tries to explain dynamic comparative advantage for new products and new production processes, as opposed to the basic H-O model, which explains static comparative advantage.

We will return to this source of growth and change in comparative advantage over time in Chapter 7.

The product life cycle model can be visualized with Figure 6.8, which identifies five different stages in the life cycle of a product (according to one version of the model) from the point of view of the innovating and the imitating country. In Stage I, or new-product phase (referring to OA on the horizontal axis), the product (at this time a specialty) is produced and consumed only in the innovating country.

In Stage II, or product-growth phase (AB), production is perfected in the innovating country and increases rapidly to accommodate rising demand at home and abroad. At this stage, there is not yet any foreign production of the product, so that the innovating country has a monopoly in both the domestic and export markets.

In Stage III, or product-maturity phase (BC), the product becomes standardized, and the innovating firm may find it profitable to license other domestic and foreign firms to also manufacture the product. Thus, the imitating country starts producing the product for domestic consumption.

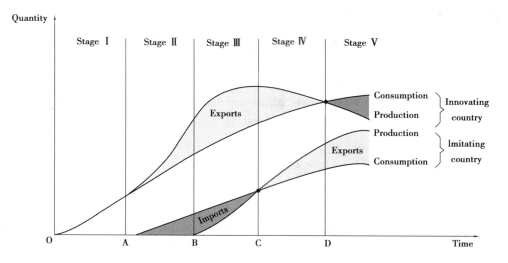

Figure 6.8　Product life cycle model

In Stage Ⅳ (CD), the imitating country, facing lower labor and other costs that the product has become standardized and no longer requires development and engineering skills, begins to undersell the innovating country in third markets, and production of the product in the innovating country declines. Brand competition now gives way to price competition.

Finally, in Stage Ⅴ (i.e., past point D), the imitating country starts underselling the innovating country in the latter's market as well, and production of the product in the innovating country declines rapidly or collapses.

Stages Ⅳ and Ⅴ are often referred to as the product-decline stage. Technological diffusion, standardization, and lower costs abroad thus bring the end of the life cycle for the product. It is time for the innovating country to concentrate attention on new technological innovations and to introduce new products.

We can see that the factor density of products in different stages of their life cycle is different. This theory is an improvement of H-O theory for focusing on dynamic instead of static comparative advantage. And it explains the reasons for the emergence and disappearance of technology gap mentioned by Posner.

Examples of products that seem to have gone through such product cycles are radios, stainless steel, razor blades, television sets, and semiconductors. In recent years, the diffusion lag of new technologies has shortened considerably, so that we have witnessed a time compression of the product life cycle. That is, the time from the introduction of a new product in the innovating country to the time when the imitating country displaces the innovating country in third markets and in the innovating country itself has become shorter and shorter. This may spell trouble for a country like the United States, which relies on new technologies and new products to remain internationally competitive. The benefits that the United States can reap from the new technologies and new products that it introduces are ever more quickly copied by other countries, especially Japan. The developing countries, on the contrary, should seize the opportunity of industrial transfer from developed countries and introduce relatively advanced industries. The developing countries, however, should not just be satisfied with attracting mature technologies transferred from developed countries, but more importantly, they should strengthen innovation and attract multinational companies to set up R&D centers locally, or will always lag behind.

6.6　The overlapping demand theory

According to H-O theory, inter-industry trade is the main form among countries with different resource endowments, mainly between developed countries and developing countries. However, after the Second World War, trade between developed countries increased, and most of them were intra-industry trade. To find out the causes for this new phenomenon, Staffan B Linder, a Swedish economist, proposed the overlapping demand theory to explain, from the perspective of demand, not supply. This theory is also called the theory of preference similarity, or Linder hypothesis.

Linder proposed the concept of overlapping demand. He assumed that in a country, consumers of different income levels have different preferences. Consumers with higher income prefer luxury goods, while consumers with lower income prefer necessities. At the same time, suppose that if consumers in different countries in the world have the same income level, their consumption preferences and demand structure are also the same. According to these two basic assumptions, it can be inferred that the relationship between the demand structure and income level is consistent for the two countries. If the average income level is taken as the main factor affecting the demand structure, the closer the income levels of the two countries are, the more similar the demand preference and structure will be, or the greater the overlap of the demand will be.

The overlapping demand is an independent condition for international trade. The closer the demand structure between the two countries is, the stronger the trade foundation between the two countries will be. When the per capita income level of the two countries is closer, the scope of overlapping demand will be larger, and the commodities repeatedly needed by the two countries are likely to become trade goods. If the national income of each country continues to increase, new commodities with repeated needs will continue to emerge due to the increase of income level, and trade will correspondingly expand, and new varieties in trade will continue to emerge. Therefore, countries with similar income levels may have closer trade relations with each other. On the contrary, if the income level is very different, there may be few goods that are needed repeatedly between the two countries, and the trade possibility is also very small.

Linder believes that whether a product is produced depends on the effective demand from the domestic market first, and if it wants to export, there is also the effective demand from the foreign markets. The decision of a manufacturer on what product to produce depends entirely on how much it can profit, and to make the manufacturer profitable, the prerequisite is that the product has a domestic market first. Manufacturers are unlikely to find a demand that does not exist at home and only exists abroad. Even if there is a demand abroad, it is hard to imagine a product that meets it. Even if he imagined the product, it would cost too much to make it suitable for foreign markets that he was unfamiliar with. Therefore, enterprises are motivated to produce certain industrial products, often designed to meet the needs of the domestic market, and the innovation in industrial products is also often designed to solve the domestic problems encountered. Therefore, only domestic products in demand will become relatively favorable products. For example, Japan is good at making small and economical and fuel-saving cars, while the United States is good at producing spacious and comfortable luxury cars, which are all related to its domestic market demand.

Therefore, Linder further pointed out that if the demand structure of the two countries is relatively similar, a product with a large demand domestically usually has a large demand in the other country, so that the trade volume between the two countries may be large.

In short, manufacturers decide their production direction and content according to the average income level and demand structure of consumers, and the necessary condition for production is that there is an effective demand for products.

When two countries have similar income levels, the closer the demand structure is, and the stronger the foundation for trade between them is. If the demand structure of Country A and Country B is the same, for the manufacturer of any country, he will find the demand for its products not only coming from domestic market but also from abroad. Then, choosing to expand production and make more profits through export trade becomes a natural choice.

Linder actually analyzes the trade between contemporary industrial countries and the two-way trade in the same industry from the perspective of demand. According to his theory, differences in per capita income levels are a potential barrier to international trade. Although a country has a comparative advantage in the production of a certain commodity, international trade will not happen if other countries have little demand for their per capita income levels by being too different. This is why trade between industrial developed countries is large, while trade between developed and developing countries is small.

If the technology gap theory and the product life cycle theory enrich and improve the H-O model from the supply side, the theory of preference similarity makes up for the lack of the H-O model from the demand side. In today's buyer's market, where the supply of goods is generally greater than the demand, demand has a more important decisive force. Therefore, the study of demand will make the theory more instructive in practice.

6.7　Trade based on different tastes

If two nations have identical production possibility frontiers (which is unlikely), there will still be a basis for mutually beneficial trade if tastes, or demand preferences, in the two nations differ. The nation with the relatively smaller demand or preference for a commodity will have a lower autarky-relative price for, and a comparative advantage in, that commodity. The process of specialization in production and trade would then follow, exactly as described in the previous section.

Trade based solely on differences in tastes is illustrated in Figure 6.9. Since the production frontiers of the two nations are now assumed to be identical, they are represented by a single curve. With indifference curve Ⅰ tangent to the production frontier at point A for Nation 1 and indifference curve Ⅰ′ tangent at point A′ for Nation 2, the pre-trade-relative price of X is lower in Nation 1. Thus, Nation 1 has a comparative advantage in commodity X and Nation 2 in commodity Y.

With the opening of trade, Nation 1 specializes in the production of X (and moves down its production frontier), while Nation 2 specializes in Y (and moves up its own production frontier). Specialization continues until P_X/P_Y is the same in both nations and trade is balanced. This occurs at point B (which coincides with point B′), where $P_B = P'_B = 1$. Nation 1 then exchanges 60X for 60Y with Nation 2 (see trade triangle BCE) and ends up consuming at point E on its indifference curve Ⅱ. Nation 1 thus gains 20X and 20Y as compared with point A. Similarly, Nation 2 exchanges 60Y for 60X with Nation 1 (see trade triangle B′C′E′) and ends up consuming at point E′ on its indifference curve Ⅲ′ (also gaining 20X and 20Y from point A′). Note that when trade is based solely on taste differences, the patterns of production become more similar as both nations depart from autarky.

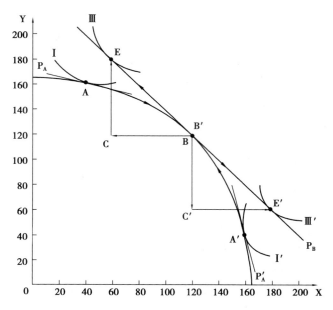

Figure 6.9 Trade based on differences in tastes

Thus, mutually beneficial trade can be based exclusively on a difference in tastes between two nations. In Chapter 5, we have examined the opposite case, where trade between the two nations is based exclusively on a difference in factor endowments and production frontiers. (This is referred to as the H-O model.) Only if the production frontier and the indifference curves are identical in both nations (or the difference in production frontiers is exactly neutralized, or offset, by the difference in the indifference curves) will the pre-trade-relative commodity prices be equal in both nations, ruling out the possibility of mutually beneficial trade.

6.8   Costs of transportation and environmental standards

6.8.1   Transportation and trade

So far, we have assumed that costs of transportation are zero. In this section, we relax this assumption. We will see that costs of transportation affect international trade directly by affecting the price of the traded commodity in the exporting and importing countries, and indirectly by affecting the international location of production and industry.

Costs of transportation include freight charges, warehousing costs, costs of loading and unloading, insurance premiums, and interest charges while goods are in transit. We will use the term transport or logistics costs to include all the costs of transferring goods from one location (nation) to another.

A homogeneous good will be traded internationally only if the pre-trade price difference in the two nations exceeds the cost of transporting the good from one nation to the other. Consideration of transport and logistics costs explains why most goods and services are not traded at all internationally. These are referred to as non-traded goods and services. They are the goods and services for which transport costs exceed price differences across nations. Thus, cement is not traded internationally except in border areas because of its high weight-to-value ratio. Similarly, the average person does not travel from New York to London simply to get a haircut.

In general, the price of non-traded commodities is determined by domestic demand and supply conditions, while the price of traded commodities is determined by world demand and supply conditions. The great reduction in transport costs that resulted from using new technologies. Now, many fruits and vegetables found in many Boston, Chicago, New York, and Philadelphia stores during winter are shipped from South America. In the past, high transport costs and spoilage prevented this. Similarly, the development of containerized cargo shipping (i.e., the packing of goods in very large, standardized containers) greatly reduced the cost of handling and transporting goods, turning many previously non-traded commodities into traded ones.

There are two ways of analyzing transport costs. One is by general equilibrium analysis, which utilizes the nation's production frontiers or offer curves and expresses transport costs in terms of relative commodity prices. A more straightforward method is to analyze the absolute, or money, cost of transport with partial equilibrium analysis. This holds constant the rate of exchange between the two currencies, the level of income, and everything else in the two nations, except the amount produced, consumed, and traded of the commodity under consideration. This is shown in Figure 6.10.

In Figure 6.10, the common vertical axis measures the dollar price of commodity X in Nation 1 and in Nation 2. Increasing quantities of commodity X are measured by a movement to the right from the common origin (as usual) for Nation 2. Increasing quantities of commodity X for Nation 1 are instead measured by a movement to the left from the common origin. Note that Nation 1's demand curve for commodity X (D_X) is negatively inclined (slopes downward), while its supply curve of commodity X (S_X) is positively inclined, as we move from the origin to the left, as we should, for Nation 1.

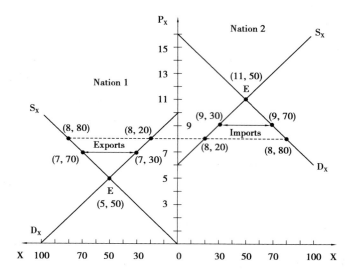

Figure 6.10　Partial equilibrium analysis of transport costs

In the absence of trade, Nation 1 produces and consumes 50X at the equilibrium price of $P_X = \$5$ (given by the intersection of D_X and S_X in Nation 1). Nation 2 produces and consumes 50X at $P_X = \$11$. With the opening of trade, Nation 1 will export commodity X to Nation 2. As it does, P_X rises in Nation 1 and falls in Nation 2. With a transport cost of $2 per unit, P_X in Nation 2 will exceed P_X in Nation 1 by $2. This cost will be shared by the two nations so as to balance trade. This occurs in Figure 6.10 when $P_Y = \$7$ in Nation 1 and $P_X = \$9$ in Nation 2. At $P_X = \$7$, Nation 1 will produce 70X, consume domestically 30X, and export 40X to Nation 2. At $P_X = \$9$, Nation 2 will produce 30X, import 40X, and consume 70X.

Note that in the absence of transport costs, $P_X = \$8$ in both nations and 60X are traded. Thus, transport costs reduce the level of specialization in production and also the volume and gains from trade. Furthermore, since with transport costs the absolute (and relative) price of commodity X differs in the two nations, its factor price will not be completely equalized even if all the other assumptions of the H-O model hold.

Finally, because of the way Figure 6.10 was drawn, the cost of transportation is shared equally by the two nations. In general, the more steeply inclined D_X and S_X are in Nation 2 relative to Nation 1, the greater is the share of transport costs paid by Nation 2, as shown in Figure 6.11.

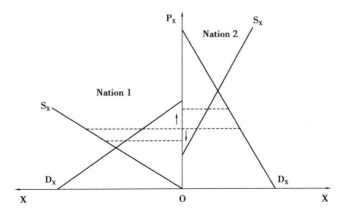

Figure 6.11   Change in transport costs

 ## 6.8.2   Environment and trade

We also examine the effect of environmental pollution on the location of industry and international trade.

Industrial location and international trade are also affected by different environmental standards in different nations. Environmental standards refer to the levels of air pollution, water pollution, thermal (i. e., heat) pollution, and pollution resulting from garbage disposal that a nation allows. Environmental pollution results whenever the environment is used (abused) as a convenient and cheap dumping ground for all types of waste products arising from the production, consumption, or disposal of goods and services.

Environmental pollution can lead to serious trade problems because the price of traded goods and services often does not fully reflect social environmental costs. A nation with lower environmental standards can, in effect, use the environment as a resource endowment or as a factor of production in attracting polluting firms from abroad and achieving a comparative advantage in polluting goods and services. In fact, US labor opposed North American Free-Trade Agreement (NAFTA) out of fear that many jobs would be lost in the United States as a result of US firms migrating to Mexico to take advantage of much more lax environmental laws and lower cleanup costs. Environmental considerations were so strong that a side agreement on the environment had to be added to ensure the passage of NAFTA by the US Congress. The High-Level Symposium on Trade and the Environment held in Geneva in March 1999 strongly recommended that trade agreements be subjected to environmental impact assessments.

A World Bank study by Low indicated that polluting or dirty industries and their exports have expanded faster than clean industries and their exports in poor developing countries than in rich developed countries. However, the study also found that as nations become richer, they voluntarily adopt more environmentally friendly approaches to economic development and become increasingly concerned about sustainable development.

In July 2001, a historic accord that set targets for industrialized countries to cut emission of greenhouse gases that contribute to global warming was signed as part of the implementation of the Kyoto Protocol on climate change signed in 1997. The United States refused to sign the agreement, calling its targets arbitrary and too costly to comply. At the UN conference on climate change held in Bali in December 2007, 190 nations (including the United States) signed an agreement to negotiate a new treaty to succeed the Kyoto Protocol (which was due to expire in 2012), calling for the halving of the emission of heat-trapping gases by 2050.

At the UN Climate Change Conference in Durban, South Africa, in December 2011, it was decided to extend the life of the Kyoto Protocol and to negotiate a new pact at the 2015 conference to be held in France to take effect by 2020 that would include emission curbs also by developing countries, which now account for almost three-fifths of global emissions. The new pact is also to establish a $100 billion "green climate fund" through which developed nations help developing nations offset the impact of environmental change. The major achievement of the 2012 UN conference held in December 2012 in Doha, Qatar, was only to remove some procedural obstacles to the setting up of the 2015 conference.

—— *China-perspective case study* ——

Analysis of the effect of technological innovation on China's foreign trade in the Internet era

With the rapid development of globalization, especially in the ten years after China's accession to the WTO, the majority of foreign trade enterprises in China have made rapid development and made remarkable achievements on the whole, thus establishing a broad consensus that foreign trade, investment and consumption drive GDP growth. In the past decade or more, the contribution of foreign trade enterprises to our economic growth is obvious to all. A large number of manufacturing enterprises have made outstanding contributions to China's economic growth. At the same time, a large number of foreign enterprises have established production bases in China. Taking advantage of China's comparative advantages of low land and labor costs, foreign trade has once again become an important way to enhance China's comprehensive national strength, and China has been given the reputation of "the world factory".

However, after the financial crisis in 2008, China's foreign trade has experienced 30 years of rapid growth and entered a period of moderation. China's economic development has generally shown an "L" type of growth. Therefore, at this stage, China will face the choice of changing the growth mode of foreign trade. Since the reform and opening-up, the total amount of export commodities has increased by nearly 240 times from $9,750 million in 1978 to $2,342,292.70 million in 2014. However, there are still many problems under the high-speed development. China is a big trading country but not a strong trading country. In 2014, the export volume of goods exceeded that of Germany, which established China's position as a big trading country. However, the development of foreign trade mainly depends on China's extensive development mode of rich resources, cheap labor and environmental factors. However, with the emergence of a new batch of cheap labor in Southeast Asia, it is no longer our advantage to rely on cheap labor to exchange orders. The extensive foreign trade development mode of high energy consumption and high pollution is not a sustainable trade development mode, which is not conducive to the optimization and upgrading of industrial structure and the improvement of national trade welfare. The majority of foreign trade enterprises are struggling due to many factors such as unreasonable domestic industrial structure, changes in the international exchange rate, and the decline in the level of enterprise competitiveness. The lack of technological innovation further leads to business difficulties, and even directly leads to the closure of many enterprises. It is a serious blow to China's foreign trade enterprises, which has become the primary problem to be solved.

From the perspective of international trade resource endowment theory and comparative advantage theory, foreign trade enterprises can gain competitive advantage only by making continuous progress in resource-intensive and technology-intensive aspects. Therefore, technological innovation backwardness is the main direct factor that directly affects the lack of product competitiveness, business decline, and deterioration of business conditions. Recognize the profound impact of technological innovation on Chinese foreign trade enterprises, prescribe the right medicine for the case, and implement targeted strategies. It is an urgent task to enhance the core competitiveness of China's foreign trade enterprises and reverse the decline of foreign trade development.

Key concepts

increasing returns to scale

differentiated products

offshoring

index of the intra-industry trade (IIT)

outsourcing

external economies

product life cycle model

monopolistic competition

technological gap model

environmental standards

imperfect competition

international economies of scale

intra-industry trade

oligopoly

monopoly

partial equilibrium analysis

general equilibrium analysis

increasing returns to scale

non-traded goods and services

transport costs

Summary

1. H-O theory based comparative advantage on the difference in factor endowments among nations. This theory, however, leaves a significant portion of today's international trade unexplained. To fill this gap, we need new, complementary theories that base international trade on economies of scale, imperfect competition, and differences in technological changes among nations.

2. Even if two nations are identical in every respect, there is still a basis for mutually beneficial trade based on economies of scale. When each nation specializes in the production of one commodity, the combined total world output of both commodities will be greater than without specialization when economies of scale are present. With trade, each nation then shares in these gains. Outsourcing and offshoring are the source of new and significant international economies of scale but also lead to complaints that a significant number of high-paying jobs are transferred abroad.

3. A large portion of international trade today involves the exchange of differentiated products. Such intra-industry trade arises in order to take advantage of important economies of scale in production, which occur when each firm or plant produces only one or a few styles or varieties of a product. Intra-industry trade can be measured by an index. With differentiated products, the firm faces a downward-sloping demand curve, produces in the downward-sloping portion of its average cost curve, and breaks even. The larger the number of firms in a monopolistically competitive industry, the lower the

product price and the higher the average cost for a given level of output. With the enlargement of the market that trade brings about, the commodity price will then be lower and the number of firms greater. The more similar nations are in factor endowments, the greater is the importance of intra-relative to inter-industry trade.

4. According to the technological gap model, a firm exports a new product until imitators in other countries take away its market. In the meantime, the innovating firm will have introduced a new product or process. According to the related product life cycle model, a product goes through five stages: the introduction of the product, expansion of production for export, standardization and beginning of production abroad through imitation, foreign imitators underselling the nation in third markets, and foreigners underselling the innovating firms in their home market as well.

5. With transport costs, only those commodities whose pre-trade price difference exceeds the cost of transporting them will be traded. When trade is in equilibrium, the relative price of traded commodities in the two nations will differ by the cost of transporting them. Transport costs also affect international trade by affecting the location of production and industry. Industries can be classified as resource-oriented, market-oriented, or footloose. Environmental standards also affect the location of industry and international trade.

Exercises

1. Find the degree of intra-industry trade if exports and imports are _____, respectively.
   A. 1,000 and 1,000
   B. 1,000 and 750
   C. 1,000 and 500
   D. 1,000 and 25
   E. 1,000 and 0

2. Do the same as in Exercise 1, but interchange the values of exports and imports.

3. Using the same AC and MC curves as in Figure 6.3, draw a figure similar to Figure 6.3 but showing that the firm can earn a profit before other firms imitate its product and reduce its market share.

4. A. In what way does monopolistic competition resemble monopoly?
   B. How is monopolistic competition different from monopoly?
   C. Why is the difference between monopolistic competition and monopoly important for consumer welfare in the intra-industry trade model?

5. How do the demand curves facing a perfectly competitive firm, a monopolistically competitive firm, and a monopolist firm differ from one another? Why?

6. Draw a figure showing the exports of the innovating and of the imitating country during the various stages of the product life cycle.

7. Indicate how increased pirating or production and sale of counterfeit American goods without paying royalties by foreign producers might affect the product life cycle in the United States.

8. Show how transport costs can be analyzed with production frontiers. (Hint: Relative commodity prices with trade will differ by the cost of transportation.)

9. Draw a figure similar to Figure 6.10, showing that transport costs fall more heavily on the nation with the steeper demand and supply curves for the traded commodity.

10. A. Explain why the H-O model needs to be extended.

    B. Indicate in what important ways the H-O model can be extended.

    C. Explain what is meant by differentiated products and intra-industry trade.

Chapter 7 | Economic Growth and International Trade

Changes in the supply of factors of production, advances in technical knowledge, income levels, demand levels and demand structures of countries will have an impact on the original form and pattern of international trade. This proposition about economic growth and changes in international trade is called dynamic international trade theory. The relationship between economic growth and international trade includes two aspects: the restriction and impact of international trade on economic growth, and the restriction and impact of economic growth on international trade. This chapter focuses on the latter aspect—how economic growth restricts and affects the development of international trade.

7.1 What is economic growth?

There are three most common definitions of economic growth. The first definition refers to the increase in the real total output of an economy. The second definition refers to the increase in real output per capita of an economy. The third definition refers to the long-term growth of the ability to provide people with a variety of economic goods. The continuous growth of this ability stems from the increase of production factors, technological progress and the corresponding adjustment of systems and concepts.

7.1.1 Labor growth and capital accumulation

We assume that the nation experiencing growth is producing two commodities (commodity X, which is L-intensive, and commodity Y, which is K-intensive) under constant returns to scale.

An increase in the endowment of labor and capital over time causes the nation's production frontier to shift outward. The type and degree of the shift depend on the rate at which L and k grow. If L and K grow at the same rate, the nation's production frontier will shift out evenly in all directions at the rate of factor growth. As a result, the slope of the old and new production frontiers (before and after factor growth) will be the same at any point where they are cut by a ray from the origin. This is the case of balanced growth.

If only the endowment of L grows, the output of both commodities grows because L is used in the production of both commodities and L can be substituted for K to some extent in the production of both commodities. However, the output of commodity X (the L-intensive commodity) grows faster than the output of commodity Y (the K-intensive commodity). The opposite is true if only the endowment of K grows. If L and K grow at different rates, the outward shift in the nation's production frontier can similarly be determined.

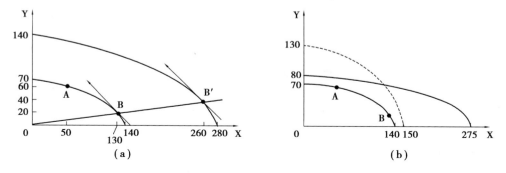

Figure 7.1　Growth of labor and capital over time

Figure 7.1 shows various types of hypothetical factor growth in Nation 1. The left panel of Figure 7.1 shows the case of balanced growth under the assumption that the amounts of L and K available to Nation 1 double. With constant returns to scale, the maximum amount of each commodity that Nation 1 can produce also doubles, from 140X to 280X or from 70Y to 140Y. Note that the shape of the expanded production frontier is identical to the shape of the production frontier before growth, so that the slope of the two production frontiers, or P_X/P_Y, is the same at such points as B and B', where they are cut by a ray from the origin.

The right panel repeats Nation 1's production frontier before growth (with intercepts of 140X and 70Y) and shows two additional production frontiers—one with only L doubling (solid line) and the other with only K doubling (dotted line). When only L doubles, the production frontier shifts more along the X-axis, measuring the L-intensive commodity. If only K doubles, the production frontier shifts more along the Y-axis, measuring the K-intensive commodity. Note that when only L doubles, the maximum output of commodity X does not double (i.e., it only rises from 140X to 275X). For X to double, both L and K must double. Similarly, when only K doubles, the maximum output of commodity Y less than doubles (from 70Y to 130Y).

When both L and K grow at the same rate and we have constant returns to scale in the production of both commodities, the productivity, and therefore the returns to L and K, remain the same after growth as they were before growth took place. If the dependency rate (i.e., the ratio of dependents to the total population) also remains unchanged, real per capita income and the welfare of the nation tend to remain unchanged. If only L grows (or L grows proportionately more than K), K/L will fall and so will the productivity of L, the returns to L, and real per capita income. If, on the other contrary, only the endowment of K grows (or K grows proportionately more than L), K/L will rise and so will the productivity of L, the returns to L, and real per capita income.

7.1.2 The Rybezynski theorem

The Rybezynski theorem postulates that at constant commodity prices, an increase in the endowment of one factor will increase by a greater proportion the output of the commodity intensive in that factor and will reduce the output of the other commodity. For example, if only L grows in Nation 1, then the output of commodity X (the L-intensive commodity) expands more than proportionately, while the output of commodity Y (the K-intensive commodity) declines at constant P_X and P_Y.

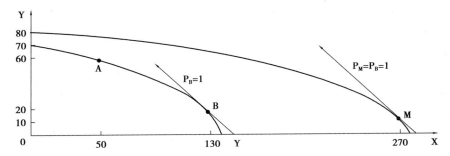

Figure 7.2 Growth of labor only and the Rybezynski theorem

Figure 7.2 shows the production frontier of Nation 1 before and after only L doubles. With trade but before growth, Nation 1 produces at point B (i.e., 130X and 20Y) at

$P_X/P_Y = P_B = 1$. After only L doubles and with P_X/P_Y remaining at $P_B = 1$, Nation 1 would produce at point M on its new and expanded production frontier. At point M, Nation 1 produces 270X but only 10Y. Thus, the output of commodity X more than doubled, while the output of commodity Y declined (as predicted by the Rybezynski theorem). Doubling L and transferring some L and K from the production of commodity Y more than doubles the output of commodity X.

For commodity prices to remain constant with the growth of one factor, factor prices (i.e., w and r) must also remain constant. But factor prices can remain constant only if K/L and the productivity of L and K also remain constant in the production of both commodities. The only way to fully employ all of the increase in L and still leave K/L unchanged in the production of both commodities is for the output of commodity Y (the K-intensive commodity) to fall in order to release enough K (and a little L) to absorb all of the increase in L in the production of commodity X (the L-intensive commodity). Thus, the output of commodity X rises while the output of commodity Y declines at constant commodity prices. In fact, the increase in the output of commodity X expands by a greater proportion than the expansion in the amount of labor because some labor and capital are also transferred from the production of commodity Y to the production of commodity X. This is called the magnification effect.

Point A on Nation 1's production frontier (in the bottom part of Figure 7.3) is derived from point A in Nation 1's Edgeworth box diagram (in the top of Figure 7.3) before the amount of labor doubles. After the amount of labor doubles, Nation 1's Edgeworth box doubles in length but remains the same height (because the amount of capital is kept constant).

For commodity prices to remain constant, factor prices must remain constant. But relative factor prices can remain constant only if K/L and the productivity of L and K remain constant in the production of both commodities. The only way for K/L to remain constant, and for all of L and K to remain fully employed after L doubles, is for production in Nation 1 to move from point A to point A^*. At points A and A^*, K/L in the production of commodity X is the same because point A^* lies on the same ray from origin O_X as point A. Similarly, K/L in the production of commodity Y at point A^* is the same as at point A because the dotted ray from origin O_Y^* to point A^* has the same slope as the ray from origin O_Y to point A. Point A^* is the only point in the Edgeworth box consistent with full employment of all resources after L has doubled and with K/L constant in the production of both commodities. Note that isoquants have the same slope at points A and A^*, indicating that w/r is the same at both points.

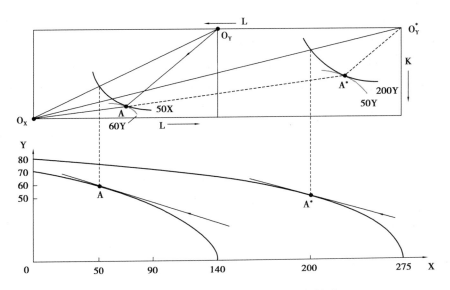

Figure 7.3 Graphical proof of the Rybezynski theorem

Since point A^* is much farther from origin O_X than point A in the Edgeworth box, Nation 1's output of commodity X has increased. On the contrary, since point A^* is closer to origin O_Y^*; than point A is to origin O_Y^*, Nation 1's output of commodity Y has declined. These events are reflected in the movement from point A on Nation 1's production frontier before L doubled to point A^* on its production frontier after L doubled. That is, at point A on its production frontier before growth, Nation 1 produced 50X and 60Y, whereas at point A^* on its production frontier after growth, Nation 1 produced 200X but only 50Y at $P_A/P_A^* = 1/4$. Doubling L more than doubles (in this case, it quadruples) the output of commodity X. That is the growth of L has a magnified effect on the growth of the output of commodity X (the L-intensive commodity).

7.1.3 Technical progress

Technical progress is usually classified into neutral, labor-saving (L-saving), or capital-saving (K-saving). All technical progress (regardless of its type) reduces the amount of both labor and capital required to produce any given level of output. The different types of Hicksian technical progress specify how this takes place.

Neutral technical progress increases the productivity of L and K in the same proportion, so that K/L, remains the same after the neutral technical progress as it was before at unchanged relative factor prices (w/r). That is, with unchanged w/r, there is no substitution of L for K (or vice versa) in production so that K/L remains unchanged. All that happens is that a given output can now be produced with less L and less K.

L-saving technical progress increases the productivity of K proportionately more than the productivity of L. As a result, K is substituted for L in production and K/L rises at unchanged w/r. Since more K is used per unit of L, this type of technical progress is called L-saving. Note that a given output can now be produced with fewer units of L and K but with a higher K/L.

K-saving technical progress increases the productivity of L proportionately more than the productivity of K. As a result, L is substituted for K in production and L/K rises (K/L falls) at unchanged w/r. Since more L is used per unit of K, this type of technical progress is called K-saving. Note that a given output can now be produced with fewer units of L and K but with a higher L/K (a lower K/L).

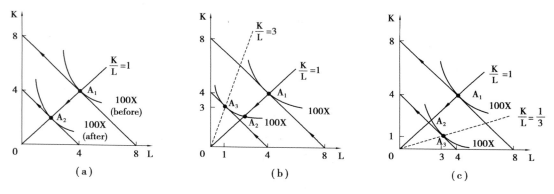

Figure 7.4   Hicksian neutral, L-saving, and K-saving technical progress

In all three panels of Figure 7.4, we begin at point A_1, where 100X is produced with 4L and 4K before technical progress occurs. After neutral technical progress, the same 100X can be produced with 2L and 2K (point A_2 in the left panel), leaving K/L = 1 at unchanged w/r = 1 (the absolute slope of the isocosts). With L-saving technical progress, the same 100X can be produced with 3K and 1L (point A_3 in the middle panel) and K/L = 3 at unchanged w/r = 1. Finally, with K-saving technical progress, the same 100X can be produced with 1K and 3L (point A_3 in the right panel) and K/L = 1/3 at unchanged w/r = 1.

7.1.4   Technical progress and production possibility frontier

As in the case of factor growth, all types of technical progress cause the nation's production frontier to shift outward. The type and degree of the shift depend on the type and rate of technical progress in either or both commodities. Here we will deal only with neutral technical progress. Non-neutral technical progress is extremely complex and can only be handed mathematically in the most advanced graduate texts.

With the same rate of neutral technical progress in the production of both commodities, the nation's production frontier will shift out evenly in all directions at the same rate at which technical progress takes place. This has the same effect on the nation's production frontier as balanced factor growth. Thus, the slope of the nation's old and new production frontiers (before and after this type of technical progress) will be the same at any point where they are cut by a ray from the origin.

For example, suppose that the productivity of L and K doubles in the production of commodity X and commodity Y in Nation 1 and constant returns to scale prevail in the production of both commodities. The graph for this type of technical progress is identical to the left panel of Figure 7.1, where the supply of both L and K doubled, and so the graph is not repeated here.

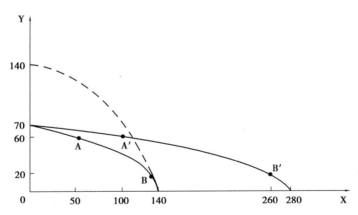

Figure 7.5   Neutral technical progress

Figure 7.5 shows Nation 1's production frontier before technical progress and after the productivity of L and K doubled in the production of commodity X only, or in the production of commodity Y only (the dotted production frontier).

When the productivity of L and K doubles in the production of commodity X only, the output of X doubles for each output level of commodity Y. For example, at the unchanged output of 60Y, the output of commodity X rises from 50X before technical progress to 100X afterward (points A and A', respectively, in the figure). Similarly, at the unchanged output of 20Y, the output of commodity X increases from 130X to 260X (points B and B'). When all of Nation 1's resources are used in the production of commodity X, the output of X also doubles (from 140X to 280X). Note that the output of commodity Y remains unchanged at 70Y if all of the nation's resources are used in the production of commodity Y and technical progress took place in the production of commodity X only.

Finally, it must be pointed out that, in the absence of trade, all types of technical progress tend to increase the nation's welfare. The reason is that with a higher production frontier and the same L and population, each citizen could be made better off after growth than before by an appropriate redistribution policy.

7.2 Trade effect of economic growth

7.2.1 Trade effect of consumption growth

Generally speaking, with the continuous improvement of per capita income, the level and structure of people's demand for commodities will change accordingly, which will affect international trade. The impact of demand change on international trade can be discussed from Engel's law and demand biased growth.

Trade goods can be divided into exportable goods and importable goods. With the growth of national income, if the nation's consumption of its importable commodity increases proportionately more than the nation's consumption of its exportable commodity at constant prices, then the consumption effect tends to lead to a greater than proportionate expansion of trade and is said to be pro-trade. If the nation's consumption of both imports and exports increases at the same rate, then impact of this consumption growth on trade is neutral. Otherwise, the expansion in consumption is anti-trade.

At the same time, according to the principle of comparative advantage, the nation exports commodity X and imports commodity Y.

According to Figure 7.6, the straight-line OC represents the neutral trade consumption effect, because consumers have not changed their relative consumption structure with economic growth. Region Ⅲ represents the anti-trade consumption effect, because product X has a greater consumption growth than product Y. Region Ⅳ represents the extreme anti-trade consumption effect. Region Ⅱ represents the pro-trade consumption effect. Region Ⅰ represents the extreme pro-trade consumption effect.

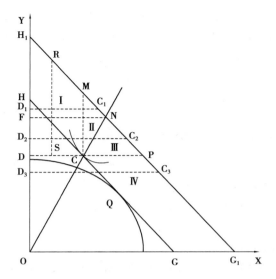

Figure 7.6　Trade effect of consumption growth

7.2.2　Trade effect of production growth

If the output of the nation's exportable commodity grows proportionately more than the output of its importable commodity at constant relative commodity prices, then growth tends to lead to greater than proportionate expansion of trade and is said to be pro-trade. Otherwise, it is anti-trade or neutral. The expansion of output has a neutral trade effect if it leads to the same rate of expansion of trade.

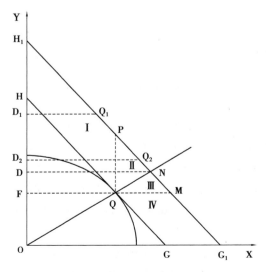

Figure 7.7　Trade effect of production growth

According to Figure 7.7, OQ ray represents the trade neutral production effect, because in this line, producers have not changed the product structure. Region I represents the extreme anti-trade production effect. Region Ⅱ represents the anti-trade production effect. Region Ⅲ represents the pro-trade production effect. Region Ⅳ represents the extreme pro-trade production effect.

 ### 7.2.3 Total trade effect of economic growth

Growth is pro-trade if output of a nation's export commodity grows proportionately more than the output of its import commodity at constant relative commodity prices, leading to greater than proportionate expansion of trade. Otherwise, growth is anti-trade, or neutral.

What happens to the volume of trade in the process of growth depends on the net result of production and consumption effects.

Table 7.1 Impact of production and consumption effects

Pro-trade	Anti-trade	Neutral	Impact on trade volume
Production Consumption			Trade expands proportionately faster than output.
	Production Consumption		Trade expands proportionately less than output.
Production	Consumption		Trade growth depends on net effect of opposing forces.
Consumption	Production		Trade growth depends on net effect of opposing forces.
		Production Consumption	Trade expands at the same rate as output.

Thus, production and consumption can be pro-trade (if they lead to a greater than proportionate increase in trade at constant relative commodity prices), anti-trade, or neutral. Production is pro-trade if the output of the nation's exportable commodity increases proportionately more than the output of its importable commodity. Consumption is pro-trade if the nation's consumption of its importable commodity increases proportionately more than consumption of its exportable commodity.

What in fact happens to the volume of trade in the process of growth depends on the net result of these production and consumption effects. If both production and consumption are pro-trade, the volume of trade expands proportionately faster than output. If production and consumption are both anti-trade, the volume of trade expands proportionately less than output and may even decline absolutely. If production is pro-trade and consumption anti-trade or vice versa, what happens to the volume of trade depends on the net effect of these two opposing forces. In the unlikely event that both production and consumption are neutral, trade expands at the same rate as output.

7.3   Growth and trade: the small-country case

A "small country" is too small to affect the relative commodity prices at which it trades (so the nation's terms of trade remain constant).

7.3.1   Factor growth, trade and welfare

If the influence of demand is not considered for the time being, the influence of the supply of factors of production on international trade mainly depends on whether the factors of production used to produce imported goods grow or the factors of production used to produce exportable goods grow. It is still assumed that the country exports X products and imports Y products. X products are L-intensive and Y products are K-intensive.

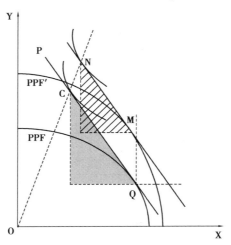

Figure 7.8   Capital increase and trade effect of small countries

We will examine the growth of production factors used to produce imported goods, that is, the growth of capital factors. Suppose that the amount of capital in the country is growing, but the production factors of X (export goods) are not growing. In this way, the increase in the amount of capital will reduce the monetary yield of capital, thus reducing the interest rate. Since capital is cheaper than before, some manufacturers will use capital to expand production, and since the production of Y uses capital more intensively than X, manufacturers of Y products will benefit more from low health capital than those of X products. Therefore, the output of Y will increase compared with X, and the import of Y will be less. This shows that the growth of production factors used to produce importable goods will lead to a decrease in the number of imports.

Figure 7.8 illustrates this situation. If the country uses the increased capital to produce X, the output of X will not increase much, but if it is used to expand the production of Y, the output of Y will increase greatly. Therefore, its shape has changed during the outward shift of its production possibility curve. The increase of its intercept on the vertical axis is greater than that on the horizontal axis, which is called biased growth.

When the price level remains unchanged, the production point is Q and the consumption point is C before the growth of factor K. After the growth of production factors, the production point is M, and the consumption point is N. This shows that both the export quantity of X and the import quantity of Y decrease after the increase of production factor K. The trade triangle has become smaller.

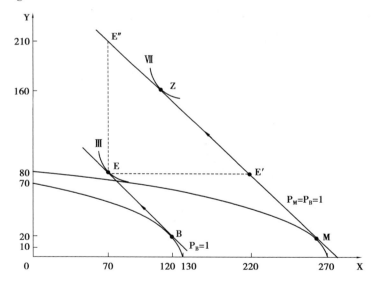

Figure 7.9　Labor increase and the trade effect of small countries

Figure 7.9 shows that L doubles in Nation 1 and that Nation 1's terms of trade do not change with growth and trade. That is, before growth, Nation 1 produced at point B, traded 60X for 60Y at $P_B = 1$, and reached indifference curve III. When L doubles in Nation 1, its production frontier shifts outward. If Nation 1 is too small to affect relative commodity prices, it will produce at point M, where the new expanded production frontier is tangent to $P_M = P_B = 1$. At point M, Nation 1 produces more than twice as much of commodity X than at point B but less of commodity Y, as postulated by the Rybezynski theorem. At $P_M = P_B = 1$, Nation 1 exchanges 150X for 150Y and consumes at point Z on its community indifference curve Ⅶ.

Since the output of commodity X (Nation 1's exportable commodity) increases while the output of commodity Y declines, the growth of output is pro-trade. Similarly, since the consumption of commodity Y (Nation 1's importable commodity) increases proportionately more than the consumption of commodity X (i.e., point Z is to the left of a ray from the origin through point E), the growth of consumption is also pro-trade. With both production and consumption pro-trade, the volume of trade expands proportionately more than the output of commodity X.

Note that Nation 1 is worse off after growth because its labor force (and population) doubled while its total consumption less than doubled (compare point Z with 120X and 160Y after growth to point E with 70X and 80Y before growth). Thus, the consumption and welfare of Nation 1's representative citizen decline as a result of this type of growth. A representative citizen is one with the identical tastes and consumption pattern of the nation as a whole but with quantities scaled down by the total number of citizens in the nation.

➤ 7.3.2   Technical progress, trade and welfare

We have seen that neutral technical progress at the same rate in the production of both commodities leads to a proportionate expansion in the output of both commodities at constant relative commodity prices. If consumption of each commodity also increases proportionately in the nation, the volume of trade will increase at the same rate at constant terms of trade. That is, the neutral expansion of production and consumption leads to the same rate of expansion of trade. With neutral production and pro-trade consumption, the volume of trade would expand proportionately more than production. With neutral production and anti-trade consumption, the volume of trade would expand proportionately less than production. However, regardless of what happens to the volume of trade, the welfare of the representative citizen will increase with constant L and population and constant terms of trade.

Neutral technical progress in the production of the exportable commodity only is pro-trade. For example, if neutral technical progress takes place only in the production of commodity X in Nation 1, then Nation 1's production frontier expands only along the X-axis, as indicated in Figure 7.10. At constant terms of trade, Nation 1's output of commodity X will increase, while the output of commodity Y declines. Nation 1 will reach an indifference curve higher than before, and the volume of trade will expand even more. What is even more important is that with a constant population and labor force, the welfare of the representative citizen now rises.

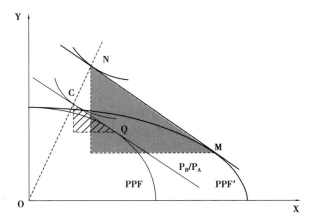

Figure 7.10　Trade effect of technological progress of exportable goods

On the contrary, neutral technical progress only in the production of commodity Y (the importable commodity) is anti-trade, and Nation 1's production frontier will expand only along the Y-axis (the dotted production frontier in Figure 7.11). If the terms of trade, tastes, and population also remain unchanged, the volume of trade tends to decline, but national welfare increases.

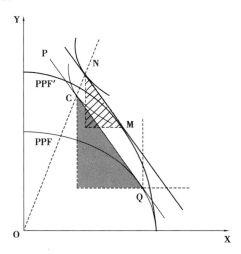

Figure 7.11　Trade effect of technological progress of importable goods

The case where neutral technical change occurs at different rates in the two commodities may lead to a rise or fall in the volume of trade but always increases welfare.

The same is generally true for non-neutral technical progress. Thus, technical progress, depending on the type, may increase or decrease trade, but it will always increase social welfare in a small nation.

7.4　Growth and trade: the large-country case

A "large country" is sufficiently large to affect the relative commodity prices at which it trades (so the nation's terms of trade can change).

❯ 7.4.1　Terms-of-trade effect

If growth, regardless of its source or type, expands the nation's volume of trade at constant prices, then the nation's terms of trade tend to deteriorate. Conversely, if growth reduces the nation's volume of trade at constant prices, the nation's terms of trade tend to improve. This is referred to as the terms-of-trade effect of growth.

The effect of growth on the nation's welfare depends on the net result of the terms-of-trade effect and a wealth effect. The wealth effect refers to the change in the output per worker or per person as a result of growth. A positive wealth effect, by itself, tends to increase the nation's welfare. Otherwise, the nation's welfare tends to decline or remain unchanged. If the wealth effect is positive and the nation's terms of trade improve as a result of growth and trade, the nation's welfare will definitely increase. If they are both unfavorable, the nation's welfare will definitely decline. If the wealth effect and the terms-of-trade effect move in opposite directions, the nation's welfare may deteriorate, improve, or remain unchanged depending on the relative strength of these two opposing forces.

For example, if only L doubles in Nation 1, the wealth effect, by itself, tends to reduce Nation 1's welfare. This was the case shown in Figure 7.9. Furthermore, since this type of growth tends to expand the volume of trade of Nation 1 at $P_M = P_B = 1$, Nation 1's terms of trade also tend to decline. Thus, the welfare of Nation 1 will decline for both reasons. This case is illustrated in Figure 7.12.

Figure 7.12 except that now Nation 1 is assumed to be large enough to affect relative commodity prices. With the terms of trade deteriorating from $P_M = P_B = 1$ to $P_N = 1/2$ with growth and trade, Nation 1 produces at point N, exchanges 140X for 70Y with Nation 2, and consumes at point T on indifference curve Ⅳ. Since the welfare of Nation 1 declined (i.e., the wealth effect was negative) even when it was too small to affect its terms of trade, and now its terms of trade have also deteriorated, the welfare of Nation 1 declines even more. This is reflected in indifference curve Ⅳ being lower than indifference curve Ⅶ.

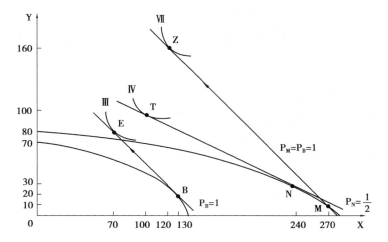

Figure 7.12　Growth and trade: the large-country case

7.4.2　Immiserizing growth

If the wealth effect is positive, but the terms of trade deteriorates so much that the nation's welfare declines, nation experiences immiserizing growth. It is more likely to occur in developing nations, although not prevalent in the real world.

Even if the wealth effect, by itself, tends to increase the nation's welfare, the terms of trade may deteriorate so much as to lead to a net decline in the nation's welfare. This case was termed immiserizing growth by Jagdish Bhagwati and is illustrated in Figure 7.13.

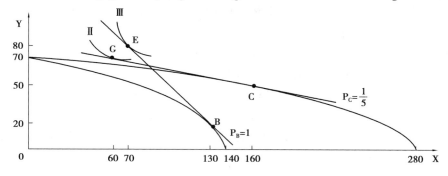

Figure 7.13　Immiserizing growth

The production frontier of Nation 1 before and after neutral technical progress doubled the productivity of L and K in the production of commodity X only. The wealth effect, by itself, would increase Nation 1's welfare at constant prices because Nation 1's output increases while its labor force (L) and population remain constant. However, since this type of technical progress tends to increase the volume of trade, Nation 1's terms of trade tend to deteriorate. With a drastic deterioration in its terms of trade, for example, from $P_A =$ 1 to $P_C = 1/5$, Nation 1 would produce at point C, export 100X for only 20X, and consume at point G on indifference curve I (which is lower than indifference curve III, which Nation 1 reached with free trade before growth).

Immiserizing growth is more likely to occur in Nation 1 when ① growth tends to increase substantially Nation 1's exports at constant terms of trade; ②Nation 1 is so large that the attempt to expand its exports substantially will cause a deterioration in its terms of trade; ③the income elasticity of Nation 2's (or the rest of the world's) demand for Nation 1's exports is very low, so that Nation 1's terms of trade will deteriorate substantially; and ④Nation 1 is so heavily dependent on trade that a substantial deterioration in its terms of trade will lead to a reduction in national welfare.

Immiserizing growth does not seem very prevalent in the real world. When it does take place, it is more likely to occur in developing than in developed nations. Even though the terms of trade of developing nations seem to have deteriorated somewhat over time, increases in production have more than made up for this, and their real per capita incomes and welfare have generally increased.

7.5 Growth and trade in both nations

Until now, we have assumed that growth took place only in Nation 1. As a result, only Nation 1's production frontier and offer curve shifted. We now extend our analysis to incorporate growth in both nations. When this occurs, the production frontiers and offer curves of both nations shift. We will now use offer curves to analyze the effect of growth and change in tastes in both nations.

Figure 7.14 shows the effect on the volume and terms of trade of various types of growth in either or both nations. We assume that both nations are large. The offer curves labeled "1" and "2" are the original (pre-growth) offer curves of Nation 1 and Nation 2, respectively. Offer curves "1*" and "2*" and offer curves "1'" and "2'" are the offer curves of Nation 1 and Nation 2, respectively, with various types of growth. A relative commodity price line is not drawn through each equilibrium point in order not to clutter the figure. However, Nation 1's terms of trade (i.e., P_X/P_Y) at each equilibrium point are obtained by dividing the quantity of commodity Y by the quantity of commodity X traded at that point. Nation 2's terms of trade at the same equilibrium point are then simply the inverse, or reciprocal, of Nation 1's terms of trade.

With the original pre-growth offer curves 1 and 2, Nation 1 exchanges 60X for 60Y with Nation 2 at $P_B = 1$ (see equilibrium point E_1). If L doubles in Nation 1, its offer curve rotates clockwise from 1 to 1^* and Nation 1 exports 140X for 70Y (point E_2). In this case, Nation 1's terms of trade deteriorate to $P_X/Pr = 70Y/140X = 1/2$, and Nation 2's terms of trade improve to $P_Y/P_X = 2$.

If growth occurs only in Nation 2 and its offer curve rotates counterclockwise from 2 to 2^*, we get equilibrium point E_3. This might result, for example, from a doubling of K (the abundant factor) in Nation 2. At E_3, Nation 2 exchanges 140Y for 70X with Nation 1; thus, Nation 2's terms of trade deteriorate to $P_Y/P_X = 1/2$, and Nation 1's terms of trade improve to $P_X/P_Y = 2$. With growth in both nations and offer curves 1^* and 2^*, we get equilibrium point E_4. The volume of trade expands to 140X for 140Y, but the terms of trade remain at 1 in both nations.

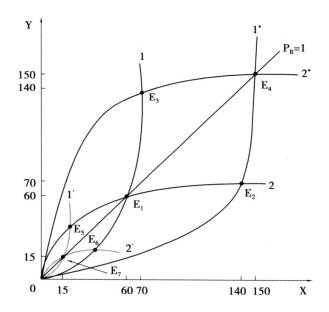

Figure 7.14　Growth and trade in both nations

On the contrary, if K doubled in Nation 1, its offer curve would rotate counterclockwise from 1 to $1'$ and give equilibrium point E_5. Nation 1 would then exchange 20X for 40Y with Nation 2 so that Nation 1's terms of trade would improve to 2 and Nation 2's terms of trade would deteriorate to 1/2. If instead Nation 2's labor only grows in such a manner that its offer curve rotates clockwise to $2'$, we get equilibrium point E_6. This might result, for example, from a doubling of L (the scarce factor) in Nation 2. Nation 2 would then exchange 20Y for 40X with Nation 1, and Nation 2's terms of trade would increase to 2 while Nation 1's terms of trade would decline to 1/2. If growth occurred in both nations in such a way that offer curve 1 rotated to 1′ and offer curve 2 rotated to 2′, then the volume of trade would be only 15X for 15Y, and both nations' terms of trade would remain unchanged at the level of 1 (see equilibrium point E_7).

With balanced growth or neutral technical progress in the production of both commodities in both nations, both nations' offer curves will shift outward and move closer to the axis measuring each nation's exportable commodity. In that case, the volume of trade will expand and the terms of trade can remain unchanged or improve for one nation and deteriorate for the other, depending on the slope (i.e., the curvature) of each nation's offer curve and on the degree by which each offer curve rotates.

——— *China-perspective case study* ———

Case 1　China's high-level opening-up has achieved remarkable results

The National Bureau of Statistics released on October 9 that since the 18th National Congress of the Communist Party of China, China's opening-up has reached an unprecedented level. The scale of foreign trade has grown steadily, and the status of a major trading country has been consolidated.

From 2013 to 2021, China's accumulated import and export of goods trade reached 262.3 trillion yuan, with an average annual growth of 5.4%. The total import and export of general trade was 149.8 trillion yuan, accounting for 57.1% of the total import and export value of goods in the same period.

From 2014 to 2021, China's service import and export scale has remained the second largest in the world for eight consecutive years. From 2013 to 2021, China's cumulative imports and exports of knowledge-intensive services reached $2.1 trillion, with an average annual growth of 9.3%.

From 2013 to 2021, China's non-financial sector has accumulated $1.2 trillion of foreign direct investment. In 2021, the amount of foreign direct investment will increase by 55.3% over 2012, with an average annual growth of 5%.

From 2013 to 2021, China's foreign investment flow will be among the top in the world, with a cumulative foreign direct investment flow of $1.4 trillion, with an average annual growth of 8.2%. In the past decade, the number of free trade agreements signed by China with foreign countries has increased from 10 to 19, and the proportion of trade volume with free trade partners in China's total trade volume has increased from 17% in 2012 to 35% in 2021.

Case 2　World Insights: China's recipe for bigger pie of global development in new blueprint

BEIJING, October 28 (Xinhua)—The world has been keeping tabs on one of China's most important meetings in its political calendar concluded last week to gauge the direction China will take in the next half-decade and beyond.

The Communist Party of China (CPC) on Sunday unveiled its new top leadership, which will take the world's most populous nation on a new journey of high-quality and inclusive development, with far-reaching significance to the region and the world.

Reviewing China's development success, Chinese President Xi Jinping, also general secretary of the CPC Central Committee, reaffirmed China's commitment to further opening-up and the common values of humanity.

Observers believe that as global recovery progresses in fits and starts, China, under the leadership of the CPC, will remain an indispensable stabilizing force and an inexhaustible source of development wisdom.

Oasis of growth

China's economic rise and modernization from a primarily agricultural country decades ago is an inspiring rags-to-riches story. From 2013 to 2021, China's GDP grew at an average annual rate of 6.6 percent, beating the global level of 2.6 percent.

The country now boasts the world's most extensive social welfare system, the largest high-speed railway network, as well as the largest and fastest growing middle-income group, which is sure to translate into massive opportunities for China and the wider world.

According to the United Nations Development Programme (UNDP)'s human development index (HDI), from 1990 to 2019, China is the only country to have moved from low human development category to high human development category since UNDP first began analyzing global HDI trends in 1990.

Earlier in May, UN Secretary-General Antonio Guterres called on the international community to rescue and prioritize the Sustainable Development Goals (SDGs).

"The multiple crises facing the world raise the bar even higher... The years ahead will demand much stronger leadership and ambition at all levels," said the secretary-general.

Against such a backdrop, the most populous nation's miraculous, people-centered development represents a motivation for an anxious world.

China's development is not only illustrated by economic figures, but also by the sense of happiness shared by its people, and the results of the CPC's people-centered endeavors in various fields have been tested by practice and recognized by the people, said Ang Teck Sin, a political commentator in Singapore.

Now that sense of fulfillment has been shared by a wider crowd across the world. China's contribution to global economic growth during the 2013−2021 period averaged 38.6 percent, outstripping that of the Group of Seven (G7) countries combined.

The world's second largest economy has become a major trading partner for over 140 countries and regions, leading the world in total volume of trade in goods, and emerging as a mainstay in building an open world economy.

Meanwhile, Chinese modernization is widely inspiring in the way that it does not comply with a fixed or a Westernized storyline, but rather adapts to its national conditions and evolving circumstances at home and abroad.

As British scholar Martin Jacques once put it, China proves that the Western belief that "as countries modernize, they also Westernize" is simply an illusion.

China's modernization has provided an important reference for m   's that are facing economic and social development problems and are e   t paths suited to their national conditions, said Luis Delgado, a research Venezuela's Center for Advanced Studies in Development and Eme.

Senegalese sociologist Mamadou Diouf said, "Chinese modernizat   ount the living environment, ecosystem and natural environment, and puts p   the center, which is key to achieving sustainable modernization."

Seed of hope

In the mostly arid, desert-capped Sub-Saharan Africa, locals have been planting a small grass from China for livestock feed, mushroom production, or even as a green barrier to fight climate change.

The "magic" plant called Juncao, which uses grass instead of wood to cultivate edible fungi, has worked wonder in 100-plus countries as a cash cow and the source of tens of thousands of jobs.

Debunking the myth that to produce edible mushrooms, trees must be chopped down, the small grass has offered a green alternative and a boon for a shared future.

First cultivated in China, the plant has taken root in the far-flung, poverty-stricken fields in Papua, New Guinea, Tanzania, Rwanda and Fiji, its mushrooms gracing the tables of an increasing number of households.

Petty in size, Juncao has become "grass of happiness" and "grass of prosperity" for people in developing countries and a signboard for China's foreign assistance and poverty-alleviation endeavors overseas.

In Iraq's Mesopotamia, desertification and soil salinization have long threatened to bury this cradle of one of humanity's earliest civilizations in dust.

"My dream is to transfer what I learned from China to Iraq and turn deserts into oases," said Sarmad Kamil Ali, deputy chief agricultural engineer of Iraq's State Board of Combating Desertification, who studied in China nearly 10 years ago to learn about sand control.

In tropical Ethiopia, China's climate remote sensing satellite, orbiting more than 600 km above the ground, is working like a guardian angel for this "hometown of coffee," to cushion the impact of climate change on coffee planting.

China's green energy projects and technical assistance overseas have not only worked as a magic wand turing barren, tropical areas into energy oases, but also helped fully harness the natural endowment of many countries.

China has been a true practitioner of its vision to build a human community with a shared future. Its invaluable experience in poverty alleviation has also taken root elsewhere as a seed of hope for locals.

The China-proposed Belt and Road Initiative (BRI) puts developing nations on the right track to achieving their long-term development goals, said Khairy Tourk, a professor of economics with the Stuart School of Business at the Illinois Institute of Technology in Chicago.

"The BRI has drawn world attention to the importance of infrastructure as an essential pillar of economic development," Tourk said.

Tea and beer

"The Chinese people are fond of tea and the Belgians love beer. To me, the moderate tea drinker and the passionate beer lover represent two ways of understanding life and knowing the world, and I find them equally rewarding," Xi said in a speech delivered at the College of Europe in Belgium in 2014.

Xi used this metaphor to elaborate on China's vision of civilization featuring diversity, equality and inclusiveness.

On multiple occasions, including the just-concluded CPC national congress, China has vowed to hold dear humanity's common values of peace, development, fairness, justice, democracy, and freedom, doubling down on the joint building of an open, inclusive, clean, and beautiful world that enjoys lasting peace, universal security, and common prosperity.

This is also the bedrock value of the country, which has long been committed to an independent foreign policy of peace, safeguarding a UN-centered international system and promoting a human community with a shared future.

China, in its earnest pursuit of national rejuvenation, knows all too well that peace is the prerequisite for development, and inclusive development requires an inclusive vision of security, in which humanity works as an indivisible whole.

To help fix global deficits in peace, development, trust, and governance, China has walked its talk to pool resources and consensus, crack security puzzles, and boost sustainable and inclusive development.

Since 1990, China has dispatched over 50,000 peacekeepers to nearly 30 UN peacekeeping missions. It is the second largest contributor to the UN regular budget and peacekeeping assessments. It has supported the United Nations' work in various fields through establishing the Peace and Development Trust fund with the UN.

The vision of a shared future largely reflects the core values of China's traditional culture such as harmony and equality, said B R Deepak, chairperson of the Center of Chinese and Southeast Asian Studies at the New Delhi-based Jawaharlal Nehru University.

The Global Development Initiative and the Global Security Initiative, both proposed by China and based on mutual respect and win-win cooperation, are like an antidote to hegemony, unilateralism, exclusion and the Cold War mentality in today's world, he said.

Unlike some Western countries' unilateral pursuits of their safety, the Global Security Initiative seeks common security, which underlines peace and cooperation, said Bambang Suryono, chairman of the Indonesian think tank Asia Innovation Study Center.

The global future "is an issue which commands the attention of people everywhere in the world, not just people of this country or that country," said Martin Albrow, a fellow of the British Academy of Social Sciences.

Tackling such big global issues as climate change, nuclear security and deforestation needs the focus on "collective activities, which go beyond national boundaries," he said, hoping that China can take the lead.

Key concepts

anti-trade production and consumption   neutral production and consumption

pro-trade production and consumption   balanced growth

Rybczynski theorem   labor-saving technical progress

capital-saving technical progress   terms-of-trade effect

wealth effect   immiserizing growth

Summary

1. Changes in factor endowments, technology and tastes affect a nation's production frontier, offer curve, volume and terms of trade, and gains from trade.

2. Increases in labor (L) and capital (K) shift the production frontier outward. Type and degree of shift depend on rate of growth.

3. The Rybczynski theorem: At constant commodity prices, an increase in the endowment of one factor will increase by a greater proportion the output of the commodity intensive in that factor and will reduce the output of the other commodity.

4. All technical progress reduces the amount of both labor and capital required to produce any given level of output.

5. Growth is pro-trade if output of a nation's export commodity grows proportionately more than the output of its import commodity at constant relative commodity prices, leading to greater than proportionate expansion of trade. Otherwise, growth is anti-trade, or neutral.

6. Production is pro-trade if output of a nation's export commodity grows proportionately more than the output of its import commodity. Otherwise, production is anti-trade, or neutral.

7. Consumption is pro-trade if the nation's consumption of its import commodity increases proportionately more than consumption of its export commodity. Otherwise, consuption is anti-trade, or neutral.

Exercises

1. Dynamic factors in trade theory refer to changes in _____.

    A. factor endowments   B. technology

    C. tastes   D. all of the above

2. Doubling the amount of L and K under constant returns to scale _____.

   A. doubles the output of the L-intensive commodity

   B. doubles the output of the K-intensive commodity

   C. leaves the shape of the production frontier unchanged

   D. all of the above

3. The Rybczynski theorem postulates that doubling L at constant relative commodity prices

   _____.

   A. doubles the output of the L-intensive commodity

   B. reduces the output of the K-intensive commodity

   C. increases the output of both commodities

   D. any of the above

4. Technical progress that increases the productivity of L proportionately more than the productivity of K is called _____.

   A. K-saving   B. L-saving

   C. neutral   D. any of the above

5. If, at unchanged terms of trade, a nation wants to trade more after growth, then the nation's terms of trade can be expected to _____.

   A. deteriorate   B. improve

   C. remain unchanged   D. any of the above

6. Briefly describe the impact of economic growth on the terms of trade of agricultural products.

7. What does the Rybczynski theorem show?

8. What are the impacts of technological progress on international trade?

Chapter 8 | Trade Restrictions: Tariffs

Learning goals

After learning this chapter, you should be able to:

✓ describe the effects of a tariff on consumers and producers.

✓ identify the costs and benefits of a tariff on a small and a large nation.

✓ understand the meaning and importance of tariff structure.

We have seen that free trade maximizes world output and benefits all nations. However, practically all nations impose some restrictions on the free flow of international trade. Since these restrictions and regulations deal with the nation's trade or commerce, they are generally known as trade or commercial policies. The most important type of trade restriction has historically been the tariff.

8.1 What is a tariff?

A tariff is a tax or duty levied on the traded commodity as it crosses a national boundary. An import tariff is a duty on the imported commodity, while an export tariff is a duty on the exported commodity. Import tariffs are more important than export tariffs, and most of our discussion will deal with import tariffs.

Export tariff is the tariff imposed by the customs of the export country on the exporters when their products are exported abroad. At present, most countries do not impose export tariff on most exports. Because the collection of export tariff is bound to increase the sales price of domestic goods in foreign markets, reduce the competitiveness of goods, which is not conducive to the expansion of exports. After the Second World War, export tariffs were mainly levied by the developing countries. The purpose of the export tariff is either for fiscal revenue, or to ensure domestic production or supply in the domestic market.

Export tariff for the purpose of fiscal revenue is generally not high. For example, some countries in Latin America generally levy 1% to 5%.

Export tariff for the purpose of protecting domestic production is usually levied on the export of raw materials in short supply. Its purpose is to ensure the needs of domestic production and increase the production cost of foreign products to strengthen the ability of domestic products. Sweden and Norway, for example, impose a tariff on timber exports to protect their pulp and paper industries. Export tariff, designed to ensure the supply of the domestic market, in addition to certain export raw materials, are levied for certain daily necessities with domestic underproduction and large needs, to curb price increases. In addition, after the Second World War, in order to safeguard their own economic rights and interests, some developing countries used the export tariff as a weapon to oppose multinational companies from buying primary products at low prices locally. Guinea, for example, once imposed a special export tariff on its bauxite and agricultural and sideline products.

Case 8.1   Tariffs: more bindings and closer to zero

The bulkiest results of Uruguay Round are the 22,500 pages listing individual countries' commitments on specific categories of goods and services. These include commitments to cut and "bind" their customs duty rates on imports of goods. In some cases, tariffs are being cut to zero. There is also a significant increase in the number of "bound" tariffs — duty rates that are committed in the WTO and are difficult to raise.

Tariff cuts

Developed countries' tariff cuts were for the most part phased in over five years from 1 January 1995. The result is a 40% cut in their tariffs on industrial products, from an average of 6.3% to 3.8%. The value of imported industrial products that receive duty-free treatment in developed countries will jump from 20% to 44%.

There will also be fewer products charged high duty rates. The proportion of imports into developed countries from all sources facing tariff rates of more than 15% will decline from 7% to 5%. The proportion of developing country exports facing tariffs above 15% in industrial countries will fall from 9% to 5%.

The Uruguay Round package has been improved. On 26 March 1997, 40 countries accounting for more than 92% of world trade in information technology products, agreed to eliminate import duties and other charges on these products by 2000 (by 2005 in a handful of cases). As with other tariff commitments, each participating country is applying its commitments equally to exports from all WTO members (i.e., on a most-favored-nation basis), even from members that did not make commitments.

More bindings

Developed countries increased the number of imports whose tariff rates are "bound" (committed and difficult to increase) from 78% of product lines to 99%. For developing countries, the increase was considerable: from 21% to 73%. Economies in transition from central planning increased their bindings from 73% to 98%. This all means a substantially higher degree of market security for traders and investors.

Import tariffs are the duties levied by the customs of the importing country on the domestic importer when foreign goods are imported. Import tariff is levied when foreign goods enter the customs territory directly, or when foreign goods are proposed to be transported to the domestic market of the importing country for sale through free ports, free trade zones or customs-bonded warehouses, it is levied when customs formalities are handled.

According to differential treatment, formal import taxes can be divided into the following types: ordinary tariffs, the MFN tariffs, GSP tariffs, and preferential tariffs.

Ordinary tariff is generally applicable to non-diplomatic relations between countries. Sometimes it is used between countries that have no bilateral trade agreement and are not under a multilateral trade agreement. The ordinary tariff rate is the highest tax rate, which is 1 to 20 times higher than the most-favored-nation (MFN) tax rate, which is a tariff rate with the nature of an import ban. So now only a few countries have imposed such discriminatory tariff rates on imports from a very small number of other countries.

The MFN tax applies to goods imported from a country or region with a trade agreement with the MFN treatment clauses with that country. The MFN rate is lower than the ordinary rate, and the difference is often large. For example, the United States imposes a MFN rate of 6.8% and an ordinary rate of 70%. After the Second World War, most countries joined the GATT (WTO) or signed bilateral trade treaties or agreements, providing the principle of MFN treatment, and applying the MFN tax rate. So the MFN tariffs are usually called normal tariffs.

The Generalized System of Preferences (GSP) was adopted after the adoption of the United Nations Conference on Trade and Development in 1968 (UNCTAD). It is a universal, non-discriminatory and non-reciprocal preferential tariff given by 32 developed countries to exports from developing countries. It is a preferential tariff of further tax reduction and even tax exemption on the basis of the MFN tariff.

Universal, non-discrimination and non-reciprocity are regarded as the three principles of GSP. The so-called universal means that developed countries should give universal preferential treatment to the manufactured products and semi-finished products exported by developing countries or regions. The so-called non-discrimination means that all developing countries or regions should enjoy the GSP treatment without discrimination and without exception. The so-called non-reciprocity means that developed countries should unilaterally grant tariff preferences to developing countries or regions without requiring them to provide reverse preferences.

The goal of the GSP is to increase the foreign exchange income of developing countries or regions, promote their industrialization, and accelerate the economic growth rate of developing countries or regions.

According to the decision of the UN conference on trade and development, the implementation of the GSP deadline for 10 years, 1979, GATT parties in Tokyo Round multilateral trade negotiations and agreed on an "authorization clause" that has laid a more solid legal foundation for the extension of the implementation period of the GSP. Since then, the GSP has been developing in the decade. At the end of each stage, the Special Committee on Preferences of UNCTAD will conduct a comprehensive review of the GSP to determine the implementation of the GSP in the next stage. The GSP is now in its fourth decade phase.

The countries offering GSP are normally developed countries that gives GSP treatment to developing countries. The beneficiary countries are developing countries (or regions) receiving GSP treatment, including the least developed countries. The basic principles of the GSP (non-discriminatory) have not yet been fully implemented. Some countries are both for the beneficiary countries and for the beneficiary countries.

The GSP program is a specific implementation program of the GSP formulated in the light of the principles and objectives of the EU and in accordance with the national conditions, which is regularly or irregularly published in the form of government decrees.

Although the contents of the GSP programs are different, they generally contain six basic elements according to the relevant provisions of UNCTAD.

Preferential tariffs refer to the special preferential low tariff or tax exemption treatment for all the commodities or part of the goods imported in a certain country or region. However, it does not apply to goods imported from non-preferential countries or regions. Some preferential taxes are reciprocal or non-reciprocal. The preferential tax began with trade between the metropolitan state and the colonial vassal. After the Second World War, the common market was also practiced between Western Europe and some developing countries in Africa, the Caribbean and the Pacific.

At present, the preferential tax mainly includes the preferential tariffs granted to more than 60 countries and regions in Africa, the Caribbean and the Pacific region. Because the preferential tariff agreement was signed in Lome, the capital of Togo, so it is called the Lome Agreement (Lome Convention). The provisions of the Lome Agreement on preferential taxes mainly include the following three points: First, the European countries will accept all the industrial products and 96% of the agricultural products of these developing countries into the EU market under the condition of tax exemption and unlimited, without requiring these developing countries to give "reverse preferences". Those agricultural products that are not duty-free are the agricultural and livestock products included in the EU's agricultural policy and some temperate horticulture products that the EU can produce. Second, the EU has made special arrangements for the import of beef, sweet wine and bananas from these countries. A certain amount of duty-free import quotas shall be given to the import of these commodities every year, and customs duties shall be imposed on imports exceeding the quota. Third, in the rules of origin, a system of "full accumulation" is established, that is, products originating from these developing countries or EU countries, such as the country of origin, when further produced or processed in any other country of these developing countries. This provision allows these countries to produce and process products in this way.

In addition to the formal import duties on imported goods, a country often imposes import duties according to some special purpose, namely import surtaxes.

Import surtaxes is usually a specific temporary measure. The main objectives are to maintain the balance of imports and exports, to prevent low dumping of foreign goods, and to impose trade discrimination or retaliation against a country. Therefore, the import surtax is also called the special tariff.

Import surtax is an important means to restrict the import of goods. For example, in the first half of 1971, the United States suffered its first trade deficit in many years, and its international balance of payments deteriorated. In order to cope with the balance of payment crisis, on August 15 of the same year, US President Nixon announced the implementation of the new economic policy, imposing a 10% import surcharge of 10% on foreign imports, that is, a 10% surcharge on the general import duty to restrict the import of goods.

Similar to the above, the case of import surtax on all imported goods is rarely occurred, and the import surtax is often levied only for individual countries and individual goods. Its main forms have the following two kinds.

First is the counter-vailing duties, also known as offset tax or compensation tax, which are an import surcharge levied on foreign imports, directly or indirectly, receiving any subsidy.

Second is the anti-dumping duty, an import surcharge levied on imported goods that are dumped. The aim is to resist commodity dumping and protect domestic goods and the domestic market.

The so-called dumping is that a country's export manufacturers sell goods abroad at a price lower than the domestic market, or even lower than the production cost of goods, so as to attack competitors and occupy the foreign market. With regard to dumping, the 1979 Tokyo Round trade negotiations chaired by GATT clearly stipulates, "When a national product is exported to another country, the export price of the product is lower than the comparable price of similar products used for domestic consumption in normal trade business, it is regarded as dumping." In order to prevent the abuse of anti-dumping duties, the GATT (WTO) has made strict provisions on them. According to the relevant provisions of GATT (WTO), the anti-dumping duties must meet three basic conditions: dumping; dumping to the domestic industry or to the construction of a domestic industry; and the dumping must have a causal relationship between the two. That is, according to the first two conditions, if the foreign exporter has dumping, but the government of the importing country does not harm its import competitive industries or impose anti-dumping duties.

The regulatory effect of import tariffs on imported goods is mainly shown in the following aspects:

①For products that can be produced in large quantities domestically or cannot be produced in large quantities for the time being but may develop in the future, higher import tariffs shall be stipulated to weaken the competitiveness of imported goods and protect the production and development of similar domestic products.

②For the import of non-essential goods or luxury goods, set higher tariffs to restrict or even prohibit the import.

③For the import of raw materials, semi-finished products, necessities or urgently needed products in production that cannot be produced or insufficient in China, lower tax rates or tax exemption shall be formulated to encourage import to meet domestic production and living needs.

④Adjust the balance of trade through tariffs. When the trade deficit is too large, increase tariffs or impose import surcharges to restrict the import of goods and narrow the trade deficit. When the trade surplus is too large, the trade frictions and contradictions with the relevant countries can be alleviated by reducing tariffs and narrowing the trade surplus.

Case 8.2   Shenzhen Customs issued 190,000 Certificates of Origin in the first half of 2019, helping exporters gain duty relief about 1.71 billion yuan

With commitment to improving business climate and policy support, Shenzhen Customs District has been promoting the certification on origin of export goods and helping exporters to gain duty reliefs abroad. In the first half of 2019, this Customs District provided Shenzhen-based exporters with Certificates of Origin (C/O) totaling 190,000 pieces, involving 34.14 billion yuan worth of goods, which enabled the exporters to enjoy duty relief, about 1.71 billion yuan in total, from the countries/regions of imports.

OMRON Shenzhen Ltd., a high-tech company of semi-conductor products, found it difficult to convert huge product-development cost into original product value. Regarding this problem, Shenzhen Customs assigned a team of experts to calculate the non-original value of the company's products (sensors, relays, connectors and other ICs) and make pre-assessment on its exports to South Korea, making them compliant with the origin rules under China-Korea Free Trade Agreement so as to gain import-duty relief provided by South Korea. In the first half year, OMRON Shenzhen Ltd. received 97 pieces of C/O under China-Korea FTA, involving 72.868 million yuan worth of goods, and saved a duty amount of 4,816,000 yuan.

Additionally, Shenzhen Customs has achieved online processing and self-help printing of export C/O. By statistics, in the first half year, local exporters printed by themselves 36,000 pieces of C/O, involving 4.84 billion yuan worth of goods.

Tariffs can be ad valorem, specific, or compound. The ad valorem tariff is expressed as a fixed percentage of the value of the traded commodity. The specific tariff is expressed as a fixed sum per physical unit of the traded commodity. Finally, a compound tariff is a combination of an ad valorem and a specific tariff. For example, a 10 percent ad valorem tariff on bicycles would result in the payment to customs officials of the sum of $10 on each $100 imported bicycle and the sum of $20 on each $200 imported bicycle. Meanwhile, a specific tariff of $10 on imported bicycles means that customs officials collect the fixed sum of $10 on each imported bicycle regardless of its price. Finally, a compound duty of 5 percent ad valorem and a specific duty of $10 on imported bicycles would result in the collection by customs officials of the sum of $15 on each $100 bicycle and $20 on each $200 imported bicycle.

Case 8.3　Duty-free sales in Hainan island exceed $7.78 billion in 9 years

HAIKOU, April 20 (Xinhua)—China's island province of Hainan raked in 55.07 billion yuan (about $7.78 billion) in duty-free sales in the past nine years, according to customs of the provincial capital city of Haikou.

The State Council gave Hainan permission to run a pilot offshore duty-free program on April 20, 2011, in an effort to make the island a world-class tourist destination.

Statistics showed that duty-free shops in Hainan received over 16.09 million customers and sold over 72 million duty-free goods over the past nine years.

In January last year, Hainan opened two new offshore duty-free shops in Haikou and Qionghai, adding to the previous two in Haikou and Sanya.

The province opened two duty-free experience shops in Sanya last week where customers are allowed to visit the bricks-and-mortar stores and place orders online.

Tariffs are the oldest form of trade policy and have traditionally been used as a source of government income. Their true purpose, however, has usually been twofold: both to provide revenue and to protect particular domestic sectors. In the early 19th century, for example, the United Kingdom used tariffs (the famous Corn Laws) to protect its agriculture from import competition. In the late 19th century, both Germany and the United States protected their new industrial sectors by imposing tariffs on imports of manufactured goods. The importance of tariffs has declined in modern times because modern governments usually prefer to protect domestic industries through a variety of non-tariff barriers, such as import quotas (limitations on the quantity of imports) and export restraints (limitations on the quantity of exports—usually imposed by the exporting country at the importing country's request). Nonetheless, an understanding of the effects of a tariff remains vital for understanding other trade policies.

8.2 Nominal tariff and effective protection rate

The rate of effective protection (calculated on the domestic value added, or processing, that takes place in the nation) exceeds the nominal tariff rate (calculated on the value of the final commodity). Domestic value added equals the price of the final commodity minus the cost of the imported inputs going into the production of the commodity. While the nominal tariff rate is important to consumers (because it indicates how much the price of the final commodity increases as a result of the tariff), the effective tariff rate is important to producers because it indicates how much protection is actually provided to the domestic processing of the import-competing commodity. An example will clarify the distinction between the nominal and effective tariff rates.

Suppose that $80 of imported wool goes into the domestic production of a suit. Suppose also that the free trade price of the suit is $100 but the nation imposes a 10 percent nominal tariff on each imported suit. The price of suits to domestic consumers would then be $110. Of this, $80 represents imported wool, $20 is domestic value added, and $10 is the tariff. The $10 tariff collected on each imported suit represents a 10 percent nominal tariff rate since the nominal tariff is calculated on the price of the final commodity (i.e., $10/$100 = 10 percent) but corresponds to a 50 percent effective tariff rate because the effective tariff is calculated on the value added domestically to the suit (i.e., $10/$20 = 50 percent).

While consumers are only concerned with the fact that the $10 tariff increases the price of the suits they purchase by $10 or 10 percent, producers view this $10 tariff as being 50 percent of the $20 portion of the suit produced domestically. To them, the $10 tariff provides 50 percent of the value of domestic processing. This represents a much greater degree of protection (five times more) than the 10 percent nominal tariff rate seems to indicate. It is this effective rate of tariff protection that is important to producers in stimulating the domestic production of suits in competition with imported suits. Whenever the imported input is admitted duty-free or a lower tariff rate is imposed on the imported input than on the final commodity produced with the imported input, the effective rate of protection will exceed the nominal tariff rate.

Case 8.4　Lower tariffs, faster customs clearance
—China, ASEAN share bounty of RCEP trade facilitation package

* The booming economic and trade cooperation between China and ASEAN countries has further gained steam as the RCEP agreement provided faster customs clearance and other trade facilitation measures.

* The RCEP will eventually eliminate tariffs on as much as 90 percent of goods traded within the region.

* Besides boosting trade growth, a more integrated regional supply chain under the RCEP agreement has also benefited China and ASEAN countries.

* The RCEP seeks to promote e-commerce and a digital economy which would be increasingly relevant in the post-pandemic world.

BANGKOK, July 7 (Xinhua)—During Thailand's durian season every year, orders from China for the thorny "king of fruits" always surge, driving up shipments from the world's top fresh durian exporter.

This year, after the Regional Comprehensive Economic Partnership (RCEP), the world's largest free trade deal that entered into force in January, Thailand's durian sales to China have been further boosted.

"Up to 100 percent of our durians are shipped to China, and the demand is increasing year by year," said Silaphon Thongrot, who has managed a durian orchard for 15 years in east Thailand's Chanthaburi Province growing durian, mangosteen, rambutan and other fruits.

Faster customs clearance and other trade facilitation measures provided by the RCEP agreement, as well as the launch of the "Durian Express" and special fruit train services to China, helped boost the trade of Thai durians and reduce exporters' costs, said Narongsak Putthapornmongkol, president of the Thai-Chinese Chamber of Commerce.

Nuttakij Oranhirunruk, vice president of the Thai-Chinese Agribusiness Association, said he has full confidence in the substantial growth of Thailand's durian exports to China this year, expecting the eastern agricultural zone to export 35,000 containers this year, compared to 25,000 last year.

The hot sale of Thai durians is just an example of the booming economic and trade cooperation between China and countries of the Association of Southeast Asian Nations (ASEAN), which has further gained steam after the RCEP agreement took effect.

Chinese customs data showed that in the first quarter of this year, trade between China and ASEAN accounted for 47.2 percent—or nearly half—of China's foreign trade with RCEP partners. With the RCEP agreement, ASEAN has once again overtaken the EU to become China's largest trading partner.

The momentum continued despite disruptions from COVID-19, with bilateral trade volume expanding 10.2 percent year-on-year during the January-May period.

Cambodian Commerce Minister Pan Sorasak considered the RCEP as a key driver for economic recovery in the participating countries both during and after the pandemic.

The minister said that under the RCEP, Cambodia is expected to see an annual export growth between 9.4 percent and 18 percent, which will contribute to national economic growth between 2 percent and 3.8 percent. Cambodia is the ASEAN chair this year.

The RCEP will eventually eliminate tariffs on as much as 90 percent of goods traded within the region. A study by the World Bank said the East Asia and Pacific region can reap significant benefits through further liberalization, with Cambodia, Vietnam and other lower-middle-income countries gaining the most from the RCEP.

"The region will also see an additional 'kick' in productivity as greater openness brings additional skills, technology and capital," the bank's research report said.

Besides boosting trade growth, a more integrated regional supply chain under the RCEP agreement has also benefited China and ASEAN countries.

Businesses with global supply chains might face tariffs even within a free trade area if their products contain components that are made elsewhere. Under the RCEP's common rules of origin, parts from any member would be treated equally, which might give companies in RCEP countries an incentive to look within the region for suppliers.

Himile (Thailand) Co., a tire mold supplier in eastern Thailand's Rayong Province, has already experienced the benefits.

The RCEP's tariff concessions, common rules of origin and simplification of customs procedures "enable us to purchase raw materials and equipment as well as distribution of products more efficiently and at a lower cost," said Qiu Jinliang, managing director of Himile (Thailand).

The company, which sources raw materials from China, Japan and South

Korea while exporting products to the United States, European and ASEAN markets, has seen the customs clearance time shortened by three days to a week per shipment while the costs of raw material imports have also been reduced, Qiu said.

Ong Tee Keat, founding chairman of the Center for New Inclusive Asia, a Malaysia-based think tank, said ASEAN countries can benefit greatly from the harmonized rules of origin under the RCEP as intermediate goods can be sourced across any of the 15 RCEP countries. Only a certain proportion of regional value content is required for goods to meet the RCEP rules of origin requirements for tariff concessions.

This could help lower the production costs of companies operating in the region, enhance the resilience of regional supply chains, and generate more investment, job opportunities and economic growth, he said.

The RCEP seeks to promote e-commerce and a digital economy which would be increasingly relevant in the post-pandemic world. "It will have implications not only on trade and economic growth, but also on promoting digital inclusiveness and a more level playing field," said Wichai Kinchong Choi, senior vice president of Kasikorn Bank, a leading Thai bank.

The RCEP is crucial for regional small and medium-sized enterprises, which took a big hit from COVID-19, as their capacity and competitiveness could be enhanced, enabling them to emerge stronger from an improved access to a larger RCEP market, he said.

Since the RCEP came into force, the development of cross-border e-commerce between China and ASEAN countries has been further enhanced.

As an important hub for China's cross-border e-commerce import and export business to ASEAN, south China's Zhuang Autonomous Region of Guangxi has attracted more than 100 cross-border e-commerce enterprises, including the first cross-border innovation center of Southeast Asia's flagship e-commerce platform Lazada and the ASEAN cross-border e-commerce logistics center of Shopee.

"It (RCEP) is not just a simple trade agreement that provides enhanced market access and stable business environment. It is a strategic tool to sustain the region's economic advantage," said former Philippine Trade Secretary Ramon Lopez, calling for the country's early ratification of the mega trade deal, which he believed is "for the future of the economy".

8.3 Costs and benefits of a tariff

8.3.1 Import demand and export supply

Let's suppose there are two countries, Home and Foreign, both of which consume and produce wheat, which can be costlessly transported between the countries. In each country, wheat is a simple competitive industry in which the supply and demand curves are functions of the market price. Normally, Home supply and demand will depend on the price in terms of Home currency, and Foreign supply and demand will depend on the price in terms of Foreign currency. However, we assume that the exchange rate between the currencies is not affected by whatever trade policy is undertaken in this market. Thus we quote prices in both markets in terms of Home currency.

Trade will arise in such a market if prices are different in the absence of trade. Suppose that in the absence of trade, the price of wheat is higher in Home than it is in Foreign. Now let's allow foreign trade. Since the price of wheat in Home exceeds the price in Foreign, shippers begin to move wheat from Foreign to Home. The export of wheat raises its price in Foreign and lowers its price in Home until the difference in prices has been eliminated.

To determine the world price and the quantity traded, it is helpful to define two new curves: the Home import demand curve and the Foreign export supply curve, which are derived from the underlying domestic supply and demand curves. Home import demand is the excess of what Home consumers demand over what Home producers supply. Foreign export supply is the excess of what Foreign producers supply over what Foreign consumers demand.

Figure 8.1 shows how the Home import demand curve is derived. At the price P_1, Home consumers demand D_1, while Home producers supply only S_1. As a result, Home import demand is D_1-S_1. If we raise the price to P_2, Home consumers demand only D_2, while Home producers raise the amount they supply to S_2, so import demand falls to D_2-S_2. These price-quantity combinations are plotted as points 1 and 2 in the right panel of Figure 8.1. The import demand curve MD is downward sloping because as price increases, the quantity of imports demanded declines. At P_A, Home supply and demand are equal in the absence of trade, so the Home import demand curve intercepts the price axis at P_A (import demand = zero at P_A).

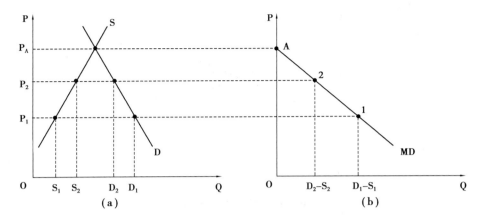

Figure 8.1 Deriving Home's import demand curve

Figure 8.2 shows how the Foreign export supply curve XS is derived. At P_1 Foreign producers supply S_1^*, while Foreign consumers demand only D_1^*, so the amount of the total supply available for export is $S_1^* - D_1^*$. At P_2 Foreign producers raise the quantity they supply to S_2^* and Foreign consumers lower the amount they demand to D_2^*, so the quantity of the total supply available to export rises to $S_2^* - D_2^*$. Because the supply of goods available for export rises as the price rises, the Foreign export supply curve is upward sloping. At P_A^*, supply and demand would be equal in the absence of trade, so the Foreign export supply curve intersects the price axis at P_A^* (export supply = zero at P_A^*).

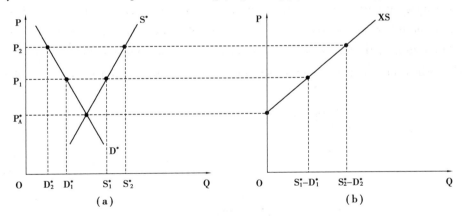

Figure 8.2 Deriving Foreign's export supply curve

World equilibrium occurs when Home import demand equals Foreign export supply (Figure 8.3). At the price P_W where the two curves cross, world supply equals world demand. At the equilibrium point 1 in Figure 8.3.

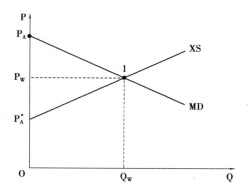

Figure 8.3   World equilibrium

8.3.2   Consumer and producer surplus

A tariff raises the price of a good in the importing country and lowers it in the exporting country. As a result of these price changes, consumers lose in the importing country and gain in the exporting country. Producers gain in the importing country and lose in the exporting country. In addition, the government imposing the tariff revenue. To compare these costs and benefits, it is necessary to quantify them. The method for measuring costs and benefits of a tariff depends on two concepts common to much microeconomic analysis: consumer and producer surplus.

Consumer surplus measures the amount a consumer gains from a purchase by computing the difference between the price he actually pays and the price he would have been willing to pay. If, for example, a consumer would have been willing to pay $8 for a bushel of wheat but the price is only $3, the consumer surplus gained by the purchase is $5.

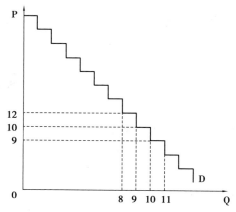

Figure 8.4   Deriving consumer surplus from the demand curve

Consumer surplus can be derived from the market demand curve (Figure 8.4). For example, suppose that the maximum price at which consumers will buy 10 units of a good is $10. Then the 10th unit of the good purchased must be worth $10 to consumers. If it were worth less, they would not purchase it; if it were worth more, they would have been willing to purchase it even if the price were higher. Now suppose that in order to get consumers to buy 11 units, the price must be cut to $9. Then the 11th unit must be worth only $9 to consumers.

Suppose that the price is $9. Then consumers are willing to purchase only the 11th unit of the good and thus receive no consumer surplus from their purchase of that unit. They would have been willing to pay $10 for the 10th unit, however, and thus receive $1 in consumer surplus from that unit. They would also have been willing to pay $12 for the 9th unit; in that case, they would have received $3 of consumer surplus on that unit, and so on.

Generalizing from this example, if P is the price of a good and Q the quantity demanded at that price, then consumer surplus is calculated by subtracting P times Q from the area under the demand curve up to Q (Figure 8.5). If the price is P_1, the quantity demanded is D_1 and the consumer surplus is measured by the areas labeled a plus b. If the price rises to P_2, the quantity demanded falls to D_2 and consumer surplus falls by b to equal just a.

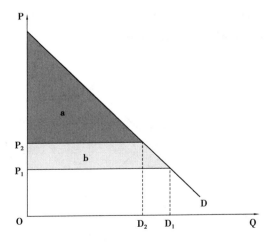

Figure 8.5　Geometry of consumer surplus

Producer surplus is an analogous concept. A producer willing to sell a good for $2 but receiving a price of $5 gains a producer surplus of $3. The same procedure used to derive consumer surplus from the demand curve can be used to derive producer surplus from the supply curve. If P is the price and Q the quantity supplied at that price, then producer surplus is P times Q minus the area under the supply curve up to Q (Figure 8.6). If the price is P_1, the quantity supplied will be S_1, and producer surplus is measured by area c. If the price rises to P_2, the quantity supplied rises to S_2, and producer surplus rises to equal c plus the additional area d.

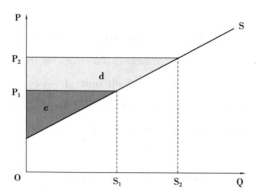

Figure 8.6   Geometry of producer surplus

8.4   Partial equilibrium effect of a tariff

From the point of view of someone shipping goods, a tariff is just like a cost of transportation. If Home imposes a tax of $2 on every bushel of wheat imported, shippers will be unwilling to move the wheat unless the price difference between the two markets is at least $2.

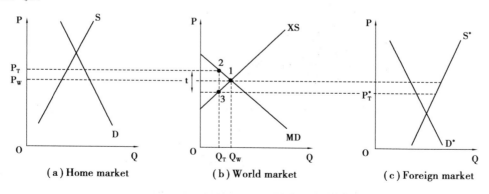

(a) Home market   (b) World market   (c) Foreign market

Figure 8.7   Effects of a tariff

Figure 8.7 illustrates the effects of a specific tariff of t per unit of wheat (shown as t in the figure). In the absence of a tariff, the price of wheat would be equalized at P_W in both Home and Foreign, as seen at point 1 in the middle panel, which illustrates the world market. With the tariff in place, however, shippers are not willing to move wheat from Foreign to Home unless the Home price exceeds the Foreign price by at least t. If no wheat is being shipped, however, there will be an excess demand for wheat in Home and an excess supply in Foreign. Thus, the price in Home will rise and that in Foreign will fall until the price difference is t.

Introducing a tariff, then, drives a wedge between the prices in the two markets. The tariff raises the price in Home to P_T and lowers the price in Foreign to $P_T^* = P_T - t$. In Home, producers supply more at the higher price, while consumers demand less, so that fewer imports are demanded (as you can see in the move from point 1 to point 2 on the MD curve). In Foreign, the lower price leads to reduced supply and increased demand, and thus a smaller export supply (as seen in the move from point 1 to point 3 on the XS curve). Thus, the volume of wheat traded declines from Q_W, the free trade volume, to Q_T, the volume with a tariff. At the trade volume Q_T, Home import demand equals Foreign export supply when $P_T - P_T^* = t$.

8.4.1 The small-country case

The increase in the price in Home, from P_W to P_T, is less than the amount of the tariff, because part of the tariff is reflected in a decline in Foreign's export price and thus is not passed on to Home consumers. This is the normal result of a tariff and of any trade policy that limits imports. The size of this effect on the exporters' price, however, is often very small in practice. When a small country imposes a tariff, its share of the world market for the goods it imports is usually minor to begin with, so that its import reduction has very little effect on the world (foreign export) price.

The effects of a tariff in the "small country" case where a country cannot affect foreign export prices are illustrated in Figure 8.8. In this case, a tariff raises the price of the imported goods in the country imposing the tariff by the full amount of the tariff, from P_W to $P_W + t$. Production of the imported goods rises from S_1 to S_2, while consumption of the goods falls from D_1 to D_2. As a result of the tariff, then, imports fall in the country imposing the tariff.

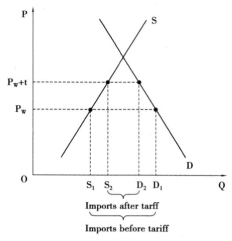

Figure 8.8　Tariff in a small country

8.4.2　The large-country case

Figure 8.9 illustrates the costs and benefits of a tariff for the importing country. The tariff raises the domestic price from P_W to P_T but lowers the foreign export price from P_W to P_T^* (refer back to Figure 8.7). Domestic production rises from S_1 to S_2 while domestic consumption falls from D_1 to D_2. The costs and benefits to different groups can be expressed as sums of the areas of five regions, labeled a, b, c, d, and e.

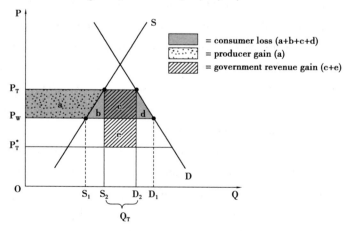

Figure 8.9　Tariff in a large country

Consider first the gain to domestic producers. They receive a higher price and therefore have higher producer surplus. As we see in Figure 8.6, producer surplus is equal to the area below the price but above the supply curve. Before the tariff, producer surplus is equal to the area below P_W but above the supply curve; with the price rising to P_T, this surplus rises by the area labeled a. That is, producers gain from the tariff.

Domestic consumers also face a higher price, which makes them worse off. As we see in Figure 8.5, consumer surplus is equal to the area above the price but below the demand curve. Since the price consumers face rises from P_W to P_T, the consumer surplus falls by the area indicated by a+b+c+d. So, consumers are hurt by the tariff.

There is a third player here as well: the government. The government gains by collecting tariff revenue. This is equal to the tariff rate t times the volume of imports $Q_T = D_2 - S_2$. Since $t = P_T - P_T^*$, the government's revenue is equal to the sum of the two areas c and e.

Since these gains and losses accrue to different people, the overall cost-benefit evaluation of a tariff depends on how much we value a dollar's worth of benefit to each group. If, for example, the producer gain accrues mostly to wealthy owners of resources, while consumers are poorer than average, the tariff will be viewed differently than if the good is a luxury bought by the affluent but produced by low-wage workers. Further ambiguity is introduced by the role of the government: Will it use its revenue to finance vitally needed public services or waste that revenue on $1,000 toilet seats? Despite these problems, it is common for analysts of trade policy to attempt to compute the net effect of a tariff on national welfare by assuming that at the margin, a dollar's worth of gain or loss to each group is of the same social worth.

Let's look, then, at the net effect of a tariff on welfare. The net cost of a tariff is:

consumer loss − producer gain = government revenue,

or, replacing these concepts by the areas in Figure 8.9,

$$(a + b + c + d) - a - (c + e) = b + d - e.$$

That is, there are two "triangles" whose area measures loss to the nation as a whole and a "rectangle" whose area measures an offsetting gain. A useful way to interpret these gains and losses is the following: The triangles represent the efficiency loss that arises because a tariff distorts incentives to consume and produce, while the rectangle represents the terms of trade gain that arise because a tariff lowers foreign export prices.

⟩ 8.4.3　The net welfare effects of a tariff

The gain depends on the ability of the tariff-imposing country to drive down foreign export prices. If the country cannot affect world prices (the "small country" case illustrated in Figure 8.8), region e, which represents the terms of trade gain, disappears, and it is clear that the tariff reduces welfare. A tariff distorts the incentives of both producers and consumers by inducing them to act as if imports were more expensive than they actually are. The cost of an additional unit of consumption to the economy is the price of an additional unit of imports, yet because the tariff raises the domestic price above the world price, consumers reduce their consumption to the point at which that marginal unit yields them welfare equal to the tariff-inclusive domestic price. This means that the value of an additional unit of production to the economy is the price of the unit of imports it saves, yet domestic producers expand production to the point at which the marginal cost is equal to the tariff-inclusive price. Thus the economy produces at home additional units of the goods that it could purchase more cheaply abroad.

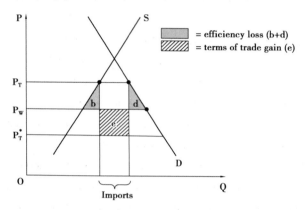

Figure 8.10　Net welfare effects of a tariff

The net welfare effects of a tariff are summarized in Figure 8.10. The negative effects consist of the two triangles b and d. The first triangle is the production distortion loss resulting from the fact that the tariff leads domestic producers to produce too much of this good. The second triangle is the domestic consumption distortion loss resulting from the fact that a tariff leads consumers to consume too little of the goods. Against these losses must be set the terms of trade gain measured by the rectangle e, which results from the decline in the foreign export price caused by a tariff. In the important case of a small country that cannot significantly affect foreign prices, this last effect drops out, and thus the costs of a tariff unambiguously exceed its benefits.

8.5　The optimum tariff

In this section, we examine how a large nation can increase its welfare over the free trade position by imposing a so-called optimum tariff. However, since the gains of the nation come at the expense of other nations, the latter are likely to retaliate, and in the end, all nations usually lose.

When a large nation imposes a tariff, the volume of trade declines but the nation's terms of trade improve. The decline in the volume of trade, by itself, tends to reduce the nation's welfare. On the contrary, the improvement in its terms of trade, by itself, tends to increase the nation's welfare.

The optimum tariff is the rate of tariff that maximizes the net benefit resulting from the improvement in the nation's terms of trade against the negative effect resulting from reduction in the volume of trade. That is, starting from the free trade position, as the nation increases its tariff rate, its welfare increases up to a maximum (the optimum tariff) and then declines as the tariff rate is raised past the optimum. Eventually, the nation is pushed back toward the autarky point with a prohibitive tariff.

However, as the terms of trade of the nation imposing the tariff improve, those of the trade partner deteriorate, since they are the inverse, or reciprocal, of the terms of trade of the tariff-imposing nation. Facing both a lower volume of trade and deteriorating terms of trade, the trade partner's welfare definitely declines. As a result, the trade partner is likely to retaliate and impose an optimum tariff of its own. While recapturing most of its losses with the improvement in its terms of trade, retaliation by the trade partner will definitely reduce the volume of trade still further. The first nation may then itself retaliate. If the process continues, all nations usually end up losing all or most of the gains from trade.

Even when the trade partner does not retaliate when one nation imposes the optimum tariff, the gains of the tariff-imposing nation are less than the losses of the trade partner, so that the world as a whole is worse off than under free trade. It is in this sense that free trade maximizes world welfare.

Figure 8.11 repeats free trade offer curves 1 and 2, defining equilibrium point E at $P_W = 1$. Suppose that with the optimum tariff, Nation 2's offer curve rotates to 2^*. If Nation 1 does not retaliate, the intersection of offer curve 2^* and offer curve 1 defines the new equilibrium point E^*, at which Nation 2 exchanges 25Y for 40X so that $P_X/P_Y = P_W = 0.625$ on the world market and for Nation 2 as a whole. As a result, Nation 1's (the rest of the world's) terms of trade deteriorate from $P_X/P_Y = P_W = 1$ to $P_X/P_Y = P_W^* = 0.625$, and Nation 2's terms of trade improve to $P_Y/P_X = 1/P_Y = 1/0.625 = 1.6$.

With the tariff associated with offer curve 2, not only does the improvement in Nation 2's welfare resulting from its improved terms of trade exceed the reduction in welfare due to the decline in volume of trade, but it represents the highest welfare that Nation 2 can achieve with a tariff (and exceeds its free trade welfare).

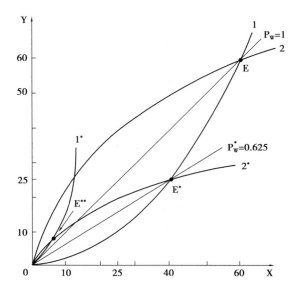

Figure 8.11 Optimum tariff and retaliation

However, with deteriorated terms of trade and a smaller volume of trade, Nation 1 is definitely worse off than under free trade. As a result, Nation 1 is likely to retaliate and impose an optimum tariff of its own, shown by offer curve 1^*. With offer curves 1^* and 2^* equilibrium moves to point E^{**}. Now Nation 1's terms of trade are higher and Nation 2's are lower than under free trade, but the volume of trade is much smaller. At this point, Nation 2 is itself likely to retaliate, and in the end, both nations may end up at the origin of Figure 8.11, representing the autarky position for both nations. By so doing, all of the gains from trade are lost.

——— *China-perspective case study* ———

China to exempt import tariffs for exhibits at services trade fair

BEIJING, September 5 (Xinhua)—Chinese authorities issued a circular on September 4, announcing the exemption of import tariffs on certain imported exhibits at the 2020 China International Fair for Trade in Services.

During the trade fair, exhibits within the sales quota of \$20,000 will be exempt from import duties, import value-added tax, and consumption tax, said the circular, jointly issued by the Ministry of Finance, the General Administration of Customs, and the State Taxation Administration.

The exemption, approved by the State Council, excludes prohibited imports, endangered animals, plants and their byproducts, as well as cigarettes, wines, and automobiles.

The sales quota of the favorable tax policy on seven items will be subject to further notice, according to the circular.

Exhibits exceeding the sales quota, or unsold exhibits that will not be returned after the trade fair, will not enjoy the preferential policy and will be subject to taxation, according to the regulations.

The 2020 China International Fair for Trade in Services, held in Beijing from September 4 to 9, will see over 2,000 offline exhibitors and more than 4,000 online companies showcase their products and services.

Key concepts

consumer surplus	rent or producer surplus
import tariff	export tariff
protection cost or deadweight loss of a tariff	ad valorem tariff
nominal tariff	specific tariff
rate of effective protection	compound tariff
domestic value added	consumption effect of a tariff
production effect of a tarifft	trade effect of a tariff

Summary

1. While it is generally accepted that free trade maximizes world output and benefits all nations, most nations impose some restrictions on the free flow of international trade.

2. An import tariff is a tax or duty levied on imported commodities. This is the most common form of tariff.

3. According to differential treatment, formal import taxes can be divided into the following types: ordinary tariffs, MFN tariffs, GSP tariffs, and preferential tariffs.

4. In addition to the formal import duties on imported goods, a country often imposes import duties according to some special purpose, namely import surtaxes.

5. An export tariff is a tax on exported commodities, which prohibited by the US Constitution, but occasionally practiced in developing countries to generate government

revenue.

6. Ad valorem tariff is a fixed percentage on the value of the traded commodity.

7. Specific tariff is a fixed sum per physical unit of a traded commodity.

8. A compound tariff is a combination of an ad valorem and specific tariff.

9. Consumer surplus is the difference between what consumers would be willing to pay and what they actually pay. Imposition of a tariff reduces consumer surplus.

10. Increase in producer surplus, or rent, is the payment that need not be made in the long run to induce domestic producers to supply additional goods with the tariff. Also called subsidy effect of tariff.

11. Tariff redistributes income from domestic consumers (who pay higher price for the commodity) to domestic producers (who receive the higher price), and from nation's abundant factor (producing exports) to the scarce factor (producing imports).

Exercises

1. Which of the following statements is incorrect?

   A. An ad valorem tariff is expressed as a percentage of the value of the traded commodity.

   B. a specific tariff is expressed as a fixed sum of the value of the traded commodity.

   C. export tariffs are prohibited by the US Constitution.

   D. The United States uses exclusively the specific tariff.

2. If a small nation increases the tariff on its import commodity, its _____.

   A. consumption of the commodity increases

   B. production of the commodity decreases

   C. imports of the commodity increase

   D. none of the above

3. The increase in producer surplus when a small nation imposes a tariff is measured by the area _____.

   A. to the left of the supply curve between the commodity price with and without the tariff

   B. under the supply curve between the quantity produced with and without the tariff

   C. under the demand curve between the commodity price with and without the tariff

   D. none of the above

4. The imposition of an import tariff by a nation results in:

   A. an increase in relative price of the nation's import commodity

   B. an increase in the nation's production of its importable commodity

C. reduces the real return of the nation's abundant factor

D. all of the above

5. What is a tariff? What is the role of tariffs?

6. Please briefly describe the main types and functions of import tariffs.

7. When small trading countries impose tariffs on imported products, what changes will happen to their economic welfare? If it is a big trading country, what is the situation?

Chapter

Non-tariff Trade Barriers

> **Learning goals**
>
> After learning this chapter, you should be able to:
>
> ✓ know the meaning and effect of quotas and other non-tariff trade barriers.
>
> ✓ describe the effect of dumping and export subsidies.
>
> ✓ explain the political economy of protectionism and strategic and industrial policies.

Tariffs are the simplest trade policy tools, but in the modern world, most government intervention in international trade takes other forms, such as import quotas, export subsidies, voluntary export restraints, and local content requirements.

9.1 Import quotas

An import quota is a direct restriction on the quantity of some good that may be imported. The restriction is usually enforced by issuing licenses to some group of individuals or firms. For example, the United States has a quota on imports of foreign cheese. The only firms allowed to import cheese are certain trading companies, each of which is allocated the right to import a maximum number of pounds of cheese each year; the size of each firm's quota is based on the amount of cheese it imported in the past. In some important cases, notably sugar and apparel, the right to sell in the United States is given directly to the governments of exporting countries.

It is important to avoid having the misconception that import quotas somehow limit imports without raising domestic prices. The truth is that an import quota always raises the domestic price of the imported goods. When imports are limited, the immediate result is that at the initial price, the demand for the goods exceeds domestic supply plus imports. This causes the price to be bid up until the market clears. In the end, an import quota will raise domestic prices by the same amount as a tariff that limits imports to the same level.

The difference between a quota and a tariff is that with a quota, the government receives no revenue. When a quota instead of a tariff is used to restrict imports, the sum of money that would have appeared with a tariff as government revenue is collected by whoever receives the import licenses. License holders are thus able to buy imports and resell them at a higher price in the domestic market. The profits received by the holders of import licenses are known as quota rents. In assessing the costs and benefits of an import quota, it is crucial to determine who gets the rents. When the rights to sell in the domestic market are assigned to governments of exporting countries, as is often the case, the transfer of rents abroad makes the costs of a quota substantially higher than the equivalent tariff.

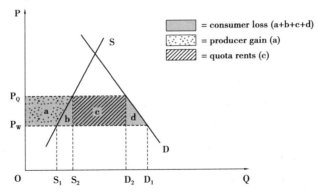

Figure 9.1   Effects of the import quota

Figure 9.1 shows those forecasted effects of the import quota. The quota would restrict imports, and the price in the nation would be above the price in the outside world. The figure is drawn with the assumption that the nation is "small" in the world market. That is, removing the quota would not have a significant effect on the world price. The welfare effects of the import quota are indicated by the areas a, b, c, and d. Consumers lose the surplus (a+b+c+d). Part of this consumer loss represents a transfer to the producers, who gain the producer surplus (a). Part of the loss represents the production distortion b and the consumption distortion d. The rents to the foreign governments that receive import rights are summarized by area c. The net loss to the nation is equal to the distortions (b+d) plus the quota rents (c). Notice that much of this net loss comes from the fact that foreigners get the import rights.

9.2 Export subsidies

An export subsidy is a payment to a firm or individual that ships a good abroad. Like a tariff, an export subsidy can be either specific (a fixed sum per unit) or ad valorem (a proportion of the value exported). When the government offers an export subsidy, shippers will export the goods up to the point at which the domestic price exceeds the foreign price by the amount of the subsidy.

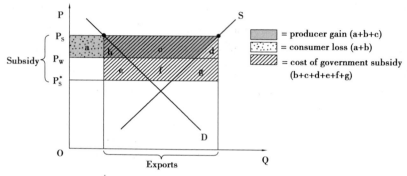

Figure 9.2　Effects of an export subsidy

The effects of an export subsidy on prices are exactly the reverse of those of a tariff (see Figure 9.2). The price in the exporting country rises from P_W to P_S, but because the price in the importing country falls from P_W to P_S^*, the price increase is less than the subsidy.

In the exporting country, consumers are hurt, producers gain, and the government loses because it must expend money on the subsidy. The consumer loss is the area a+b; the producer gain is the area a+b+c; the government subsidy (the amount of exports times the amount of the subsidy) is the area b+c+d+e+f+g. The net welfare loss is therefore the sum of the areas b+d+e+f+g. Of these, b and d represent consumption and production distortion losses of the same kind that a tariff produces. In addition, and in contrast to a tariff, the export subsidy worsens the terms of trade because it lowers the price of the export in the foreign market from to P_W to P_S^*. This leads to the additional terms of trade loss e+f+g, which is equal to $(P_W - P_S^*)$ times the quantity exported with the subsidy. So an export subsidy unambiguously leads to costs that exceed its benefits.

Case 9.1　China says US EV subsidy provisions "suspected of violating WTO rules"

BEIJING, September 22 (Xinhua)—The electric vehicle (EV) subsidy provisions in the US Inflation Reduction Act are discriminatory and suspected of violating the World Trade Organization (WTO) rules, the Chinese Ministry of Commerce (MOC) said Thursday.

The relevant provisions, granting tax credits for EVs on the condition of final assembly in North America, discriminate against other similar imported products and are suspected of violating the WTO principles of the MFN treatment and national treatment, MOC spokesperson Shu Jueting told a press conference.

Shu said China is concerned about the US move, and also takes note that some other WTO members have also expressed serious concerns over it.

As a WTO member, the United States should implement relevant investment policies in a manner consistent with the WTO rules and safeguard a trade order that upholds fair competition, Shu said.

China will continue to follow and evaluate the subsequent implementation of the act and take measures to safeguard the country's legitimate rights and interests when necessary, the MOC spokesperson added.

9.3   Voluntary export restraints

A variant on the import quota is the voluntary export restraint (VER), also known as a voluntary restraint agreement (VRA). These refer to the case where an importing country induces another nation to reduce its exports of a commodity "voluntarily", under the threat of higher all-around trade restrictions, when these exports threaten an entire domestic industry. A VER is a quota on trade imposed from the exporting country's side instead of the importers'. The most famous example is the limitation on auto exports to the United States enforced by Japan after 1981.

Voluntary export restraints are generally imposed at the request of the importer and are agreed to by the exporter to forestall other trade restrictions. However, a voluntary export restraint is exactly like an import quota where the licenses are assigned to foreign governments and is therefore very costly to the importing country.

When voluntary export restraints are successful, they have all the economic effects of equivalent import quotas, except that they are administered by the exporting country, and so the revenue effect or rents are captured by foreign exporters.

A VER is always more costly to the importing country than a tariff that limits imports by the same amount. The difference is that what would have been revenue under a tariff becomes rents earned by foreigners under the VER, so that the VER clearly produces a loss for the importing country.

Voluntary export restraints are less effective in limiting imports than import quotas because the exporting nations agree only reluctantly to curb their exports. Foreign exporters also tend to fill their quota with higher-quality and higher-priced units of the product over time. Furthermore, as a rule, only major supplier countries are involved, leaving the door open for other nations to replace part of the exports of the major suppliers and also for transshipments through third countries.

9.4　Dumping and anti-dumping

Trade barriers may also result from dumping. Dumping is the export of a commodity at below cost or at least the sale of a commodity at a lower price abroad than domestically. Dumping is classified as persistent, predatory, and sporadic.

Persistent dumping, or international price discrimination, is the continuous tendency of a domestic monopolist to maximize total profits by selling the commodity at a higher price in the domestic market (which is insulated by transport costs and trade barriers) than internationally (where it must meet the competition of foreign producers).

Predatory dumping is the temporary sale of a commodity at below cost or at a lower price abroad in order to drive foreign producers out of business, after which prices are raised to take advantage of the newly acquired monopoly power abroad.

Sporadic dumping is the occasional sale of a commodity at below cost or at a lower price abroad than domestically in order to unload an unforeseen and temporary surplus of the commodity without having to reduce domestic prices.

Trade restrictions to counteract predatory dumping are justified and allowed to protect domestic industries from unfair competition from abroad. These restrictions usually take the form of anti-dumping duties to offset price differentials, or the threat to impose such duties. However, it is often difficult to determine the type of dumping, and domestic producers invariably demand protection against any form of dumping. By so doing, they discourage imports and increase their own production and profits (rents). In some cases of persistent and sporadic dumping, the benefit to consumers from low prices may actually exceed the possible production losses of domestic producers.

In practice, those anti-dumping laws can then be used to erect barriers to trade by discriminating against exporters in a market. In the United States and a number of other countries, dumping is regarded as an unfair competitive practice. US firms that claim to have been injured by foreign firms that dump their products in the domestic market at low prices can appeal, through a quasi-judicial procedure, to the Department of Commerce for relief. If their complaint is ruled valid, an "anti-dumping duty" is imposed, equal to the calculated difference between the actual and the "fair" price of imports.

The legal definition of dumping deviates substantially from the economic definition. Since it is often difficult to prove that foreign firms charge higher prices to domestic than to export customers, the United States and other nations instead often try to calculate a supposedly fair price based on estimates of foreign production costs. This "fair price" rule can interfere with perfectly normal business practices: A firm may well be willing to sell a product for a loss while it is lowering its costs through experience or breaking into a new market.

Formal complaints about dumping have been filed with growing frequency since about 1970. China has attracted a particularly large number of anti-dumping suits, for two reasons. One is that China's rapid export growth has raised many complaints. The other is the fact that the United States officially considers China still a non-market economy.

Case 9.2   Dumping in the GATT (WTO)

What is dumping?

Dumping is, in general, a situation of international price discrimination, where the price of a product when sold in the importing country is less than the price of that product in the market of the exporting country. Thus, in the simplest of cases, one identifies dumping simply by comparing prices in two markets. However, the situation is rarely, if ever, that simple, and in most cases it is necessary to undertake a series of complex analytical steps in order to determine the appropriate price in the market of the exporting country (known as the "normal value") and the appropriate price in the market of the importing country (known as the "export price") so as to be able to undertake an appropriate comparison.

Article VI of GATT and the Anti-Dumping Agreement

The GATT 1994 sets forth a number of basic principles applicable in trade between members of the WTO, including the most-favored-nation principle. It also requires that imported products not be subject to internal taxes or other changes in excess of those imposed on domestic goods, and that imported goods in other respects be accorded treatment no less favorable than domestic goods under domestic laws and regulations, and establishes rules regarding quantitative restrictions, fees and formalities related to importation, and customs valuation. Members of the WTO also agreed to the establishment of schedules of bound tariff rates. Article Ⅵ of GATT 1994, on the contrary, explicitly authorizes the imposition of a specific anti-dumping duty on imports from a particular source, in excess of bound rates, in cases where dumping causes or threatens injury to a domestic industry, or materially retards the establishment of a domestic industry.

The Agreement on Implementation of Article Ⅵ of GATT 1994, commonly known as the Anti-Dumping Agreement, provides further elaboration on the basic principles set forth in Article Ⅵ itself, to govern the investigation, determination, and application, of anti-dumping duties.

9.5 Local content requirements

A local content requirement is a regulation that requires some specified fraction of a final good to be produced domestically. In some cases, this fraction is specified in physical units, like the US oil import quota in the 1960s. In other cases, the requirement is stated in value terms, by requiring that some minimum share of the price of a good represent domestic value added. Local content laws have been widely used by developing countries trying to shift their manufacturing base from assembly back into intermediate goods.

From the point of view of the domestic producers of parts, a local content regulation provides protection in the same way an import quota does. From the point of view of the firms that must buy locally, however, the effects are somewhat different. Local content does not place a strict limit on imports. Instead, it allows firms to import more, provided that they also buy more domestically. This means that the effective price of inputs to the firm is an average of the price of imported and domestically produced inputs.

Consider, for instance, the earlier automobile example in which the cost of imported parts is $6,000. Suppose that purchasing the same parts domestically would cost $10,000 but that assembly firms are required to use 50 percent domestic parts. Then they will face an average cost of the parts, which will be reflected in the final price of the car.

The important point is that a local content requirement does not produce either government revenue or quota rents. Instead, the difference between the prices of imports and domestic goods in effect gets averaged in the final price and is passed on to consumers.

9.6 Technical, administrative, and other regulations

International trade is also hampered by numerous technical, administrative, and other regulations. These include safety regulations for automobiles and electrical equipment, health regulations for the hygienic production and packaging of imported food products, and labeling requirements showing origin and contents. Many of these regulations serve legitimate purposes, but some (such as the French ban on Scotch advertisements and the British restriction on the showing of foreign films on British television) are only thinly veiled disguises for restricting imports.

Other trade restrictions have resulted from laws requiring governments to buy from domestic suppliers (the so-called government procurement policies). For example, under the Buy American Act passed in 1933, the US government agencies gave a price advantage of up to 12 percent (50 percent for defense contracts) to domestic suppliers. As part of the Tokyo Round of trade liberalization, the United States and other nations agreed on a government procurement code to bring these practices and regulations into the open and give foreign suppliers a fair chance.

International commodity agreements and multiple exchange rates also restrict trade. However, as the former ones are of primary concern to developing nations and the latter ones relate to international finance.

Case 9.3 Chinese political advisors discuss people-to-people connectivity along the Belt and Road

BEIJING, November 25 (Xinhua)—Chinese political advisors on Friday discussed measures to strengthen people-to-people connectivity on the Belt and Road at a consultation session in Beijing.

The biweekly session was held by the National Committee of the Chinese People's Political Consultative Conference (CPPCC), China's top political advisory body. Wang Yang, chairman of the CPPCC National Committee, presided over the session.

To lay a solid social foundation for high-quality Belt and Road development, cooperation in all fields should attach importance to enhancing friendships between countries and strengthening people-to-people bonds, and a problem-oriented approach should be adopted for work in all areas, Wang said.

Ten political advisors made proposals at the session, and 30 political advisors voiced their opinions via a CPPCC working platform.

Cooperation between China and the Belt and Road countries has brought tangible benefits to countries along the Belt and Road and built a sound foundation for people-to-people connectivity, the political advisors said. The COVID-19 pandemic and the complex external environment pose new challenges to people-to-people exchanges between the countries, they said.

They called for the promotion of policy coordination, infrastructure connectivity, unimpeded trade and financial integration. This promotion should be based on the principles of extensive consultation, joint contributions, shared benefits, and integrating economic and social benefits, in order to focus cooperation on improving people's livelihoods and increasing solidarity.

9.7　The infant industry argument

According to the infant industry argument, developing countries have a potential comparative advantage in manufacturing, but new manufacturing industries in developing countries cannot initially compete with well-established manufacturing in developed countries. To allow manufacturing to get a toehold, then, governments should temporarily support new industries until they have grown strong enough to meet international competition. Thus it makes sense, according to this argument, to use tariffs or import quotas as temporary measures to get industrialization started. It is a historical fact that some of the world's largest market economies began their industrialization behind trade barriers: The United States had high tariff rates on manufacturing in the 19th century, while Japan had extensive import controls until the 1970s.

The infant industry argument seems highly plausible. Yet economists have pointed out many pitfalls in the argument, suggesting that it must be used cautiously.

First, it is not always a good idea to try to move today into the industries that will have a comparative advantage in the future. Suppose that a country that is currently L-abundant is in the process of accumulating capital. When it accumulates enough capital, it will have a comparative advantage in K-intensive industries. However, that does not mean it should try to develop these industries immediately. In the 1980s, for example, South Korea became an exporter of automobiles; it would probably not have been a good idea for South Korea to have tried to develop its auto-industry in the 1960s, when capital and skilled labor were still very scarce.

Second, protecting manufacturing does no good unless the protection itself helps make industry competitive. For example, Pakistan and India have protected their manufacturing sectors for decades and have recently begun to develop significant exports of manufactured goods. The goods they export, however, are light manufactures like textiles, not the heavy manufactures that they protected; a good case can be made that they would have developed their manufactured exports even if they had never protected manufacturing. Some economists have warned of the case of the "pseudo infant industry", in which an industry is initially protected, then becomes competitive for reasons that have nothing to do with the protection. In this case, infant industry protection ends up looking like a success, but may actually have been a net cost to the economy.

More generally, the fact that it is costly and time-consuming to build up an industry is not an argument for government intervention unless there is some domestic market failure.

The infant-industry argument for protection is correct but requires several important qualifications which, together, take away most of its significance. First of all, it is clear that such an argument is more justified for developing nations (where capital markets may not function properly) than for industrial nations. Second, it may be difficult to identify which industry or potential industry qualifies for this treatment, and experience has shown that protection, once given, is difficult to remove. Third, and most importantly, what trade protection (say, in the form of an import tariff) can do, an equivalent production subsidy to the infant industry can do better. The reason is that a purely domestic distortion such as this should be overcome with a purely domestic policy (such as a direct production subsidy to the infant industry) rather than with a trade policy that also distorts relative prices and domestic consumption. A production subsidy is also a more direct form of aid and is easier to remove than an import tariff. One practical difficulty is that a subsidy requires revenues, rather than generating them as, for example, an import tariff does. But the principle remains.

Case 9.4　China expands pilot zones for promoting cross-border e-commerce

BEIJING, November 26 (Xinhua)—China has approved the establishment of comprehensive pilot zones for cross-border e-commerce in another 33 cities and regions, in its latest bid to boost foreign trade growth.

This is the seventh batch of such pilot areas, which lifted the tally to 165 across the country.

Many of the latest batch of comprehensive pilot zones for cross-border e-commerce are located in central and western China as well as the country's border areas.

The pilot zones are expected to help facilitate the transformation and upgrading of traditional industries, and optimize and upgrade foreign trade.

China's cross-border e-commerce has been growing fast in recent years. Its trade volume has ballooned by nearly 10 times in the past five years, reaching 1. 92 trillion yuan (about $269.14 billion) in 2021. In the first half of 2022, the market registered a 28.6-percent year-on-year growth in trade volume.

China-perspective case study

China launches anti-dumping probe into EU, US and Singapore rubber imports

China's Ministry of Commerce on Wednesday announced the launch of anti-dumping investigations into imported hydrogenated butyl rubber from the United Sates, the European Union and Singapore.

The request for anti-dumping measures was formally submitted to the ministry by Zhejiang Cenway New Materials Co., Ltd. and Panjin Heyun New Materials Co., Ltd. on August 14, 2017, according to a statement posted on the ministry's website.

The two companies said that producers from the three regions have been dumping butyl rubber through unfair pricing, hurting margins and sales in China's domestic industry.

The ministry will hold a year-long investigation, beginning from Wednesday. The probe will look at products imported between April 1, 2016, and March 31, 2017.

The move comes amid heightened trade tensions between China and the US over products including steel and aluminum foil. US President Donald Trump has vowed to use trade policies to more aggressively protect American economic interests.

Butyl rubber has high impermeability to gases and high resistance to heat, making it suitable for a variety of rubber products, such as tire inner tubes and protective clothing.

US giant ExxonMobil, which was formerly headed by current US Secretary of State Rex Tillerson, is the world's largest producer of butyl rubber.

Zhejiang Cenway earlier this year (2017) announced expansion plans to boost capacity by 150 kilotons per annum by 2018 as part of a 200-million-euro (239 million US dollars) project, according to the *European Rubber Journal*.

Key concepts

quota

new protectionism

voluntary export restraints

technical, administrative and other regulations

persistent dumping

sporadic dumping

export-import bank

counter-vailing duties

infant-industry argument

industrial policy

non-tariff trade barrier

most-favored-nation principle

bilateral Trade

dumping

predatory dumping

export subsidies

foreign sales corporations

scientific tariff

strategic trade policy

Summary

1. As tariffs were negotiated down after the Second World War, the importance of non-tariff barriers was greatly increased.

2. A quota is a direct quantitative restriction on the amount of a commodity allowed to be imported or exported.

3. Import quotas are used to protect domestic industry and agriculture, and/or for balance of payments reasons.

4. Import quota involves distribution of import licenses, while tariff does not.

5. Since import quotas are more restrictive than equivalent import tariffs, society should resist domestic producers' efforts to use quotas instead of tariffs.

6. With voluntary export restraints, an importing country induces another nation to reduce its exports voluntarily, under threat of higher trade restrictions.

7. Health and safety regulations may serve as barriers to international trade by raising the costs of imported products.

8. Government purchasing restrictions may be biased against foreign goods.

9. Rebates for indirect taxes may be given to exporters and imposed on importers of a commodity.

10. Persistent dumping is the continuous tendency of a domestic monopolist to maximize total profits by selling the commodity at a higher price in the domestic market.

11. Predatory dumping is the temporary sale of a commodity at below cost or a lower price

abroad to drive foreign producers out of business.

12. Sporadic dumping is the occasional sale of a commodity at a below cost or lower price abroad to unload surplus of the commodity without reducing domestic prices.

13. Export subsidies are the granting of tax relief to exporters or subsidized loans to foreign buyers to stimulate a nation's exports. 14. Export subsidies are illegal by international agreement, but often used in disguised form.

14. Temporary trade protection is justified to establish and protect a domestic industry during its "infancy" until it can meet foreign competition, achieve economies of scale, and reflect the nation's comparative advantage.

Exercises

1. An import quota _____.

    A. increases the domestic price of the imported commodity

    B. reduces domestic consumption

    C. increases domestic production

    D. all of the above

2. An increase in the demand of the imported commodity subject to a given import quota

    _____.

    A. reduces the domestic quantity demanded of the commodity

    B. increases the domestic production of the commodity

    C. reduces the domestic price of the commodity

    D. reduces the producers' surplus

3. The temporary sale of a commodity at a below cost or lower price abroad in order to drive foreign producers out of business is called _____.

    A. predatory dumping   B. sporadic dumping

    C. continuous dumping   D. voluntary export restraints

4. A fallacious argument for protection is _____.

    A. the infant industry argument

    B. protection for national defense

    C. the scientific tariff

    D. to correct domestic distortions

5. Industrial policy refers to _____.

    A. an activist policy by the government of an industrial country to stimulate the development of an industry

B. the granting of a subsidy to a domestic industry to stimulate the development of an industry

C. the granting of a subsidy to a domestic industry to counter a foreign subsidy

D. all of the above

6. What are non-tariff barriers? Compared with tariff barriers, what are their characteristics?

7. Briefly analyze the economic effects of import quotas.

8. Briefly analyze the economic effects of export subsidies.

Chapter 10 International Integration

This chapter will help you to understand an important phenomenon of the world economic development, that is, the trade restrictions adopted by a certain country only apply to a certain country, while there are no such restrictions for other countries. Such discriminatory trade restrictions mainly resulted in the rapid development of regional economic integration after the Second World War. Another characteristic of regional economic integration is the complete free trade within the region. The practice of regional economic integration, which was free in the region and protected outside the region, had a significant impact on the international economy and trade at that time. Regional economic integration and its impact on the world economy are the key issues discussed in this chapter.

10.1 Main forms of regional economic integration

Regional economic integration is a process in which two or more countries or regions agree to eliminate economic barriers, with the end goal of enhancing productivity and achieving greater economic interdependence. At the initial stage, members in the region adopt discriminatory policies to reduce or eliminate trade barriers, while non-members outside the region continue to retain trade barriers. With the gradual improvement of the degree of integration, the members will, under the coordination of a supranational common institution composed of members authorized by them, work out unified policies to remove obstacles to the development of economic and trade among members, achieve common development in the region, optimize the allocation of resources, promote economic and trade development, and finally form a highly coordinated whole of economy and trade.

The forms of regional economic integration are divided into different types according to different ways.

10.1.1　Divided by the dynamic development process of regional economic integration from low level to high level

(1) Preferential trade arrangement

This is the lowest and loosest form of organization in regional economic integration. At this stage, members reached an agreement to give each other special tariff or non-tariff preferences for all or part of the goods. However, for non-members, their own foreign trade barriers are still maintained. For example, in the early 20th century, Britain and its former colonial countries implemented the Commonwealth preferential tax.

(2) Free trade area

In this stage of regional economic integration, free trade agreements are usually signed when members ask. Eliminate tariff and non-tariff barriers in trade between members to achieve free circulation of goods, but at this stage, tariff and non-tariff barriers for non-members are also retained. For example, the European Free Trade Area established in 1960 and the North American Free Trade Area established in 1994 are examples of regional economic integration at this stage. Economists generally believe that the establishment of free trade areas will produce trade deflection effects. That is, the products of non-members will be imported by members with lower tariffs, and then transferred to the markets of members with higher tariffs. This leads to unfair distribution of tariff revenue. In order to solve this problem, they generally use the certificate of origin for management and strengthen customs supervision. But even so, it is still unable to completely eliminate the occurrence of trade deflection effect.

(3) Customs union

At this stage of regional economic integration, members eliminated tariff and non-tariff barriers to each other, realized the free flow of goods, and established common tariff and non-tariff barriers to non-members. This is the biggest difference between a customs union and a free trade area. Due to the establishment of common foreign trade barriers, there is no trade deflection effect in the customs union stage. The European Economic Community, which was formally established in 1958, is an example of a customs union.

(4) Common market

From the customs union to the common market, the biggest difference between the two is in hand. In addition to implementing the customs union system and realizing the complete free flow of commodities among members, the latter also realizes the free flow of tea production. The European Common Market approached this stage in the 1970s.

(5) Economic union

At this stage of regional economic integration, in addition to meeting the requirements of the common market, that is, the free flow of goods and factors of production among members, some unified foreign economic and social policies have been formulated and implemented, and differences in economic and trade policies have been gradually abolished, so that the scope of integration has expanded from production and exchange of goods to distribution and other fields. After its completion in 1993, the EU has basically entered this stage.

(6) Complete economic integration

This is the highest level of economic integration and the ultimate goal of the EU. At this stage, all countries in the region have fully coordinated their economic, fiscal, financial and trade policies and implemented a unified economic policy.

10.1.2 Divided by the economic development level of countries and regions composed of regional economic integration

(1) Horizontal economic integration

Horizontal economic integration refers to an integrated organization composed of countries and regions with similar economic development levels. This is the main form of early regional economic integration, such as the European Community, the US-Canada Free Trade Area, etc.

(2) Vertical economic integration

Vertical economic integration refers to an integration organization composed of countries and regions with large differences in economic development levels and stages. For a long time, this form of regional economic integration organization is difficult to establish. It was not until the early 1990s that changes began to take place. In 1994, the US-Canada Free Trade Area absorbed Mexico, a new member of the developing country, and formally established the North American Free Trade Area, turning it from a horizontal economic integration organization to a vertical economic integration organization. The development of vertical economic integration has become more obvious with the completion of EU's eastern expansion. In April 2003, the 15 members of the EU signed the People's League Treaty with 10 candidate countries, and formally accepted the 10 newly added members in 2004. The addition of these 10 new members has transformed the EU from a horizontal economic integration organization to a vertical economic integration organization.

10.2   The development of regional economic integration

10.2.1   The development of regional economic integration in different stages after the Second World War

Regional economic integration is not the product of modern economy. As early as the 18th and 19th centuries, Europe had already had a tax union. At that time, Austria and its neighboring countries established five customs unions, and Sweden and Norway also established a customs union. At the beginning of the 20th century, Belgium and Luxembourg established a customs union. These are the dimensions of regional economic integration organizations.

It should be pointed out that the rapid development of regional economic integration, which has become an important force influencing the development of the world economy, emerged after the Second World War. The development of regional economic integration after the Second World War mainly went through three stages.

The first stage is the high-speed development period from the early stage after the Second World War to the 1960s. During this period, a number of regional economic integration organizations emerged. In January 1949, the Soviet Union and Eastern European countries established the Council of Economic Exchanges; In April 1951, France, the Federal Republic of Germany, Italy, Belgium, the Netherlands and Luxembourg signed the Treaty of the European Coal and Steel Community and decided to establish a coal and steel community. In March 1957, the above-mentioned six countries signed the Treaty of Rome in Rome, and formally entered into force on January 1, 1958. In January 1960, Britain, Sweden, Denmark and other countries signed the Convention on the Establishment of the European Free Trade Association, establishing the European Free Trade Area. Since the

1960s, developing countries have also established more than 20 regional economic integration organizations. For example, the Association of Southeast Asian Nations in Asia, the West African Community in Africa, the Gulf Cooperation Council in the Arab world, and the Central American Common Market in Latin America.

The second stage is the stagnation period from the mid-1970s to the mid-1980s. During this period, due to the deterioration of the world economy, the process of regional economic integration was also properly affected. The integration
within the European Community has developed slowly, and the integration of developing countries has suffered setbacks. Some previously established integration organizations have also interrupted their activities or disintegrated.

The third stage is a period of rapid growth since the 1980s. At this stage, more than 30 regional economic integration organizations were established, and about 130 countries and regions participated in these different regional economic integration organizations. The more prominent ones are: In the early 1990s, the European Community transited to the EU, and its members continued to increase. In January 1988, the United States and Canada signed the US-Canada Free Trade Agreement. After that, the United States, Canada and Mexico established the North American Free Trade Area. In the late 1980s, the regional economic integration of developing countries such as the Asia-Pacific Economic Cooperation (APEC) was further strengthened. Since the 1990s, China has joined the ranks of regional economic integration.

With the continuous development of regional economy, its impact on the world economy and trade is growing. In particular, the European Union, the North American Free Trade Area, the Asia- Pacific Economic Cooperation and other regional economic integration organizations composed of or involving developed countries.

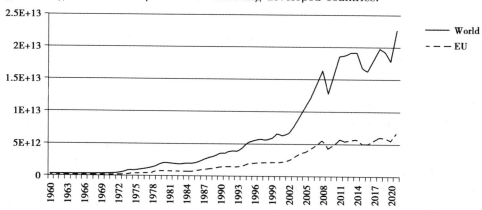

Figure 10.1   Comparison chart of global export trade and EU export trade trends (1960—2021)

⟩ 10.2.2　Major regional economic integration organizations after the Second World War

（1）European Union

①Establishment and development of the EU

European Union （EU） is developed on the basis of the European Community. The European Community includes the European Coal and Steel Community, the European Atomic Energy Community and the European Economic Community. On April 18, 1951, France, the Federal Republic of Germany, Italy, the Netherlands, Belgium and Luxembourg signed the Treaty of the European Coal and Steel Community in Paris, which entered into force on July 25, 1952. On March 25, 1957, the above-mentioned six countries signed the Treaty of the European Economic Community and the Treaty on the Framework of the European Atomic Energy Community in Rome, collectively referred to as the Treaty of Rome, and formally entered into force on January 1, 1958. According to the Treaty of Rome, it took the six members 12 years from January 1, 1958 to December 31, 1969 to complete the customs union, but actually it took only 10 years to complete it ahead of schedule in 1968. On April 8, 1965, the six countries signed the Brussels Treaty and decided to merge the institutions of the three communities, collectively referred to as the European Community （EC）. The treaty entered into force on July 1, 1967. To promote the construction of European integration. On February 17, 1986, the heads of government of the members of the European Community signed in Luxembourg. The European Single Document for large markets. In December 1991, the intergovernmental meeting of the European Community signed the Treaty of the EU in Maastricht, the Netherlands, which aims to deepen European integration and establish a political, economic and monetary union. On November 1, 1993, the treaty was ratified and entered into force by all members, and the EU was formally established.

In the course of the development of the EU, six expansions have been completed so far, while the further expansion of the EU has not yet been completed.

In 1973, the then European Community completed its first expansion, absorbing three new members from Britain, Denmark and Ireland, and developed from six countries to nine. In 1981, the European Community completed its second expansion, absorbing Greece as its new member, thereby expanding from 9 to 10 countries. In 1986, the European Community completed its third expansion, absorbing the accession of Spain and Portugal, and developed from 10 countries to 12. In 1995, the EU completed its fourth expansion, with Finland, Austria and Sweden joining, and developed into 15 members. In 2004, the EU expanded for the fifth time since its establishment, bringing 10 countries from Central and Eastern Europe into its system, thus expanding its membership to 25. The sixth expansion included the accession of three countries. Romania and Bulgaria signed a treaty of accession in Luxembourg on April 25, 2005, and formally joined the EU on January 1, 2007. So far, the EU has 27 members. Croatia's accession in 2013 expanded the EU to 28 members. With Britain exiting from the EU in 2020, the number of the members is 27 now. From the community of six countries in the 1950s to the EU of 27 countries today, European unity has achieved great success in Western Europe. The EU has become the leading political and economic force in Europe.

In the development process of the EU, the fifth enlargement has the most far-reaching significance. The fifth enlargement of the EU has transformed it from a horizontal economic integration organization into a vertical economic integration organization, and has taken an important step towards the realization of the dream of establishing a unified European market.

In the late 1980s and early 1990s, the shocked political upheaval took place in Eastern Europe. After a series of countries changed their flags and sails, the Cold War pattern in Europe came to an end. After that, Central and Eastern European countries began to return to the "Europe" dominated by Western Europe, while Western Europe expanded to Central and Eastern Europe. Against this background, the EU has begun its fifth expansion, which is also the largest expansion since its establishment—eastward expansion.

After the end of the Cold War, Central and Eastern European countries have asked for "returning to Europe" one after another, and many countries have applied to join the EU. From 1990 to 1994, at the summit meetings held in Rome, Edinburgh, Copenhagen, Corfu and Essen, the EU set the goal of establishing closer ties with Central and Eastern European countries. At the summit held in Copenhagen in 1993, the EU formulated three criteria for the admission of new members, clarified the conditions for accession politically, economically and legally, and began arduous accession negotiations with the candidate countries. After nearly 10 years of hard work, the EU basically completed the accession negotiations with 10 new members (Poland, Hungary, Slovakia, Lithuania, Latvia, Estonia, Czech Republic, Slovenia, Cyprus and Malta) at the end of 2002, and signed the accession treaty in April 2003. On May 1, 2004, these countries formally joined the EU.

②Supranational institutions of the EU

Reflected in the establishment of the EU's organizational structure and the functioning of its functions, it is to decentralize power, restrict each other and maintain balance. In terms of the organization composition and power distribution, it is emphasized that each member has a share. Its supranational institutions mainly include:

The decision-making and executive bodies of the EU are the Council of Ministers and the European Commission. These two institutions are the core institutions of the EU. The European Council of Ministers is responsible for coordinating members, formulating integration policies and promoting the development of European integration; The European Commission is the defender of the common policy and undertakes the responsibility of ensuring the smooth development of integration.

The EU's supervisory and advisory bodies are the European Parliament and the European Court of Audit. For quite a long time, the European Parliament was only a purely supervisory and advisory body, not a legislative body as its name suggests. As for the Audit Institute, it is basically a financial supervision institution.

The European Court of Justice is the judicial arbitration institution of the EU. As the defender of the Community Law, the European Court of Justice plays an irreplaceable role in the integrated development of the Community Law.

The EU's financial institution is the European Investment Bank. The European Investment Bank (EIB) is a financial institution of the European Community established in accordance with the Treaty of Rome, with independent legal status. The business focus of the EIB is mainly in three areas: to grant assistance to regional development, to fund projects that are indispensable to the establishment of the common market but lack three common financial means, and to aid projects that are beneficial to all members but lack other financing channels.

③Main contents of EU economic integration

Since the establishment of the EU, the economic goal is to achieve economic integration. In order to achieve this goal, a series of common policies have been gradually implemented from the European Community to the European Uion, coordinating the actions of members in various fields. These common policies constitute the basic content of EU economic integration.

These common policies mainly include: establishing a customs union among members to realize the free flow of goods and the unification of customs rates abroad, implementing the common agricultural policy, social policy, development policy, regional policy and science and technology policy, and being committed to the realization of monetary integration. On January 1, 1999, the euro was officially launched, bringing the monetary integration of the EU to a new stage. On December 1, 2009, the Lisbon Treaty, a simplified version of the EU Constitution, officially entered into force, making an important step forward in European integration. It can be said that the EU is an example of the best and highest degree of regional economic integration in the current world economy.

(2) NAFTA and the Free Trade Area of the Americas

The great success of the EU has made the United States greatly promote regional economic integration. In May 1985, the United States and Canada began negotiations on free trade between the two countries. In November 1988, the two governments officially signed the US-Canada Free Trade Agreement and took effect on January 1, 1989. The agreement does not require a complete free trade between the United States and Canada, but only requires that all tariffs and many non-tariff barriers in bilateral trade be gradually reduced and finally eliminated within 10 years from 1989 to 1998. For goods imported from third countries outside the region, both parties still use their own tariffs. In order to prevent third countries from using the free trade zone to evade tariffs, both parties confirmed the rules of origin.

In the mid-1980s, Mexico, which was in debt crisis, adhered to the interventionist economic policy, restricted imports and opposed foreign participation in the Mexican economy. In the 1990s, Mexico recognized that such a policy would not revitalize the economy, decided to reduce government intervention in the economy and open the market to foreign products, services and investment. Driven by this policy, Mexico and the United States have signed a broad bilateral trade agreement as the best way to strengthen the economic relationship between the United States and Mexico and deal with international competition and challenges. Subsequently, Canada, which has signed the US-Canada Free Trade Agreement with the United States, also requested to join the negotiations. The United States, Canada and Mexico signed the North American Free Trade Agreement (NAFTA) in December 1992, which came into force on January 1, 1994. During the establishment of the North American Free Trade Area, the three countries reached agreements on environmental protection, labor and employment in 1993 as supplementary documents to NAFTA. NAFTA mainly included several aspects: It would take 15 years to gradually eliminate tariffs among the three members, and at the same time reduce non-tariff barriers to a large extent; open the financial and insurance market; relax restrictions on foreign investment; protect intellectual property right.

However, the US-Mexico-Canada Agreement (USMCA) has replaced NAFTA (North American Free Trade Agreement) on July 1, 2020. USMCA has specific rules of origin that apply to each good, which are not always the same rules that applied under NAFTA. In addition, USMCA replaced the NAFTA Certificate of Origin with a USMCA certification of origin.

In order to expand the scope of North American economic integration, the United

States convened the Summit of the Americas in Miami in December 1994, which was attended by 34 countries from North and South America. At the meeting, 34 heads of state signed an agreement on the establishment of the Free Trade Area of the Americas, and set 2005 as the deadline for completing the negotiations.

Although the countries participating in the Summit of the Americas reached consensus on the establishment of the Free Trade Area of the Americas, there were obvious differences on the timetable and approach for the establishment of the Free Trade Area of the Americas, as well as on issues such as labor and environmental protection.

(3) Asia-Pacific Economic Cooperation

Asia-Pacific Economic Cooperation (APEC) was launched at a ministerial meeting held in Canberra, Australia, in November 1989. At that time, representatives of 12 countries and regions attended the meeting. China formally joined APEC in 1991. At present, the organization has 21 members: Australia, Brunei, Canada, Chile, China, China's Hong Kong, Indonesia, Japan, Malaysia, Mexico, New Zealand, Papua New Guinea, Peru, the Philippines, Russia, Singapore, South Korea, Chinese Taipei, Thailand, the United States and Vietnam. Most of them have participated in other regional economic integration organizations. In 1993, the leaders of APEC members put forward the idea of establishing the Asia-Pacific Economic Community, and planned to remove the barriers to trade and investment in the region by 2020. All countries will start liberalization on a unified date, but the progress of implementation should take into account the differences in the level of economic development among APEC members: Industrialized countries and regions should achieve free trade and investment no later than 2010, and developing countries and regions should not be later than 2020. This work is gradually being carried out through the annual ministerial meeting.

10.2.3   Regional economic integration organizations in which China participates

China's participation in regional economic integration started late, but has developed rapidly in recent years. In 1991, China formally joined the Asia-Pacific Economic Cooperation Organization and became an important member of the world's largest regional economic integration organization.

In April 1994, China formally applied to join the Asia-Pacific Trade Agreement (formerly the Bangkok Agreement). After seven years of negotiations, China officially became a member of the Asia-Pacific Trade Agreement from May 23, 2001, and implemented the Asia-Pacific Trade Agreement from January 1, 2002. The Asia-Pacific

Trade Agreement is a preferential trade arrangement between its members under the auspices of the United Nations Economic and Social Council for Asia and the Pacific. It is also the first regional trade agreement with substantive preferential tariff arrangements to which China has acceded. The core content and objective of the agreement is to expand mutual trade and promote the economic development of members by providing each other with preferential tariffs and non-tariff concessions. The existing members of the agreement include China, India, South Korea, Bangladesh, Sri Lanka and Laos. China has completed preferential tariff negotiations with South Korea, Sri Lanka, Bangladesh and India, and implemented preferential tariffs.

In November 2001, China and ASEAN reached a consensus to establish an ASEAN-China Free Trade Area within the next decade, that is, before 2010. In November 2002, leaders of China and ASEAN signed the Framework Agreement on Comprehensive Economic Cooperation between China and ASEAN in Phnom Penh, the capital of Cambodia. This marks the official start of the process of establishing the ASEAN-China Free Trade Area. After nearly ten years of efforts, ASEAN-China Free Trade Area has signed the Agreement on Trade in Goods, the Agreement on Trade in Services and the Investment Agreement, and completed the ASEAN-China Free Trade Area in 2010.

China has also signed free trade agreements with Pakistan, Chile, New Zealand, Singapore, Peru, Costa Rica, Iceland, Switzerland, South Korea and Australia. Free trade area agreements between China and GCC, Norway, Sri Lanka, Maldives, Georgia and other countries and regions are also under negotiation.

On January 1, 2022, the Regional Comprehensive Economic Partnership Agreement (RCEP) officially entered into force, and six ASEAN members, including Brunei, Cambodia, Laos, Singapore, Thailand and Vietnam, and four non-ASEAN members, including China, Japan, New Zealand and Australia, formally began to implement the agreement.

After eight years of negotiations, the RCEP was signed on November 15, 2020. Through the joint efforts of all parties, it reached the threshold of entry into force on November 2, 2021. The effective implementation of RCEP marks the official landing of a free trade area with the largest population, the largest economic and trade scale and the greatest development potential in the world. It fully reflects the confidence and determination of all parties to jointly safeguard multilateralism and free trade and promote regional economic integration, and will make important contributions to regional and even global trade and investment growth, economic recovery and prosperity.

China will fully fulfill its RCEP obligations, implement the agreement with high quality, expand foreign trade and two-way investment, constantly stabilize and strengthen the supply chain of the industrial chain, and continuously improve the business environment. We will guide local governments, industries and enterprises to make good use of the agreed market opening commitments and rules, and better grasp the market opening opportunities brought by RCEP. The Ministry of Commerce, together with relevant departments, will continue to do a good job in RCEP training, support the construction of the public service platform of the Free Trade Zone, strengthen the function of the service network of the China Free Trade Zone, and provide guidance and services for the high-level implementation of the agreement by various regions, industries and enterprises.

China will work with RCEP members to actively participate in and support the construction of the RCEP mechanism, make contributions to the economic and technical cooperation of RCEP, jointly promote the overall implementation of the agreement, continue to improve the liberalization and facilitation of regional trade and investment, and build RCEP into the main platform for economic and trade cooperation in East Asia.

10.3   Trade-creating customs union theory

This section first explains the process of trade creation, and then illustrates the effect of trade-creating customs union with examples.

10.3.1   Trade-creating customs union

The static and partial equilibrium effect of customs union can be measured by trade creation and trade diversion. Trade creation occurs when some domestic production in a country that is a member of the customs union is replaced by lower-cost imports from another member country. Assuming that all economic resources are fully utilized before/after the establishment of the customs union, trade creation will increase the welfare of members, because it will bring a greater degree of product specialization based on comparative advantage. Trade-creating customs union also increases the welfare of non-members, because the increase of a member's real income (due to the increase in the degree of specialization of production) will also increase imports from other countries in the world.

10.3.2   Description of trade-creating customs union

Figure 10.2 illustrates the effect of a trade-creating customs union. D_X and S_X in Figure 10.2 represent the domestic demand curve and supply curve of commodity X in Country 2 respectively. Assume that the free trade price of commodity X in Country 1 $P_X = \$1$, and the free trade price of commodity X in country 3 (or other countries in the world) is $P_X =$

$1.5, and that Country 2 is a small country, which cannot affect the price of these commodities. If Country 2 first imposes a non-discriminatory 100% ad valorem tax on all imported commodities, then Country 2 will import commodity X from Country 1 at a price of $P_X = \$2$. At this price, Country 2 consumes 50X (GH), of which 20X is produced domestically (GJ) and 30X (JH) is imported from Country 1. Country 2 also received a tariff income of $30 (MJHN). In the figure, S_1 is the fully elastic supply curve of commodity X from Country 1 to Country 2 under free trade. $S_1 + T$ represents the supply curve including tariff. Country 2 will not import X from country 3, because the tax inclusive price of X imported from this country is $P_X = \$3$.

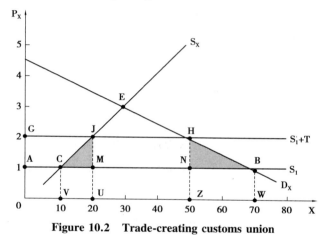

Figure 10.2　Trade-creating customs union

　If Country 2 now establishes a customs union with Country 1 (that is, only the tariff on the goods imported from Country 1 is canceled), the price of Country 2's commodity X is $P_X = \$1$. At this price, Country 2 consumes 70X (AB), including 10X (AC) produced domestically and 60X (CB) imported from Country 1. At this time, Country 2 has no tax revenue. The welfare of consumers in Country 2 due to the establishment of customs union is equal to AGHB. However, as a whole, only part of this is the net income of Country 2 as a whole. That is to say, AGJC represents the decrease of rent or producer surplus, MJHN represents the tax loss, and the sum of the remaining shadow triangular CJM and BHN areas totaling $15 is the static net welfare income of Country 2.

　The triangle CJM represents the producer surplus in the welfare income created by trade. It comes from the transformation of 10X (CM) production from the low production efficiency Country 2 (the cost is VUJC) to the import from the high production efficiency Country 1 (the cost is VUMC). Triangular BHN is the consumer surplus in the welfare income created by trade. It comes from the fact that Country 2 increases consumption (NB) by 20X, and only consumes ZWBN to obtain ZWBH benefits.

Viner took the lead in advocating the development of the theory of customs union in 1950. His research focused on the production effect created by trade and ignored the consumption effect. Meade developed the theory of customs union in 1955 and proposed to consider its consumption effect for the first time. Later, Johnson's research added the areas of the two triangles to obtain all the benefits of the customs union.

10.4   Trade-diverting customs union theory

This section first explains the meaning of trade diversion, and then explains the effect of trade-diverting customs union.

10.4.1   Trade-diverting customs union

When a country's imports are transferred from a low-cost country in outside the customs union to a high-cost country in the customs union, trade diversion occurs. It came into being because the members signed preferential trade agreements. As far as trade diversion is concerned, it reduces welfare because it transfers production from non-members with higher efficiency to members with lower efficiency. Therefore, the diversion of trade worsens the distribution of international resources and makes production deviate from the principle of comparative advantage.

Trade-diverting customs union leads to both trade creation and trade diversion, which may increase or reduce the welfare of members, depending on the relative strength of the two opposite forces. It can be expected that the welfare of non-members will decrease, because their utilization rate of economic resources is lower than when there is no trade diversion. Trade-creating customs union only leads to trade creation and will certainly increase the welfare of members and non-members, while trade-diverting customs union not only leads to trade creation but also leads to trade diversion, which may increase or reduce the welfare of members (and will reduce the welfare of other countries in the world).

10.4.2   Description of the trade-diverting customs union

Figure 10.3 illustrates the effects of trade-diverting customs union. D_X and S_X in the figure respectively represent the domestic demand curve and supply curve of commodity X of Country 2. S_1 and S_3 represent the fully elastic supply curves of Country 1 and country 3 under the free trade system, respectively. After imposing a non-discriminatory 100% tariff on commodity X, Country 2 imports commodity X from Country 1 along the $S_1 + T$ line at the price of $P_X = \$2$ (exactly the same as Figure 10.2). As mentioned above, when $P_X =$

$2, Country 2 consumes 50X (GH), of which 20X (GJ) is produced domestically, and 30X (JH) is imported from Country 1, and Country 2 receives tariff income of $30 (JMNH).

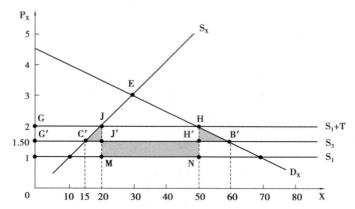

Figure 10.3   Trade-diverting customs union

If Country 2 only establishes a customs union with country 3 now (that is, only cancels the import tariff on country 3), Country 2 will find that it cheaper to import X from Country 3 at P_X = $1.50. At the price of P_X = $1.50, Country 2 consumes 60X (G′B′), including 15X (G′C′) produced domestically and 45X (C′B′) imported from country 3. In this case, Country 2 does not receive tariff revenue. The import of commodity X of Country 2 is now transferred from Country 1 with high production efficiency to country 3 with low production efficiency, because of the discriminatory import tariff charged against Country 1 (Country 1 is not a member). Note the import volume of Country 2 is 30X before the establishment of the customs union, and 45X after the establishment. In this way, the trade-diverting customs union has also caused a certain degree of trade creation.

The static welfare effect of Country 2 due to the establishment of a customs union with country 3 can be calculated through the shaded part of Figure 10.3. The welfare income of the sum of the shadow triangle C′JJ′ and B′HH′ ($3.75) only comes from trade creation, while the welfare loss of the shadow rectangle MNH′J′ ($15) is caused by the transfer of 30X imports from the lower-cost Country 1 to the higher-cost country 3. In particular, the consumer surplus of G′GHB′ is generated by the customs union. G′GJC′ represents the part of Country 2 where the surplus is transferred from producers to consumers. In this way, it is even (that is, Country 2 as a whole has neither net income nor net loss). The rectangular JMNH ($30) is the tariff revenue before the establishment of a customs union between Country 2 and Country 3. Rectangle J′JHH′ is the income of Country 2 transferred to consumers due to the decrease of X's price caused by the establishment of customs union.

In this way, only the shaded triangles C′JJ′ and B′HH′ are left as the net income of Country 2, and the shaded rectangle MNH′J′ is the loss of tariff income that has not been calculated yet.

Because the area of the shaded rectangle measuring the loss of Country 2 in trade diversion ($15) exceeds the area of the shaded triangle measuring the welfare obtained from pure trade creation ($3.75). The customs union resulted in a net loss of $11.25 for country 2. However, this is not always the case. As can be seen from Figure 10.3, the flatter the S_X curve and the D_X curve (that is, the greater the elasticity in the relevant range), and the closer S_3 is to S_1, the larger the area of the shadow triangle, the smaller the area of the shadow rectangle. In this way, even for a country that participates in a pure trade-diverting customs union, its chances of obtaining net welfare income will increase. Some scholars have tried several times to measure the static welfare effect formed by the EU, and the results all came up with surpringly small net static welfare income (only 1% – 2% of GDP).

10.5　The dynamic effect of customs union

The establishment of a customs union will not only have a static impact on the economies of its members, but also have a long-term dynamic impact.

(1) The establishment of customs union can bring economies of scale

After the establishment of the customs union, enterprises of one member can freely enter the domestic market of other members, so they can obtain economies of scale that cannot be realized in small markets under trade restrictions. The expansion of the market is conducive to improving the specialization of workers and machines. Enterprises can use the most effective equipment, make more thorough use of by-products, and improve production efficiency. A large amount of evidence shows that the EU has achieved significant economies of scale in the production of steel, automobiles and other products.

(2) The establishment of a customs union is conducive to strengthening competition

It is generally believed that trade restrictions will promote monopoly, thereby reducing efficiency. Under the protection of full trade wall, a few enterprises that control the domestic market prefer to be at peace with each other. They often reach agreements rather than compete on the basis of price. However, the possibility of successful collusion will follow the customs union. The increasing openness of the local market and the increase in the number of bright competitors have decreased. Under the conditions of free trade, domestic enterprises must participate in competition. Otherwise they will face the fate of bankruptcy.

（3）The establishment of customs union is conducive to stimulating investment

The establishment of a customs union will stimulate investors inside or outside the union to increase investment. Due to the establishment of the customs union, the structural adjustment, economic internality and externality, and the expected growth of income and demand will all lead to investment behavior. In addition, the establishment of customs union makes producers face a broader market in economy and geography, thus reducing the risk and uncertainty of investment. This will also stimulate increased investment. Finally, investors from non-members will also hope to avoid being expelled from the big market of the alliance due to trade restrictions and higher common external tariffs through investment in members.

—— *China-perspective case study* ——

RCEP officially takes effect

On January 1, 2022, the Regional Comprehensive Economic Partnership Agreement (RCEP) officially entered into force. Six ASEAN members, including Brunei, Cambodia, Laos, Singapore, Thailand and Vietnam, and four non-ASEAN members, including China, Japan, New Zealand and Australia, officially began to implement the agreement.

The effective implementation of RCEP marks the official landing of a free trade area with the largest population, the largest economic and trade scale and the greatest development potential in the world. It fully reflects the confidence and determination of all parties to jointly safeguard multilateralism and free trade and promote regional economic integration, and will make important contributions to regional and even global trade and investment growth, economic recovery and prosperity.

In an interview with our reporter, the relevant person in charge of the Ministry of Commerce said that, with the official entry into force of RCEP, from today (January 1, 2022), China will fully implement all commitments and obligations under the RCEP agreement, including the immediate implementation of zero tariffs on a large number of products.

It was reported that in terms of market opening, the proportion of immediate zero tariff between China and ASEAN, Australia and New Zealand exceeded 65%.

China and Japan have newly established a free trade relationship, and their immediate tariff free ratio has reached 25% and 57% respectively.

The relevant person in charge of the Ministry of Commerce said that the effective implementation of RCEP will become a bridge and link connecting domestic and international double cycles, strengthen China's ability to allocate resources in domestic and international markets, which is of great significance for China to build a new development pattern, and will also bring tangible benefits to enterprises and consumers.

Enterprises will benefit from "expanding the market", "fixing the chain" and "enjoying services".

"Market expansion" means that the RCEP takes effect, indicating that the regional unified market has officially started to operate, the level of trade and investment liberalization and facilitation has been significantly improved, and the market space of enterprises will be significantly expanded.

"Fixed chain" means that the cumulative rules of the region of origin and the two-way opening of service trade and investment will strengthen regional industrial cooperation, strengthen the supply chain of the regional industrial chain, and ensure more smooth business activities of enterprises.

"Access to services" means that RCEP will create a more perfect business environment and a higher level of trade facilitation to bring better support to enterprises.

For consumers, the implementation of RCEP will bring three experiences of "high quality", "substantial benefits" and "convenience"—foreign high-quality goods will enter the Chinese consumer market more under the incentive of the entry into force of the agreement, and consumers will have more choices. The realization of zero tariff will reduce the cost of imported goods, and consumers can buy foreign products at a lower price; RCEP's high-level trade facilitation measures will also help consumers receive imported goods more quickly.

Key concepts

regional economic integration

free trade zone

common market

trade creation

preferential trade arrangement

customs union

economic alliance

trade diversion

Summary

1. Economic integration refers to the commercial policies that the countries that join the alliance reduce or eliminate trade barriers differently. In preferential trade agreements

(such as the Commonwealth Preference System), trade barriers are reduced only among participating countries. Free trade areas (such as the European Free Trade Association and the North American Free Trade Area) eliminate all trade barriers among members, but each member retains barriers against non-members. Customs unions (such as the EU) have taken a step further and adopted common commercial policies for trade outside the union. Allowing labor and capital to flow freely among members is another step forward. The economic union can coordinate (such as the economic union of Belgium, Netherlands and Rwanda), or even unify (such as the United States) the monetary and fiscal policies of its members.

2. The static and partial equilibrium effect of customs union should be measured by trade creation and trade diversion. Trade creation occurs when the domestic products of one member are replaced by low-cost imported products of another member. This can increase the specialized production and welfare of customs union countries. Trade-creating customs union will also increase the welfare of non-members, because part of the increased income of members will be used for imports from other regions of the world.

3. Trade diversion occurs when lower-cost imports from outside the customs union are replaced by higher-cost imports from another union member. By itself, this reduces welfare because it shifts production away from comparative advantage. A trade-diverting customs union leads to both trade creation and trade diversion and may increase or reduce welfare, depending on the relative strength of these two opposing forces.

4. In addition to the static welfare income, the countries forming the customs union will obtain obvious dynamic benefits from the intensified competition, the expansion of economic scale, the stimulation of investment, and the better use of economic resources.

5. The EU was established in 1958 and consists of the Federal Republic of Germany, France, Italy, Belgium, the Netherlands and Luxembourg. Britain, Denmark and Ireland joined in 1973, Greece, 1986, Spain and Portugal joined in 1981, Austria, Finland and Sweden joined in 1995, Poland, Hungary, the Czech Republic, the Slovak Republic, Slovenia, Estonia, Lithuania, Latvia, Malta and Cyprus joined in 2004, Bulgaria and Romania joined in 2008, and Croatia joined in 2013. Then, Britain exited in 2020. In 1968, free trade was achieved in industrial products and a common agricultural policy was implemented, while a complete unified market was formed in 1993. The establishment of the EU led to the expansion of industrial trade but the transfer of agricultural trade. In 1993, the United States, Canada and Mexico signed the North American Free Trade Agreement. Over the past decade, free trade agreements have flourished.

Exercises

1. What is a customs union?
2. What is trade creation? What is trade diversion?
3. What are the economic effects of a customs union?
4. Briefly describe the process of China's participation in regional economic integration.
5. Briefly describe the development of EU regional economic integration.

Further Readings

BALDWIN R, WYPLOSZ C. The economies of European integration [M]. 3rd ed. New York: McGraw-Hill Higher Education, 2009.

BEHAR A, VENABLES A J. Transport costs and international trade [Z] // DE PALMA A, LINDSEY R, QUINET E, et al. A handbook of transport economics, Northampton, Massachusetts: Edward Elgar Publishing, Inc., 2011:97-115.

BERNANKE B S. Essays on the Great Depression [M]. New Jersey: Princeton University Press, 2000.

CHEN Z J. On the influence of international relations on international trade [J]. Modern economics & management forum, 2022, 3 (1):30-33.

CLARK X, DOLLAR D, MICCO A. Port efficiency, maritime transport costs, and bilateral trade [J]. Journal of development economics, 2004, 75(2):417-450.

DEVLIN J, YEE P. Trade logistics in developing countries: the case of the Middle East and North Africa [J]. World economy, 2005, 28(3):435-456.

FRANK R H, BERNANKE B S. Principles of macroeconomics [M]. 3rd ed. Boston, Massachusetts: McGraw-Hill/Irwin, 2005.

FUJITA M, KRUGMAN P, VENABLES A J. The spatial economy: cities, regions, and international trade [M]. Massachusetts: The MIT Press, 1999.

GANI A. The logistics performance effect in international trade [J]. The Asian journal of shipping and logistics, 2017, 33(4):279-288.

HAFTEL Y Z, KIM S Y, BASSAN-NYGATE L. High-income developing countries, FDI outflows and the International Investment Agreement regime [J]. World trade review, 2022, 22(1):1-17.

HAUSMAN W H, LEE H L, SUBRAMANIAN U. The impact of logistics performance on trade [J]. Production and operations management, 2013, 22(2):236-252.

HE Y G. International trade [M]. 2nd ed. Beijing: China Higher Education Press, 2021.

HUANG W P, PENG G. International economics [M]. 4th ed. Beijing: China Renmin University Press, 2022.

IWANOW T, KIRKPATRICK C. Trade facilitation, regulatory quality and export performance [J]. Journal of international development, 2007, 19(6):735-753.

ITAKURA K. Impact of liberalization and improved connectivity and facilitation in ASEAN [J]. Journal of Asian economics, 2014, 35(C):2-11.

JIN Z H. International Trade [M]. 4th ed. Beijing: China Renmin University Press, 2022.

KALI R, MéNDEZ F, REYES J. Trade structure and economic growth [J]. The Journal of international trade & economic development, 2007, 16(2):245-269.

KANEVSKAIA O. ICT Standards bodies and international trade: what role for the WTO? [J]. Journal of world trade, 2022, 56(3):429-452.

KRUGMAN P R. Increasing returns, monopolistic competition, and international trade: revisiting gains from trade [J]. Journal of international economics, 1979, 9(4):469-479.

KRUGMAN P R. The great unraveling: losing our way in the new century [M]. New York: W. W. Norton & Company, Inc., 2003.

KRUGMAN P R. The conscience of a liberal [M]. New York: W. W. Norton & Company, Inc., 2007.

KRUGMAN P R. The return of depression economics and the crisis of 2008 [M]. New York: W. W. Norton & Company, Inc., 2008.

KRUGMAN P R. Arguing with zombies: economics, politics, and the fight for a better future [M]. New York: W. W. Norton & Company, Inc., 2020.

KRUGMAN P R, OBSTFELD M. International economics: theory and policy [M]. 8th ed. New Jersey: Prentice Hall, 2008.

KRUGMAN P R, OBSTFELD M, MELITZ M J. International economics: theory and policy [M]. 12th ed. New Jersey: Pearson Education Ltd., 2022.

LEONTIEF W. Why economics needs input-output analysis? [J]. Challenge from Taylor & Francis journals, 1985, 28(1):27-35.

LEONTIEF W. When should history be written backwards? [J]. Economic history review, 1963, 16(1):1-8.

LEONTIEF W. Can economics be reconstructed as an empirical science? [J]. American journal of agricultural economics, 1993, 75(Supplement):2-5.

LIU H Y, GUO W Q, WANG Y, et al. Impact of resource on green growth and threshold effect of international trade levels: evidence from China [J]. International Journal of environmental research and public health, 2022, 19(5):2505.

LODEFALK M, SJHOLM F, TANG A. International trade and labour market integration of immigrants [J]. The world economy, 2022, 45(6):1650-1689.

MARTINEZ-ZARZOSO I, MáRQUEZ-RAMOS L. The effect of trade facilitation on sectoral trade [J]. The B.E. journal of economic analysis & policy, 2008, 8(1):1-46.

NAKOS G, DIMITRATOS P, ELBANNA S. The mediating role of alliances in the international market orientation-performance relationship of SMEs [J]. International business review, 2019, 28(3): 603-612.

NELLO S S. The European Union: economics, policies and history [M]. 3rd ed. New York: McGraw-Hill Higher Education, 2011.

OHLIN B. Interregional and international trade [M]. Rev. ed. Massachusetts: Harvard University Press, 1967.

PIZANO D. Conversations with great economists: Friedrich A. Hayek, John Hicks, Nicholas Kaldor, Leonid V. Kantorovich, Joan Robinson, Paul A. Samuelson, Jan Tinbe [M]. New York: Jorge Pinto Books Inc., 2009.

POMFRET R, SOURDIN P. Trade facilitation and the measurement of trade costs [J]. Journal of international commerce, economics and policy, 2010, 1(1):145-163.

PUGEL T. International economics [M]. 17th ed. New York: McGraw-Hill Higher Education, 2020.

RAHMAN M, ALAM K. CO_2 emissions in Asia-Pacific region: do energy use, economic growth, financial development, and international trade have detrimental effects? [J]. Sustainability, 2022, 14(9):5420.

RICARDO D. On the principles of political economy and taxation [M]. Georgetown, D.C., J. Milligan; Washington City, J. Gideon, Junior, Printer, 1819.

ROBERT J C. International economics: China student edition [M]. 17th ed. Beijing: China Renmin University Press, 2022.

SALVATORE D. Introduction to international economies [M]. New York: John Wiley & Sons, 2005.

SALVATORE D. International economics [M]. 12th ed. New York: John Wiley & Sons, 2019.

SAMUELSON P A, NORDHAUS W D. Economics [M]. 19th ed. New York: McGraw-Hill Higher Education, 2004.

SMITH A. An inquiry into the nature and causes of the wealth of nations: volume 1 [M]. London: W. Strahan and T. Cadell, London, 1776.

YANIKKAYA H. Trade openness and economic growth: a cross-country empirical investigation [J]. Journal of development economics, 2003, 72(1):57-89.